80@80
SPENCER LEIGH

First published: February 2025
Text © Spencer Leigh
This edition © Poppublishing 2025
This book is available in both paperback and ebook formats

All rights reserved. No part of this publication may be reproduced, stored in a retrieval system, or transmitted in any form or by any means, electronic, electrostatic, recording, magnetic tape, mechanical, photocopying or otherwise, without prior permission in writing from the publisher.

The right of Spencer Leigh to be identified as author of this Work has been asserted by him in accordance with sections 77 and 78 of the Copyright, Designs and Patents Act 1988.

Editor/Designer: David Roberts

For more information about this book,
or to contact the author, email David Roberts at
Poppublishing@gmail.com

This book is dedicated to the one I love

Acknowledgements

My thanks to David Roberts at Poppublishing, who has a lifetime of work in the industry and wrote and researched the brilliant *Rock Atlas* books (one for the UK, one for the USA). His company likes to publish books by old friends such as the memoirs of Beatles insider, Brian Southall.

My thanks to Tim Adams, Patrick Humphries, Mark Kelly and Pam Wolff for reading over my draft text, making comments and pointing out typos.

"I'd be the first one to agree,

I'm preoccupied with me."

(from 'I Won't Send Roses', Mack and Mabel)

Foreword by
Bob Harris & Colin Hall

Photos of Bob Harris and Colin Hall © @marcwestoxford

FOREWORD

Colin: "So, Bob …"
Bob: "Yes, Colin?"
Colin: "Spencer Leigh - in 300 words? That's what the publisher would like."
Bob: "Surely not! A feature-length radio documentary would barely suffice, given the fact the man is a broadcasting legend."
Colin: "Too true … he's a Lancastrian treasure trove of words and insights and has been on the radio for over 50 years. He's a walking encyclopaedia of the development of pop and rock music culture in the UK and USA."
Bob: "You're absolutely right, Colin. He really has achieved so much. His work for BBC Radio Merseyside alone is superb. I think it began with a series on the Liverpool poets and then he did that series, *Let's Go Down The Cavern* which was put out as a book too. That was the first history of Merseybeat."
Colin: "That's right. I didn't like to miss his weekly show *On The Beat* which was full of reviews and interviews."
Bob: "… and it ran for 35 years and 2,000 shows: that's truly remarkable, Colin."
Colin: "Undoubtedly … the figures speak for themselves … Spencer interviewed so many stars as they made their way through Liverpool, including the one and only Willie Nelson who rolled a massive spliff as they chatted away … "
Bob: "That's Willie for you! And let's not forget that Spencer is also a prolific writer and researcher whose work includes the musical, *Cavern of Dreams*, from 1984, an early milestone. He's contributed obituaries to the *Independent* and the *Guardian*, while his rock music biographies are a particular forte."
Colin: "Absolutely. His biography of the Cavern's DJ Bob Wooler, *The Best of Fellas* is an absolute classic and very funny,

while *Drummed Out* is considered by many to provide the definitive analysis on the sacking of Pete Best."

Bob: "The list goes on - for instance, did you know that Spencer was a columnist and reviewer for *Country Music People?*"

Colin: "No, I didn't know that, Bob, but I'm not surprised! Of course, Liverpool is such a fabulous and vibrant music city that it was dubbed the 'Nashville of the North'!"

Bob: "And now here we are celebrating all the career highlights and memories from Spencer's illustrious career in *80@80*, written to celebrate 80 splendid years and counting…"

Colin: "Exactly! And what better way to do this for such a kind and generous man than to be invited to contribute a foreword to his wonderful book. We feel honoured to have been asked to celebrate Spencer's in this way."

Bob: "We certainly do."

Colin: "Here's to you, Spencer Leigh, legend and all-round good fellow: thank you very, very much…"

Bob: "…and long may you rock. I'm looking forward to *90@90*."

Thanks Colin, Thanks, Bob. Much appreciated.

Colin was the custodian to John Lennon's childhood home in Menlove Avenue and indeed, lived in the house longer than John Lennon did. I have heard Bob Harris more than any other DJ and I saw them together at the Yoko Ono Centre in Liverpool for a marvellous evening of music and stories.

SL

INTRODUCTION

Please allow me to introduce myself...

It is 2024, and this book has been written and compiled for my eightieth birthday. I am 80 on 1 February 2025. Maybe I won't make it and if so, the title is unfortunate, but then again, I'm never going to know about it.

I'm married to a librarian but even so, I've written a librarian's nightmare. This is an autobiography that could also be filed under music, insurance or local history; There are 80 chapters covering the 80 years in my life. As well as new material, there are articles and book extracts that go back down the decades. The transitions are hopefully as smooth as possible, so that a reader doesn't think, "I'll skip this chapter on insurance." They're fun, I guarantee it, and if you read the book through from start to finish, then job done.

Born on Merseyside in 1945, I went to a preparatory school in Crosby, a boarding school in North Wales, and back to Crosby for my A-levels. I trained to be an actuary with Royal Life Insurance in Liverpool and became their chief underwriter, taking early retirement when they merged with Sun Alliance at the end of 1997

From the 1970s onwards, I have been writing magazine articles and books, mostly about popular music. I was also broadcasting on BBC Radio Merseyside and my weekly series *On The Beat* ran from 1985 to 2020. My final guest was Zucchero. It sounds neat to conclude with a Z but in truth, I had lined up Bucks Fizz for the following week and the show was cancelled because of Covid regulations. As a consequence, I could not enter BBC premises as I was 75 years old. Specialist shows were being axed anyway and I was lucky to have lasted as long as I did.

This book is partly autobiographical, but it is also about what I've written over the years. Although I've tried not to make it an ego trip, I enjoy writing in the first person and I'm reliving every page as I write.

Everything is described the way it was and, with one exception, names have not been changed. A lad in my class when I was 13 is here called Johnny as I didn't want to embarrass him. I realise that this in turn could embarrass anyone called Johnny in the same class but I'm sure that there wasn't a Johnny there. Come to think of it, my father kept a low profile and he would have hated to have seen tales about himself in print, but you can't go round changing the names of your parents.

The question I constantly ask myself is: who knows where the time goes? That Sandy Denny song sung by Judy Collins is a shoo-in for my funeral.

Contents

1. FAMILY MATTERS
2. YOU'LL NEVER WALK ALONE
3. DAYS IN THE LIFE, 1945-1954
4. A FOUR-LEGGED FRIEND
5. DAYS IN THE LIFE, 1955-1958
6. GOT A LOT OF LIVIN' TO DO
7. DAYS IN THE LIFE, 1958-1961
8. LOST EMPIRES
9. HOLLY DAYS
10. DAYS IN THE LIFE, 1961-1963
11. MERSEYSIDE HITMAKERS
12. THE GREATEST PACKAGE SHOW
13. DAYS IN THE LIFE, 1963-1964
14. HONEY, JUST ALLOW ME ONE MORE CHANCE
15. DAYS IN THE LIFE, 1965-1966
16. TIM ON MY HANDS
17. DAYS IN THE LIFE, 1967
18. STRANGE DAYS INDEED
19. EVERYBODY RAZZLE DAZZLE
20. DAYS IN THE LIFE, 1968-1970
21. ARE YOU PAYING FOR SCARBOROUGH FAIR?
22. ALMOST LIVERPOOL 8
23. DAYS IN THE LIFE, 1971
24. WRONGLY ACCUSED
25. DAYS IN THE LIFE, 1971-1974
26. VIVA LAS VEGAS
27. DAYS IN THE LIFE, 1974
28. JOHN STONEHOUSE – MY PART IN HIS DOWNFALL
29. DAYS IN THE LIFE, 1975-1979
30. MUSIC GAMES
31. NORTH-WEST COUNTRY
32. DAYS IN THE LIFE, 1980
33. DISASTER ARIAS
34. LET'S GO DOWN THE CAVERN
35. JUST LIKE STARTIN' OVER
36. DAYS IN THE LIFE, 1981-1983
37. CAT O' NINE TALES
38. DAYS IN THE LIFE, 1984
39. CAVERN OF DREAMS
40. SEXUALITY
41. DAYDREAM BELIEVER
42. DAYS IN THE LIFE, 1985-1986
43. THE MAN WHO WASN'T THERE
44. DAYS IN THE LIFE, 1986-1988
45. BE BOP A LULA

46. DAYS IN THE LIFE, 1988-1991
47. DR HECKLE AND MR SNIDE
48. DAYS IN THE LIFE, 1992-1994
49. COMIC GENIUS
50. DAYS IN THE LIFE, 1994
51. DON'T YOU WANT TO APOLOGISE FOR THAT AWFUL REVIEW?
52. DAYS IN THE LIFE, 1995-1996
53. A NOT SO SUNNY ALLIANCE
54. DAYS IN THE LIFE, 1997-1999
55. RUN DEVIL RUN
56. DAYS IN THE LIFE, 2000-2001
57. WHERE HAVE YOU BEEN ALL THE DAY, BILLY BOB?
58. THE BEST OF FELLAS
59. DAYS IN THE LIFE, 2002-2004
60. GERMANY CALLING
61. 1,000 UK NUMBER 1 HITS
62. DAYS IN THE LIFE, 2004-2005
63. SAM THE SHAM
64. DAYS IN THE LIFE, 2006-2007
65. AFTER BATHING AT THE ADELPHI
66. DAYS IN THE LIFE, 2008-2010
67. I'M THIS CLOSE TO COMING BACK
68. LIPA
69. DAYS IN THE LIFE, 2011-2014
70. FRANKIE AND THE MOB
71. DAYS IN THE LIFE, 2015
72. PAPERBACK WRITERS
73. DAYS IN THE LIFE, 2016-2019
74. GHOST STORIES
75. DAYS IN THE LIFE, 2020-2023
76. LOVE ACTUALLY
77. SPANNER IN THE WORKS
78. EVERYBODY'S TALKING ABOUT JAMIE
79. THE BEATLES' LEGACY
80. BOP TILL YOU DROP

CHAPTER 1

Family Matters

My grandfather, Thomas Wilson Leigh, was a paper merchant who ran the family business from School Lane in Liverpool, close to Bluecoat Chambers, only five minutes away from the building that became home to the Cavern. He lived with his wife, Ethel, at 1 Beach Road, Southport, the property changing hands for almost half a million in 2020. It had five bedrooms with a huge cupboard at the end of the landing in which my grandmother stored tins of canned food. There had been rationing during the Second World War and for five years after that. Granny was clearly preparing for another major conflict judging by the contents of that cupboard. There was a large garden and Grandpa referred to the watering can as his 'outside toilet'.

In the mid-1950s, Grandpa retired from the day-to-day running of his company, leaving it to his sons – George, Harold and Thomas (my dad). Being retired didn't come easily to him: he dressed as though for work each day and sometimes he would get up at 4am and try and get a train from Birkdale to Liverpool. It was Alzheimer's, I suppose, but people accepted it as one of his funny little ways. He died in 1961 and my granny went to live in a flat in Southport, dying herself in 1966.

The house was sold and the proceeds split between the brothers. Dad only received £2,000 and he must have been cheated. He didn't say so himself, but he never ever spoke affectionately of his brothers.

Although the company was called T W Leigh & Co, my grandad started it with John Gibbons, whose brother was the managing director of the Liverpool department store, Henderson's. Mr Gibbons died in 1969 and left £200,000, mostly to the National Trust and the Liverpool Boys' Association but I don't know how much of that was attributable to T W Leigh & Co.

My grandparents also raised a family friend, Ethel Sutcliffe, whose parents had been killed in the war. She played in amateur dramatics and, rather bizarrely, my grandparents' dachshund had a role in one of those plays at the Little Theatre in Southport, which later played host to the Beatles. Et, as she was called, went on holiday to Italy in 1959 and brought me back a copy of Conway Twitty's 'Danny Boy' which was banned for copyright reasons in the UK: that made me a real hero at school.

On the other side, my grandfather Benny Waugh, was a funeral director and church organist who died in 1939. His widow, Violet, lived in a large, gloomy house called East View on Liverpool Road, Crosby, close to Merchant Taylors' School. There was a family Bible on a lectern in the front room. On an outside wall was a large wooden board advertising John Waugh & Sons, funeral directors, although there was no longer any direct link with the firm. Vi, though I would never have called her that, would go to the Walker Art Gallery and copy paintings that she liked. I thought her watercolours were very good, but I presumed that they were completely original.

I was in two minds about Granny Waugh. When my brother was born, I was sent to live with her for a few days. She put me to bed with the tale of *Little Red Riding Hood*. We were alone in that big, gloomy house with creaky floorboards and she said slowly and spookily, "And how do you know that I am not the Big Bad Wolf?" Wooooo! I didn't sleep that night and so despite four children, her parenting skills had room for improvement.

A few years back I learnt that both Vi and Benny were buried in Birkdale Cemetery, only a mile from where I live in Ainsdale. There is a little horizontal marker with a number but no headstone and no other identification. That must be unusual for a funeral director's grave and I don't know why. Maybe I should pay for a headstone.

Vi and Benny had two sons and two daughters. Spencer had been at Liverpool College with Rex Harrison as a fellow pupil and he played the church organ at St Luke's, Crosby. In the 1960s, he became a vicar in Formby. Noel was a schoolteacher on the Wirral and in the 1930s, he played drums in a local dance band. For a short time, he was in Jim McCartney's band, Jim being Paul's father: they appreciated each other's musicianship but didn't know each other well. Noel was a stickler for precise and correct English and he encouraged the playing of chess in schools.

As I remember it, in the 50s and 60s, the two sisters - Ethel, my mother, and Dorothy (Dossie) - were usually feuding, but my mother was well used to Dossie's temperament. She said Dossie could pick an argument with herself.

Uncle Spen and my dad went to classical concerts together in the months running up to the Second World War and military service. As a result, Tom got to know Ethel and they were married in 1942. I was born Thomas Spencer Leigh, a war baby on 1 February 1945, with Chris following in 1948 and Pam in 1953.

My dad loved cricket and Chris was born at a very dramatic time in the England v Australia series. Don Bradman came out to bat at the Oval for his last ever test innings and he was out for a duck, which meant that his overall Test average fell to 99.94. Australia still won the Test.

When two of the England players, Alec Bedser and Jack Crapp, checked in at a London hotel, the receptionist said "Bed, sir?" "No, Crapp", was the reply. "Ah, yes, first door on the left." Anyway, I shouldn't get sidetracked; the Don's last innings was on 14 August and Chris arrived three days later.

I was partly named after my uncle, which was also my grandmother's maiden name, and partly because of Winston Spencer Churchill. I'm grateful I got the middle name and was not a Winston like John Lennon.

I did use my first name, Tommy, for a while but dropped that completely after the Conway Twitty fan club sent a letter addressed to Tommy Leigh to our home at 8 Mersey Road, Crosby. I wasn't a member, but I must have made an inquiry and the letter invited me to meet his plane at London Airport when he arrived for a UK tour in May 1960. Maybe they'd been amazed that someone in the UK knew the banned record of 'Danny Boy'.

As the letter was addressed to Tommy Leigh, my father opened it and, taking it seriously, he thought that he'd been invited to meet Conway Twitty. (I'd never have guessed an hour ago that Conway Twitty would be the first rocker to make an appearance in this book but here he is making his second appearance.)

In 1996 I decided to research my family tree and because I was a Leigh, I went down that side of the family. It took some months and I met relatives whom I didn't know existed. I discovered a great-aunt in West Wycombe, Berkshire, who knew a lot about my dad and yet he'd never mentioned her. I called it a day after drawing up a family tree featuring 120 people. Along the way, I came across a Cheshire saying, "As many Leighs as fleas", which seems about right.

Once or twice a year my father would go to Leeds but it was very hush-hush. When I researched the family tree, I discovered it was to visit Margaret Tookey Leigh, my grandfather's sister, who had a mental age of six but lived until 1964 when she was 84 - an astonishing age for somebody with learning difficulties in those days.

Tookey was a family name that arose when my great-great-grandfather Samuel married Letitia Tookey. In 1850 the Dental Act was passed and Samuel became one of the founders of dentistry in the UK. *The British Journal of the Dental Society* said, "He seldom took a holiday and his heart was as generous as his hands were diligent."

Four of his grandsons became dentists and one of them, Percival Tookey Leigh, was Mayor of Leeds. He and his wife Blanch had no children and they made his sister Hannah Breese an extraordinary offer. "You've got six children, we've got none so give us two of yours." They accepted this and Percival Leigh-Breese became a leading architect in London, assisting Harold MacMillan during his time as Prime Minister and was awarded the CBE.

Uncle Harold and Aunt Mary were told that if they named their son Percival Tookey, he would receive an endowment in his will. Poor Val was given the name but no payment was forthcoming.

Great-uncle Herbert practised as a dentist in Leeds until he was 90 in 1963 and he was using modern equipment too. There's your answer to this health shortage: get these old guys out of retirement! Herbert's son was probably the only Canadian Mountie to be called Cuthbert.

From time to time, Grandpa Leigh showed me an illustration of someone which had been passed down in the family for generations. He didn't know its true significance and that was as close to distant family history as I got at the time. Very much later I was able to put a name to the face. My six-times great-grandfather, Samuel Leigh, was born in 1635. When he was 25, he rewrote the Psalms as rhyming couplets. He sold his book at the Golden Lyon in St Paul's Churchyard, London. I viewed it at Lambeth Palace Library with my cousin Peter. To our astonishment the picture that our grandfather had shown me all those years ago was at the front of the book. It's a splendid portrait: in the late-1960s, he could have passed as a Rolling Stone.

The publication included fulsome praise for Charles II who had just ascended the throne:

"Hosannas only we could once aspire
But now sing Hallelujahs in the choir.
The King return'd and with him halcyon days
Turn mournful elegies to songs of praise."

His praise for Charles II is so effusive that I wonder which side he had really been on. Was he praying that those marvellous locks would remain on his shoulders?

Dad

CHAPTER 2

You'll Never Walk Alone

I was born in 1945, a momentous year by any standards:
The bombing of Dresden.
Mussolini captured and shot.
Hitler committed suicide.
Germany surrendered.
The USA dropped atomic bombs on Hiroshima and Nagasaki.
Japan surrendered.
Formation of the United Nations.
Benjamin Britten wrote his opera, *Peter Grimes*.
George Orwell wrote *Animal Farm*.
Tupperware and biros invented.

In July 1945 Lou Preager and his Dance Orchestra were featured in a new BBC radio contest, *Write a Tune*, which boasted £1,000 prize money for the best song.

It was so much money that the BBC was inundated with songs - 73,853 to be precise. The winners were Eily Beadell and Nelly Tollerton with 'Cruising Down the River on a Sunday Afternoon', which was sung and then recorded by Paul Rich. It became a standard and was the title song of a 1953 US film featuring Dick Haymes and Billy Daniels.

Incidentally, the BBC's prize money came from the

Hammersmith Palais, an early example of radio sponsorship and bypassing the BBC's rules.

Everybody wants to know what was No 1 on the day they were born. Well, there were no UK charts back then and anyway, there was a shortage of shellac because of the war. Allowing for that, in the year I was born I'm pretty certain one song stood out. So, whatever was No 1 the day you were born, I'm going to top it with 'You'll Never Walk Alone'.

Richard Rodgers and Oscar Hammerstein wrote the musical *Carousel*, the score containing 'June Is Bustin' Out All Over' and 'If I Loved You'. The inspirational ballad, 'You'll Never Walk Alone', was unusual in that the title only occurred in the final line.

In the original Broadway production, the abrasive fairground barker Billy Bigelow was played by John Raitt, father of Bonnie. He is killed when a robbery goes wrong and from beyond the grave, he comforts his wife and daughter and assures them they'll never walk alone. As a result, the judge in Purgatory allows him to return to earth to witness his daughter's graduation. After arguing with her, he is returned to Purgatory. How did Rodgers and Hammerstein get this ridiculous plot past their financial backers?

The first person to record the song was Frank Sinatra and if you hear it today, you will be surprised to hear him sing, "When you walk through a storm, keep your chin up high." By the time it had reached Gerry and the Pacemakers in 1963 it had become the superior "Hold your head up high", a better image, and with alliteration too.

'You'll Never Walk Alone' echoed the optimism that people felt now that the war was ending. Ivor Novello's 'We'll Gather Lilacs' from his lavish stage musical, *Perchance to Dream*, was also written with that in mind. Other songs of the year were 'Laura'

(Dick Haymes), 'Long Ago and Far Away' (Dick Haymes again) and 'The More I See You' (yet more Dick Haymes). I know: you're wondering if Dick Haymes ever went to bed.

In the mid-50s, several American rock'n'rollers alighted on 'You'll Never Walk Alone' - Roy Hamilton, Conway Twitty (not him again!), Gene Vincent and Johnny Preston - while the UK rocker, Tony Sheridan, performed it in beat clubs in Hamburg. "No one ever gives that man enough credit," the Searchers drummer Chris Curtis once told me, "We heard him sing it and I'm sure Gerry did too."

In 1963 Gerry and The Pacemakers added the song to their stage act and George Martin enhanced their performance with strings. Their record was No 1 when Lee Harvey Oswald shot President Kennedy.

The disc-jockey at Anfield played the Top 10 before a match and the Kop Choir soon alighted on 'You'll Never Walk Alone', singing it themselves once it had passed from the Top 10. Gerry's version would start and then the Kop would take over. Gerry, who supported Everton FC, became a staunch Liverpool supporter. Well, wouldn't you?

YNWA became Liverpool FC's anthem and was then used by the city itself. In 1985 Gerry led a new, all-star recording for the Bradford City fire appeal and naturally it is associated with Hillsborough memorials. It is a song about grief and mourning without specifically saying so.

The fact that Gerry had to strain for the final notes added to its attraction and, partly for its sentiment and partly for its ending, it is beloved by football choirs around the world, being the Germans' official anthem for Euro 2004. It has been used in different formats by Belgium, French and Italian teams.

Carousel came from a stage play by Ferenc Molnàr and because it brought fame to the area, the fans of Borussia Dortmund picked up on the song. They were managed by Jurgen Klopp from 2008 to 2015. He then took on Liverpool and should he return to football, he might consider coaching Celtic, as they also sing 'You'll Never Walk Alone'.

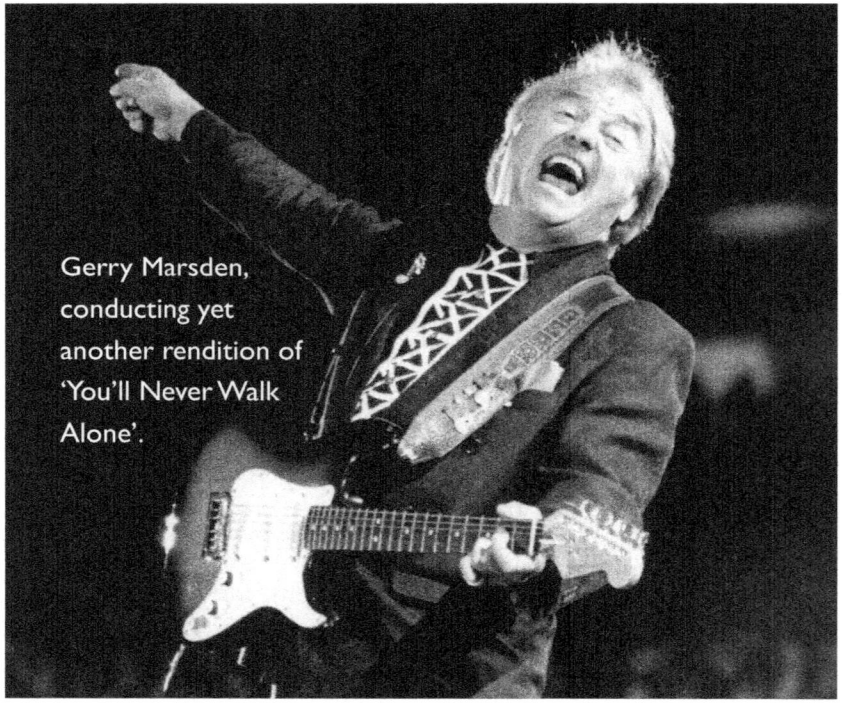

Gerry Marsden, conducting yet another rendition of 'You'll Never Walk Alone'.

CHAPTER 3

Day's In The Life: 1945-1954

The road linking Liverpool and Southport is called Liverpool Road as it passes through Waterloo and Crosby. I never appreciated how significant it has been for me until now.

There was *East View* (my grandmother's house), St Faith's Church (where the much-imitated Father Hassall ran through prayers like an express train), Merchant Taylors' School for Boys (where I studied A-levels), Crosby Preparatory School (my first school), Mr Milton's house (he visited the school as an outsider to administer corporal punishment), a girlfriend's house (Jill Stellingworth – hello, if you ever read this), Seafield Convent (where Cherie Blair went. Catholic girls were taught that you mustn't even shake hands with a boy before you were married), Bill Pattison the dentist (with suitcases full of tooth extractions. He would order his wife around: "Woman, answer the phone!"), and the turning into Kimberley Drive (my best friend Andrew Doble lived at No.9.)

Back on Liverpool Road, there was a newspaper shop on the corner of Endbutt Lane, run by a lady with bird-in-a-cage earrings and Myerscough's, an electrical store which sold 78rpm records, if chipped, for a shilling. One such purchase, and a particular favourite of mine, was 'Book of Love' by the Monotones.

Then we have the highlight of Liverpool Road: Merchant

Taylors' School for Girls, where I'd slow down my walking pace, and Lambda Records (Bernard Whitty's first shop, and after he moved, P&A Audio), the Regent Cinema (after the film, couples went round the back for a grope), the path to Coronation Park (after the film, the more athletic couples climbed over the railings), St Luke's Church (where my uncle was organist, and one night some gravestones were smashed), St Luke's Church Hall (aka the Jive Hive with its sprung dance floor), Satterthwaites Bakehouse (excellent meat pies until I met the piemaker who picked his nose), the Midland Bank (my first cheque book), and the Crown Buildings, which included a post office as silent as a bank, and Lambda Records, Bernard Whitty's second shop.

I can't remember any cafés, but my friends and I would never think of going for a coffee – we drank tea for free at home. Coffee though was a bit special.

At right angles to Liverpool Road and the Crown Buildings was Coronation Road and you could walk up to the front entrance of Coronation Park (I hope you're paying attention). As you went in, you were confronted with a huge glacial boulder and there were tennis courts and a lake for model boats. Mike Hart made a drunken date in Coronation Park, the subject of his song, 'Gliders and Parks'.

Opposite that front entrance was the unique *Newsmag* which sold comics and magazines for the previous month for tuppence each but with the first page always missing, due to the sale-or-return policy. The returns even included *Playboy*, but they charged ten pence for that.

There was also a shoe shop, A J Webster's, where the supremely polite proprietor in his unusual rimless glasses never took a blind bit of notice of what you said, and even if you were ten years old, you were still 'Mr Leigh'.

"Hello, Mr Leigh. How are you?"

"Fine, thank you. Busy day, Mr Webster?"

"Oh, I'm doing fine, thank you, Mr Leigh, and how's your mother?"

"Busy day today, Mr Webster?"

"Good, good, good, and are the rest of the family well too?"

He didn't listen to anything anyone said and these conversations show I had a streak of surrealism in me.

Of all the places I've described on Liverpool Road, the one that had the biggest early impact on me was undoubtedly Crosby Prep School. It was large enough to employ 10 teachers (no teaching assistants back then) and 120 pupils. I entered in September 1949. Like all the new boys, I was In Miss Banks' class on the right-hand side as you entered. She was a kindly mother hen who put us five-year-olds at ease.

The second year you went upstairs to Miss Fallows' class. She blinked and blinked and so we all imitated her. She had two short fingers on one hand and would drag you to the front of the class with her first and fourth fingers holding your ear. I can remember the nails from her short fingers sticking into me.

On that landing were the washrooms and the headmistress' office. The original owner and headmistress, Miss Milton, had retired but was only living a few doors away with her brother. Miss Clayton, who resembled a Beatrix Potter dormouse, did not administer corporal punishment and if any pupil had done wrong, she would ring Mr Milton who would come along, give three swishes of the cane and return home. The fact that an outsider should come into the school and administer corporal punishment sounds extraordinary, but it happened. I won't say I have the scars to prove it as I didn't get caned until I was at Rydal.

The main thing I learnt from the prep school was punctuality.

There were ribbon races in all the classrooms to see how you were doing and there was a separate ribbon race for punctuality. I didn't have much trouble as it wasn't far to walk and there was the L1 bus if it was raining.

Then there was Mrs Braithwaite, an elderly, good-natured soul, and the motherly Mrs Burkhill, who praised everybody.

Any new boy who turned left instead of right when he entered the building would get a shock. This was the top class, run by the formidable Mrs Kent. She was our Peggy Mount and she ruled her class with strict but fair discipline. Nobody crossed her. This makes me wonder why Miss Clayton would ring Mr Milton – couldn't she have asked Mrs Kent to administer the punishment and keep it in house? Maybe Mr Milton liked the exercise: it brought some variety to his morning walk.

For mid-morning breaks, a regulation small bottle of milk was provided by the Government – and continued until Mrs Thatcher stopped it.

In the basement, there was the dinner room which provided stew, stew and more stew, but sometimes mince for variety. There would be an apple or rice pudding with as much water as we could drink. After lunch, we would go onto the playground, usually for off-ground tig.

When I was about nine, Tony Wills lost his paintbox. When I opened my desk, there were two paintboxes. He accused me of stealing it and said, "I'll get you in the morning, Leigh." Tony always hung round with another boy Michael, so it would be two against one.

I hadn't taken his paintbox and I went home filled with dread. The next morning I decided not to go to school. I told Mum that I was ill. Dad said, "Ethel, he wasn't sick last night. There's nothing wrong with him."

I said, "Okay, I'm well but I won't be later on. This fucker thinks I stole his paintbox and you'll be visiting me in hospital." Of course, I didn't say those exact words, but I would have done if I'd had the vocabulary.

"And did you? If you stole his paintbox, own up to it."

"Of course not. I've got a fuckin' paintbox of my own." (Again, not my exact words.)

When I got to school, Tony Wills apologised to me. His mother worked at the school and she said that someone had been cleaning up and put his paintbox in the wrong desk. Tony Wills said I could read his *Beano*. All was well.

There isn't much more I can recall. I have no school reports, no paperwork, nothing. In my mind, it's like I was never there.

With one exception.

On Wednesday 6 February 1952 I had just passed my seventh birthday, and in the morning, I walked the mile to school. I said 'Good morning' to the milkman and his horse as I always did. Lessons were as normal but during lunch, the headmistress told us that the King had passed away and we were all to go home.

This was a bonkers decision. We were young boys and what if no one was at home? Why didn't the teachers take the opportunity to teach us about death and about the monarchy?

My mother was home but sad and tearful. After all, George VI had seen her through the war. My brother Chris was only three: he was told to be quiet which was difficult for him. We didn't have a TV and my mother was waiting for the *Liverpool Echo* to be delivered at half-past four. The headline said that the King had 'passed away' at Sandringham, and again, note the reluctance to use the word 'death'.

We returned to school the next day and assembled outside for morning exercises. We did star jumps for the new Queen, but we did those on the playground every morning anyway. I have no memories of the funeral. but we didn't have a television and following it on the wireless would have been hard for a seven-year-old. We did get a TV — black and white, 12-inch screen — for the Coronation. The marketing slogan, "Bush for perfect reproduction" would be in defiance of the trade description act today. We invited the neighbours to watch. Dad banged the top when the picture went fuzzy.

All schoolchildren were given a mug and a silver crown (a five-shilling piece): we had only ever seen half-crowns before. Winifred Atwell cheered up the nation with her 'Coronation Rag' and somebody created Coronation Chicken, which has stayed with us ever since.

As a postscript, an old boy of Crosby Prep made good in 1960. Christopher Morris (born 1940) had been born in Ormskirk, moved to Crosby and then to Birkenhead. He studied at Birkenhead High School and secured a place at Aberystwyth University. However, he made a trip to London and sang at the 2i's coffee bar. Larry Parnes liked what he heard and renamed him Lance Fortune. He had a Top 10 hit in 1960 with 'Be Mine', which was arranged by John Barry. He performed on UK package tours but his subsequent singles were only moderate sellers and he became part of a rock'n'roll entertainment band, the Stagger Lees, which often performed at holiday camps. When I met him in the early 80s, he had a mobile fruit and veg van in Barnsley. He told me that his dad had been annoyed with him as he should have stayed at Aberystwyth.

Around 1970 when I was 25, I met Miss Clayton again, who told me that Crosby Prep was closing and the building would become part of Merchant Taylors. She said, "I was always trying to get you to dress neatly but your brother was the problem. He was always doing something naughty. He once told me he had lost his dinner money," she wagged her finger, "but I knew he had spent it in one of the sweet shops in South Road."

Miss Clayton and I said our goodbyes and she added, "It's nice to see you again, Spencer, but do you still like fighting?"

CHAPTER 4

A Four-legged Friend

Jack Brooks, actually Jack Bruches, was born into a Russian family in Liverpool in 1910. As a young man, he wanted to work in Hollywood and write songs and somehow he got there and was nominated for Oscars with 'Ole Buttermilk Sky', 'Am I in Love?' (sung by Bob Hope and Jane Russell in *Son of Paleface*) and Dean Martin's calling-card, 'That's Amore'. Jack wrote Roy Rogers' 'Four-Legged Friend', also in *Son of Paleface*: it sounds absurd to say that a Scouser wrote that song, but it's true.

Every schoolboy in Britain got to know 'Four-Legged Friend' as *The Roy Rogers Show* was shown on TV and Roy was also a Saturday morning hero at children's matinees.

In 1954 the singing cowboy undertook a UK tour with his wife and cowgirl Dale Evans and his 20-year-old Palomino, Trigger. Ticket sales showed that clip clop was as popular as hip hop. When they arrived in Liverpool for a week's variety, Roy and Dale had flu and were confined to bed in the Adelphi: a photoshoot showed Trigger signing the hotel register with a pencil between his teeth and then giving the couple flowers. The press said Trigger stayed at the Adelphi, which was untrue though not beyond the bounds of possibility. Trigger was stabled with the police horses in Smithdown Road.

The Monday and Tuesday performances were cancelled,

but all was well on Wednesday when Roy announced that there would be three performances a day so that children would not be disappointed. For his first visit to the Empire, Roy Rogers rode Trigger down Lime Street while 4,000 children cheered. Gosh, it was exciting! Roy asked Trigger what two plus two was and Trigger raised a hoof and hit the ground four times. Roy asked Trigger to pray and the horse knelt on its front feet and put its head down. Okay, okay, we were easily satisfied back then.

Roy told the kids that it wasn't cissy to go to church and when the entourage reached London, they joined forces with Rev. Billy Graham.

Roy Rogers' tour was the first time that there had been mass marketing of memorabilia in the UK. There were the Roy Rogers Stetson and the Roy Rogers cap-gun and holster, not to mention the money box, the lunch box and the punch-out book (sadly, not as exciting as it sounds). Quaker Oats had a Roy Rogers competition. His cap guns came with a warning that you must never shoot to kill: all his westerns were wholesome. Roy Rogers never killed anyone. Well, he did in 1975 in *Mackintosh and C J.* but by then he wanted to break the mould.

On the whole, British fans were not attracted to cheap tat. In the mid-50s, Colonel Parker asked Hank Saperstein to visit Britain with a view to licensing Elvis products. He set himself up in a London hotel, but nobody made him an offer he couldn't refuse.

Brian Epstein at 19 would have been too old for a Roy Rogers gun and holster. However, if he had appreciated what Rogers was doing, he wouldn't have made his major blunder. The NEMS' contract with the American manufacturers for Beatle memorabilia was way too generous, but this is understandable because the merch around celebrities in Britain had been negligible by comparison with America. If only Brian had gone to see Roy Rogers...

Years later I met my wife Anne who was, and still is, very much into horses. Much to her amusement, I regarded palominos as a classic breed for competitions, but it was only because I had seen Trigger racing across the plains with Roy Rogers.

CHAPTER 5

Days In The Life: 1955-1958

My father and my uncles Harold and George had been pupils at Rydal, a public school in Colwyn Bay, North Wales. I doubt that Dad had enjoyed it all that much but for some reason, he thought his eldest child (me!) should go there. I was 10 years old, although he had only gone to Rydal when he was 13. The fees were high, so it was a sacrifice, and he was determined. When my dad wanted to do something, he couldn't be dissuaded. I don't know what my mother thought about all this, but Chris was relieved that Dad only intended to send me.

Nevertheless, my brother thought I was the privileged one in receiving this boarding-school education but really, I was the unlucky one, Chris had a much more enjoyable time and probably a better education at Bickerton House in Southport.

There was an entrance examination and I did this instead of the Eleven-plus. My father took me to a luxurious hotel, the Queen's, opposite Chester Station, for the exam. There were 20 of us and the questions were of the variety "What is next in this series?" Nothing very strenuous. I was bright enough but not bright enough to make a mess of them. Starting in September 1955, I was a Rydalian.

My mother took me to the school outfitters' Watson Prickard - known to schoolboys as Watson Hardprick - in North John

Street, Liverpool for my blazer, tie and grey short trousers as well as a coffin-sized trunk. My name was stitched into my clothing. Very few personal possessions were allowed: probably just as well in case they got stolen.

At the beginning of term, I was put on the train with several other boys heading for Rydal from Liverpool Lime Street. There was a coach reserved for us and there was a master to ensure things didn't get out of hand. The train pulled into Chester and our carriage was coupled to another train which took us to Colwyn Bay.

Getting off at Colwyn Bay, we were told to walk crocodile-style across town and up to the top of Pwllycrochan Avenue to reach Rydal Preparatory School, or Colditz as we preferred to call it.

The prep school was in one huge building with a sports wing and woods at the back. The headmaster was Kenneth Compton-Lewis and his wife had horses and a stable. If you had done something wrong (and even if you hadn't), you might be sent to the paddock to muck out the stables.

I was in Trojan House (they all had historical names and it was better than being a Barbarian) and our housemaster was Mr Furness, known as 'the blazing fiery Furness', a man who knew how to wield a cane. He hit one boy, Blackie, so hard that it snapped. Blackie pulled his short trousers down and showed us, with some pride, his stripes.

Mr Furness was a terrible history teacher. He gave the same lessons year in year out and he spouted out facts and dates in a monotone at remarkable speed. If anyone deserved the cane, it was him. These were colourless, lifeless lessons and one day when he told a joke, I thought I was the only one who'd noticed. "I'll give him a bit of support," I thought and started laughing, but sometimes you can't stop. It ended in the inevitable: "Leigh, Room 101 straight after supper." With shades of *1984,* the beatings took place in Room 101.

The beatings were usually done by Mr Furness as he enjoyed wielding the cane. Even the headmaster sent boys to Room 101 if they hadn't otherwise been given work in the stables. Beatings were administered before you went to bed and you went to Room 101 in your pyjamas and dressing-gown.

Once there, Mr Furness would say, "Leigh, take off your dressing-gown and your pyjama bottoms." This sounds excessive but he wanted to check that I hadn't put soap on my buttocks to take away the sting. Inspection over, and satisfied that he was seeing pure bottom, I could put my pyjamas back on and bend over. The chair was positioned so that he could take a run to hit you all the harder. Mercifully, I never got more than three of his stand-up swipes.

Your dormitory knew when you were being caned and they might follow behind so that they could listen at the door. This could be dangerous. Mr Furness might sense that there was somebody at the door. He would administer one hit and then rush to the door and fling it open, and a couple of kids might fall in. "Blackie, Jones, come inside and hold your hands out." They received the cane across their hands for that.

Sometimes Mr Furness might give you a choice. "You can either have the cane in Room 101 or the slipper in the dormitory." The slipper sounded better but it was a hard slipper and your mates might see you cry.

In fact, there was a lot of crying at the preparatory school as the very young boys didn't know what was going on and hated it.

Boys sometimes ran away from Junior School – especially new boys, known as natty new bugs. They never got far as Mr

Lewis (John Lewis, in fact) would be sent out on his motorbike to find them. He was very successful but instead of addressing the boy's problems, it would be a caning offence, which would make them feel even worse.

I knew of fellow pupils who went to the school sanatorium to have ointment for their stripes but I never heard of any pupil who was treated for mental health issues. If someone had complained of stress or being bullied, they were told to get over it.

The preparatory school had an impressive entrance hall with a fine staircase going to the first floor but out of bounds to pupils. As a little act of rebellion, I used to run up the stairs when no one was looking. Once I met the geography teacher Ian Newton at the top. "Where are you going, Leigh? These stairs are out of bounds to the likes of you." To which I replied, "Well, sir, my dad pays good money to send me here and I don't see why I can't use them." "You smug little git!" said Ian Newton and 'wallop!' he smashed me across the face. That hurt and I can still feel it now. To be fair to these teachers, I think that some of them were deeply troubled individuals, but they should have been managing whelk stalls on Southend Pier rather than young boys at public school.

Ian Newton, a good 18-stoner, wouldn't tolerate misbehaviour, but he had a unique way of dealing with it. He would say, "Leigh, will you hit Seddon for me?" I hit Seddon. "No, no, not hard enough. Hit him again and if you don't do it hard enough, I'll hit you." Seddon was mad when I hit him harder as I discovered when class was over. What an appalling way to run an educational system.

My parents would visit me at half-term and usually stayed at the Colwyn Bay Hotel. Once, they couldn't get in and they stayed at another hotel which only had a small screen in the TV lounge. The seats were taken and they watched TV by looking in the mirror.

I remember Dad walking up to Rydal one Sunday afternoon when everyone was on the playing field, mostly playing little games of cricket. He offered to join in and hit the first ball for 6, which made me very proud. Unfortunately, it landed in Davvy Duce's garden – he was the art teacher – and as he could hardly discipline my father, he gave me two detention marks. I was being punished for not being in control of my dad.

One lonely boy was distraught when his parents visited him. He wanted to return home and to lighten his mood, his parents took him to WH Smith and bought him the new comic annuals. He came back to his dormitory with ten annuals. He hoped this would make things better, but everybody grabbed the annuals and continued to ignore him.

Sometimes, I would wake up in the middle of the night and hear somebody crying and crying. One boy's continual crying incensed a dorm leader and he said, "Get onto the parapet" and the poor lad had to climb out of the window and stay there until 7am so that the dorm leader could get some sleep. This was both dangerous and cold. There was a door in one dormitory which led into the rafters. That dorm leader knew where the key was and some boys were punished by sitting on the rafters all night.

One dorm leader would masturbate into a jam-jar and intending to fill a jar each term. I don't know what he did with the contents.

Some lads did enjoy Rydal Preparatory School. One came from a broken home and both his parents had new partners. Neither his mum nor his dad wanted him around so what was the solution? Send him to Rydal. Astonishingly, there were a couple of lads whose parents lived abroad and didn't want them to fly over for Christmas – they stayed at the damn place during the holidays.

The dormitories were cold and the food was bog-standard and they served the lumpiest rice pudding imaginable. Those who had the misfortune to sit on Davvy Duce's table had a half-hour tirade about eating habits. "Smith, you're not eating your cabbage. Do you have a doctor's note to say you can't eat cabbage?" "No, sir." "Thought so, get it down you – all of it." I'm sure some lads were eating stuff they were allergic to, but there were no exceptions for allergies back then.

I said to Mr Duce one lunchtime, "Excuse me sir, but you are not eating your sprouts. Have you got a doctor's note?" (Immensely foolish of me, I know.) "As a matter of fact I have, Leigh," he lied, "but I do not tolerate insolence. Leave your food, it will be served up at breakfast and go to the detention room. Pick up *Tom Brown's Schooldays* and write it out." I went to the detention room and he didn't come and relieve me for a couple of hours.

Tea was at 5pm and didn't consist of very much. If possible, the school would find ways to make it even less. We had to assemble at the tables in silence, ready for grace, and nothing could be said until then. If there was any noise, Mr Furness or whoever, but Mr Furness was very good at it, would say in a loud voice, "THERE WILL BE NO JAM TODAY" and the serving staff would come to the tables and remove the jam.

This was also a time to hand out important messages and I can remember the duty master saying, "Leigh, there's a telegram for you." As he handed it to me, he said, "Your grandmother's died. Go back to your seat, no blubbing." He added, "Have you got another grandmother, Leigh?" "Yes, sir". "Well, be positive and think of her."

Tea was also the time for birthday parties, such as they were. Parents were given strict notes. There must be no more than 12 guests (the size of a table) and parents could send a birthday cake (not over four pounds in weight), 12 small cakes, one pound of biscuits, two jellies, two tins of fruit and one tin of condensed milk. Not my idea of a party.

The weekly bath night was supervised by Mrs Williams, known to us as Mrs Wom. There was a large room with four baths and we would line-up for them. Mrs Williams would inspect our ears and our hair and seemed oblivious to the fact that we had nothing on. Any high jinks were banned and we had to be silent. We did not have hairdryers and so you would ask another boy to help you dry your hair. You pull down on the towel and then he at the back would do the same and the towel would go back and forth for a couple of minutes.

The showers after sport were usually presided over by Davvy Duce (God, I hated this man). He didn't like laughter in the shower room and if he disciplined you, he would write on your bare chest with his Flomaster. If you got two bad marks, that would be 2D. "It will wash off," he said, "This is not a concentration camp." But why did he do it in the first place?

My dad and his brothers went to Rydal and I can't believe it was any different for them. Dad rarely laughed at TV comedy with one exception: Jimmy Edwards as a brutish headmaster in *Whacko!* which had the catchphrase, "Bend over, Wendover." That suggests that he knew exactly what Rydal was like, so why did he send me there?

When I was 12 or 13 and preparing for the senior school, which was at the bottom of Pwllycrochan Avenue, an extraordinary thing happened. On Sunday morning there would be a service in the chapel, followed by a letter-writing period where you wrote home - the letters could be censored but we had more sense than to express our true feelings. They had to be approved before posting, but there wasn't much discipline in the letter-writing period itself and so you could skive off.

Johnny, a rambunctious but supremely organised 13-year-old, got something going with a couple of the non-teaching staff (or 'skivvies' as they were insultingly called). In the Sunday half hour before lunch, he drew up a rota as to who could enter one of their bedrooms. Johnny would be at the bottom of the stairs keeping guard while another skivvy would be at the top. When the coast was clear, the nominated boy would go up to her room.

I'd been waiting a few weeks, hoping my turn would come, so it was probably February 1958 and I would be just 13. Johnny said, "It's your turn on Sunday." "Whoopee!", I thought and up I went. I can remember going through the bedroom door and seeing a half-naked body, but try as I may, I have no idea what happened next, if anything. There is nothing else in my life where my mind has blanked out.

I can't believe that the masters (or at least some of them) didn't know what was going on. Maybe they thought it was all part of 'growing up'. I don't know – these were very different times.

Our class moved over to the main school and presumably another lad took over Johnny's administration, and I still can't remember what happened next in that bedroom. Maybe nothing at all, maybe I ran out, but whatever happened I wanted to forget it. That was 1958 and it still lingers in my mind in 2024.

CHAPTER 6

Got a Lot of Livin' To Do

Rydal Preparatory School and then Rydal School itself were grim but one thing gave me comfort and consolation. Rock'n'roll.

I love rock'n'roll, always have, but I'm sure I loved rock'n'roll even more when I was younger for knowing that my elders hated it, really hated it. My father thought it was an abomination and for some unknown reason, particularly loathed the Everly Brothers with their high harmonies: he called them the Barmy Bats. When he said that Duane Eddy was too lazy even to write some words, I retorted that Stravinsky only wrote instrumentals: he said, "You cheeky little sod" and cuffed me.

Dad never changed his mind about rock'n'roll and indeed, I can't recall anyone over 30 who thought that the new music was good. One school chum told his house master, Mr Pilling, that he wanted to be a rock'n'roll singer and was told, "You've already got too many qualifications. You can read and write." Today, parents go out of their way to share the musical tastes of their children.

In early 1956 Elvis Presley's first RCA single, 'Heartbreak Hotel', was a game-changer. It was sent to HMV's label manager, 43-year-old Wally Ridley, in Britain, for immediate release. He told me, "RCA Victor sent me everything they released in America and I had to decide what should be released here on HMV. Steve Sholes said, 'I'm sending you six sides. You won't understand a word but do yourself a favour and release two of them because this man is gonna be very big indeed.' I released it and HMV got the worst reviews it had ever had. Radio Luxembourg wouldn't play it and nor would the BBC. Jack Payne wrote half a page for the *Daily Express* saying, 'How dare they release such rubbish'. The chiefs wanted to sack me."

In the press, the music was being treated as if it came from outer space, which had been the title of a popular science fiction film. Steve Race wrote in *Melody Maker*: "I fear for this country. It ought to have the good taste to reject music so decadent. It is not pleasant to watch a whole generation of British teenagers associate themselves with the cheapest music even America has yet produced."

Author Ray Connolly was raised in Ormskirk: "I was obsessed with rock'n'roll from the age of 15 when I first heard Elvis. It was like the scales had fallen from my eyes and I thought, 'This is my life.' It was assumed that anyone who liked rock'n'roll was semi-moronic. When I went to university, students didn't like pop music. It wasn't intellectual enough and they liked trad jazz, which I've always hated."

Folk singer Martin Carthy saw it as the start of a social revolution. "I was 14 or 15 when rock'n'roll came along, the sort of age where something is either going to leave you stone cold or knock you over – and it knocked me over. When I look back on Bill Haley, Lonnie Donegan, Elvis Presley and Gene Vincent, I can see that rock'n'roll and skiffle represented something very important – the idea that ordinary people could make music. For the first time, you didn't have to be a trained musician to make music."

It seems that nearly everybody heard it by chance. George Harrison told BBC Radio 2, "I was riding along on my bicycle and heard 'Heartbreak Hotel' coming out of somebody's house. What a sound, what a record; it changed the course of my life."

The BBC included minuscule portions of rock'n'roll in its schedules, but EMI ensured that the record was among the selections in jukeboxes in coffee bars and slot machine arcades. It could be heard on evening shows from Radio Luxembourg. Now you can hear any song you want instantly but back then, youngsters depended on luck. However, you could go into a record shop and ask to hear a record in a booth.

Paul McCartney told *Q* magazine: "I'd seen an ad for 'Heartbreak Hotel' in the *NME* and I had to go into a record shop and listen to it through headphones in one of the booths. It was a magical moment, the beginning of an era."

But you couldn't go into a listening booth if, like me, you were only 11 years old.

I saw the title 'Heartbreak Hotel' by Elvis Presley accompanied by an exciting cover picture of him in full flow in the *NME*. The title, the name and the look promised so much, and I sensed that this could be a magic kingdom, but I hadn't heard it. Then one day I had a cold and was in bed. I switched on the radio for *Housewives' Choice*, a dreary BBC programme for the good housewives of the UK which shunned rock'n'roll and preferred David Whitfield and Ronnie Hilton – and it was followed by a religious pep talk, *Five to Ten*. An irate vicar denounced the vilest, most repulsive, most appalling record he had ever heard. The singer would rot in hell and his name was Elvis Presley. I'm exaggerating but that's what he wanted to say. He played 30 seconds of 'Heartbreak Hotel' which was enough to change my whole life. And here's the important point – we knew that this was not a silly craze or teenage fad. Elvis would remain with us for the rest of our lives. The record healed the sick as I left my bed and went to a store and bought it (5/7d or 28p, should you be interested).

Pandora's box had been opened. The summer of 1956 was brilliant. EMI had first option on product from the US Capitol label and along came a record even more outrageous than 'Heartbreak Hotel', Gene Vincent and the Blue Caps with 'Be-Bop-A-Lula'. Could a girl really be called Be-Bop-A-Lula and how could she wear 'red blue jeans'? I'd never met a girl with 'flying feet'.

It wasn't until November 1956 that anything by Little Richard was released in the UK. His Specialty singles were leased to Decca and released on their London-American label. The first was the frenzied 'Rip It Up' but his thunder was stolen by Bill Haley and his Comets who took it into the Top 10. Then London-American combined Richard's first US hits on the same single, 'Long Tall Sally' and 'Tutti Frutti', which made Number 3 early in 1957. As my father used to say, "The lunatics have taken over the asylum." He wasn't right but he did have a point.

Here's the Methodist minister, Lord Soper, watching the first BBC first TV pop show to feature rock'n'roll: "I'm perplexed by *6.5 Special*. I can't understand how intelligent people can derive any sort of satisfaction from something which is emotionally embarrassing and intellectually ridiculous."

The film, *Rock Around the Clock* seems quaint today but rock'n'roll was a revolutionary force and it set the wheels in motion for Little Richard (who was in the follow-up *Don't Knock the Rock* and also *The Girl Can't Help It*) and Elvis Presley. Taking their cue from Edward VII's reign, some youths with sideburns dressed in long, velvet-collared jackets, combined with drainpipe trousers, white socks and crepe soles. They became known as

Teddy boys and they were often fighting or ripping up cinema seats. Mum said that I couldn't go to see Elvis Presley in *Loving You* on my own as I might get caught in a riot, so she took me to it. She spent every moment wondering if some Ted was about to knife her in the back.

Zealous cinema managers stopped dancing in the aisles and, in Liverpool, hundreds of exuberant fans were chased from the ABC in Lime Street to the Pier Head. Lord Boothby said on the BBC's *Any Questions*, "What worries me is that a fourth-rate film with fifth-rate music can pierce the shell of civilisation. The sooner this ridiculous film is banned the better."

Lord Boothby also said that "one of the purposes of us old fogies is to stop young people being silly". You can rely on a Lord to say something silly, especially one who knew about adult delinquency through his mates, the Krays.

In 1958 Jack Good created ITV's fast-moving *Oh Boy!* which was far slicker than its American counterparts but had to make do with British artists. Jack Good discovered Cliff Richard, who admitted, "I was a carbon copy of Elvis. All I had was a leg, a guitar and a lip. Jack didn't like that and he didn't want me to be too much like Elvis. He made me cut off my sideburns. He liked me to be moody but that wasn't because he wanted me to copy Elvis. He didn't think I looked as good when I smiled. However, I don't think that I ever did look moody. Awkward perhaps, but not moody."

CHAPTER 7

Days In The Life: 1958-1961

In September 1958 I again took the train to Colwyn Bay but this time I was 13 and old enough for the main school. I was allocated to Hathaway House on Lansdowne Road, a large, detached house with an elegant black and white timbered front. It was 300 yards from the main school buildings and opposite one of the playing fields, which was for cricket and rugby.

The housemaster was Mr Pilling who lived with his wife and two children in one side of the house. Forty boys were housed there, all aged between 13 and 18 and once a week, the best-behaved would be invited to the Pillings' living room to watch a programme, often *The Army Game* or, if we were lucky, *Sunday Night at the London Palladium*. *The Army Game* filled us with dread as conscription had yet to be abolished. All this must have been disruptive for the Pilling family's life.

Mr Pilling told us to be wary of his children's toys as we might trip over them. "Don't worry if you break them," he said, "I tread on them periodically." His default was sarcasm and he made history interesting with such *bon mots* as "Pitt is to Addington as London is to Paddington" although these lines would hardly curry favour in O-levels.

On my first day Mr Pilling had a message for me: "When you go to the main building, The Master wants to see you." The

Master was a retired teacher Donald Boumphrey whose whole life revolved around cricket and Rydal and who still lived on the premises. In his room was a bookcase full of *Wisden* annuals. He said, "Leigh, I knew your father, a right-hand batsman. Did he play after he left Rydal?" I said proudly, "Yes, sir, he played for Waterloo and once got 51 against the Maghull Home for Epileptics." "He should have done more," said The Master, "but I suppose the war stopped that." I could borrow *Wisden* anytime I wanted and I prepared statistical surveys for him, little knowing that this would hold me in good stead in later years.

In a similar way, I would play around with Top 30 statistics and I devised my own makeshift standard deviations before I knew what they were.

The Master himself had played one first class match – it was for Wales against the West Indies and he scored 10 runs but was out twice. He was far friendlier and more worldly-wise than the regular teachers but at the time I just thought, "If ever I do something wrong, here is someone who will speak in my favour."

The greatest cricketer that Wales had produced was the England and Glamorgan all-rounder, Wilf Wooller, an Old Rydalian, and he talked to the school on his annual visit. He was the commentator when Gary Sobers hit six sixes in an over. As well as occasional county cricketers, we had a visit from the supremely unfunny Mike and Bernie Winters – even unfunnier in the flesh, I can assure you – a comedy act with two straight men. I was to finish my schooling at Merchant Taylors, which we will come to, and their motivational talks were of a far higher standard – ornithology with Peter Scott; overcoming tragedy with Douglas Bader, who flew fighter planes even though he had lost his legs; and writing musical theatre with the playwright and lyricist Sir Alan Herbert, known for *The Water Gypsies*. My mother was most impressed: she used to sing his song, 'When I'm Washing Up' when she was washing up.

There were teaching brothers who connected the Rydal schools. Ebenezer Bradford – a name straight out of Dickens – taught English at the junior school. A pleasant, avuncular man, he instilled in me a love of reading although it was there anyway. Much thinner and always worried, Joe Bradford taught mathematics at the senior school. He was a good teacher but I didn't know him for long. Every morning he would take his wife a cup of tea. One day he collapsed on the stairs and died. Some other teacher then took our maths class in his place but we were better at maths than he was. The death of Joe Bradford was regrettable. Apart from the teachers I've namechecked, the rest were distinctly below par.

I couldn't tell you much about Sidney Fisher, who taught physics, as we hardly saw him. He was a local councillor and was Mayor of Colwyn Bay. He would come into class and say "Read the chapter starting on page 44. Don't make a noise" and scoot off for council business. It was good for the Head to have an insider on the council, but our fees were meant to cover a decent education. I wish I'd had more self-motivation and studied on my own but these things seem easier with hindsight.

Any teacher with a physical characteristic was ripe for satire. The Latin teacher was Big Bum Lowry and we had all sorts of songs for him. *("I sing this song as I mooch along, My name is Big Bum Lowry, I have two children, tall and thin, Because I feed them on Gordon's Gin.")* He could open a textbook at precisely the right page, or at least he pretended he was on the right page, and took it from there.

Muff Cooper taught gym and the other teachers didn't regard him as one of the team. Far better to know Latin than how to climb a rope. Muff would watch the boys climbing the ropes. "Baxter, you're wearing underpants under your shorts, take them off." In 1960 Cooper was desperate to go to the Olympic Games in Rome so he wanted a party of Rydal schoolboys he could supervise to pay his way. The only time he was nice to me was when he said, "Leigh, do you think your dad could send you to Rome? Tell him you want to see the Olympics." I didn't as a week in Rome with Muff Cooper was the last thing I wanted.

A few years after I left a pupil, Chris Hovey, fell off the rings in the gym and dislocated his neck. He would be in a wheelchair for the rest of his life. His parents sued the Governors and were awarded £70,000, a very large payment for the time.

The elderly Josh Howard had a whining voice and always seemed petrified. His teaching skills had left him, and the lessons consisted of him presiding over a class while we read textbooks. He was terrorised by a thuggish lad, Jim Mellor, who had a hand grenade – I presume it was defused but Jim maintained it wasn't. As Mr Howard was supervising the class, this hand grenade rolled to the front and landed in front of him. I'm surprised that I remember Mellor's first name as nobody ever used it: he was always 'Mellor'.

The preparatory school had been claustrophobic. Admittedly it had its own woods, embankments and playing fields, but we rarely went into town. When I was at the main school, we had more freedom. We could go into town, which meant visits to WHSmith and record shops for me. Other destinations included a walk along the prom to Rhos-on-Sea and trips to the local Odeon cinema. The school runs might be through the paths in Pwllycrochan Woods. I would never say I was happy at Rydal but at least I could explore a bit.

Take a typical Sunday. Rydal was a Methodist school and I

had been confirmed into the Church of England at St Paul's in Colwyn Bay. Because it meant leaving school premises, I would go to Holy Communion at St Paul's at 8am on Sunday morning: this was a Pyrrhic victory as everybody else was sensibly asleep in bed.

I'd return for breakfast and go to the morning service in the chapel where Rev Kenneth Underwood preached. He had a connection with a mission in Lakshittipet, India, known to us all as 'the luxury shit pit'. We would pray for the people of the town and trust that they would find God.

As in the junior school, this was followed by a letter-writing period before Sunday lunch. I wrote home and also to Granny and Grandpa Leigh as every reply from them included a ten-shilling note. Grandpa would never say "Here's a ten-shilling note": he would say, "Here's a picture of the Queen."

After lunch, I'd walk a couple of miles to Rhos Point with friends along the Prom: probably hoping to see some girls from the neighbouring Penrhos School, which was at Rhos-on-Sea. We could talk to them on Sundays in full view on the Prom. Otherwise, we would be gated for a week and if we were caught talking to a town girl at any time, it was three weeks.

We would walk to the Rhos Point Café and might have fish and chips, luxury items after school fare. We got fed up with baked beans at school and we counted the number of beans on our plates. When I was in the lead with 358, I put the number on the school noticeboard with no explanation, and then these mysterious numbers started appearing, gradually getting higher, and the masters wondered what it meant. Johnny won with 663. He knew how to talk to dinner ladies.

No wonder the tuck shop did good business. Looking back, I'm surprised that it was allowed but it was good for additional profits. School food was functional and tasteless and we longed for a Mars Bar, a Bounty or a Coca-Cola. Our relatives gave us spending money and most of it went on tuck. I have poor teeth and I blame Rydal. I should have known better but the eating came out of frustration.

I've just read a report about Domino's pizzas in *The Sunday Times*. Seems that Domino's supply 100 pizzas every Sunday to Stowe School. We had no such luxury, but doesn't it all suggest that boarding school food hasn't improved all that much?

My parents stayed at the Colwyn Bay Hotel when they came to see me. The owners allowed me to visit the television lounge on Saturdays at 6pm to see the ITV show *Oh Boy!* which was then replaced by *Boy Meets Girls*. There was rarely anybody there and it was my own, personal weekly treat. The producer Jack Good crammed 20 songs into the half-hour *Oh Boy!*, which established Cliff Richard, Billy Fury, Marty Wilde and the Vernons Girls. I raved about the shows with the American guests, Brenda Lee and Conway Twitty. (There he is again). Sometimes I'd get a full hour of music as the BBC had a rival show *Drumbeat* with Adam Faith, Vince Eager and Roy Young. All this was heaven to me. I was meant to be back on school premises by that time and could be punished, but it was worth the risk and I never got caught.

When my parents came up in 1960, my father took me to the film version of *Sons and Lovers*, the D H Lawrence novel. He thought my head was too full of silly rock'n'roll. This was exactly when the publication of D H Lawrence's *Lady Chatterley's Lover* was controversial, so I'm not sure of Dad's thinking here. He certainly thought *Lady C* was an abomination.

There were newspapers in the school library, but they would be redacted with a black ink roller over notorious stories such as Liberace's trial for defamation and whether *Lady C* was pornographic. The Headmaster said that the title of this book must not even be mentioned. When Penguin won the case and the book could be published, I went to Colwyn Bay Library to reserve it. The librarian, surely breaking rules of privacy, rang up the Head to say that a boy in a Rydal blazer had come in and reserved "that book". I was lucky to escape the cane.

A year later my mother showed me a page in her library book. It was a new novel by J B Priestley. She pointed at a sentence and said, "Is that the word?" I said, "I'm afraid it is." She was disgusted by the "fuck" Priestley had written but all authors were band wagoning after that verdict. I was surprised she had asked me but if she had asked Dad, he would have said, "Take that filth back immediately" and she would never have finished the story.

My dad was truly horrified in 1961 when they came up for speech day and I was getting the maths prize. Just before the ceremony, I went to the barber with a photograph of Adam Faith and asked for his haircut. I went up to collect my prize from Leonard Cheshire VC and made a few Adam Faith gestures on the way down which made everybody laugh. Except my dad. I had let the side down and quite remarkably for a father in 1961, he told me to grow my hair.

When it comes to sport, I recall standing on the touchline in the rain, under orders to chant "R-Y-D-A-L" when I didn't give a toss as to who won the game. I hated rugby and the skill was in trying to avoid the scrum as everybody was grabbing everybody else's balls once you got into that huddle.

I did play a bit of cricket and was a slow bowler rather than a spin bowler, but I did once take four wickets for eight runs. Once when a master was called away, I found myself the umpire and I loved sticking up my finger when someone was out. I did give someone out LBW, largely I suspect because I wanted to stick my finger up and I didn't like the batter anyway. The hapless batsman snarled, "I'll get you, Leigh!"

I offered to be one of the school scorers as that meant I'd get a few trips to other schools. I went scoring at Shrewsbury School and I ended up feeling even sorrier for their schoolboys. Not only did their toilets not have locks – they didn't have doors! There had been some jiggery-pokery so doors had been removed. When I went into the pavilion for a sandwich after the first innings, a teacher said, "Put that sandwich back. They're for the teams. You're only the scorer."

Looking back in Rydal's scorebook, I found a game against Ruthin School around 1951 where R W Barber scored 136 out of Ruthin's 160. He later played for England. When I told Donald Boumphrey, he re-lived every moment.

The only person to be excused sport was Pickersgill, who had a heart condition. The school activities would be put on the noticeboard and there would be lists of who would be playing what, but at the bottom of the team sheet, it might say, "To go for a walk - Pickersgill".

Oddly enough, poor Pickersgill was put into Trearddur House, a dormitory at the top of Pwllycrochan Avenue. He died in 1961 and the Headmaster told us what a courageous boy he was: he wanted to be in Trearddur House although the walk was steep. It sounds like the school was trying to absolve itself from any responsibility for his death.

I was the only boy who had a black tie ready for these occasions. On 3 February 1959, we woke up to the news that Buddy Holly had died in a plane crash. I hadn't got a black tie and I sneaked out in the morning break and bought one. I got it out when Mr Bradford died: I wore it when Pickersgill died. Maybe it was in my blood because my grandfather was a funeral director.

I did okay in mock O-levels in March 1961, although I was disappointed not to get 100% in Maths. I celebrated by going to see an Elvis film, but rock'n'roll films were on Rydal's banned list and I was gated for a week and had to write 500 lines.

The O-levels themselves went OK. The French orals were spread over a couple of days. I was on the second day and by then I knew the questions – "When did you last clean your shoes?", "When did you last have a bath?" I had the answers off pat and the examiner realised this and threw in a killer question, "When did you last go to the cinema?" It had been a few days before and I had been to see a controversial X film – very much out of bounds - *Victim* with Dirk Bogarde. I said *La Victime* and I hadn't expected her to ask me what it was about. It was difficult especially as I didn't know the French for blackmail, let alone homosexual. I think the examiner enjoyed seeing me squirm and probably gave me bonus points for *noir poste*.

The end of term was 27 July 1961, the day I left Rydal for good. T W Leigh and Co was a family business and Uncle George's son Randle had qualified as an accountant. George and Harold wanted him in the company and callously voted out my dad. He was unqualified but had been doing the company's books efficiently. It was heartless and my school fees were high on the agenda when it came to cutting expenses.

It turned out to be pointless as George and Randle could not work together as father and son. They could have offered Dad his job back but there were too many wounded feelings.

I had mixed feelings. I felt sorry for my dad but I was relieved that my ordeal was over. Because I had been at Rydal, I was given a shoo-in for Merchant Taylors' School in Crosby.

Once I left Rydal, that was it. I was going to carve a new life. My mother used to go Bath once a year to see an old schoolteacher,

Emily Fordham, but I would never do that. Mum used to write to her too which could lead to frenzied activity as Miss Fordham replied to every letter by return.

I was friendly with a few Rydalians who lived near me, Peter Sutch, Bob Hurd, Ian Hall (known as Henry) and I would see them from time to time. Bob Hurd was not academically minded but he tried hard. He only got one O-level but the Headmaster in front of the whole school said, "Some of you can get eight or nine O-levels without much effort, but Hurd has worked hard for his one O-level. This is much more impressive than somebody who has got 10 O-levels without any effort, so well done, Hurd." The Head was telling those in lower classes to apply themselves, but could anything have been more humiliating?

Peter Sutch used to spell out his name 's ,u, T, c, h'. His dad Joe was a local builder in Crosby and Peter would join his company. Joe said that a builder should stand for the Council as that is where you hear about building plans, and you can spot your opportunities. Peter was to become the youngest councillor on Merseyside.

If there was any boy I looked up to it would be Nigel McCulloch. His father was killed in the war and he lived with his mother, Audrey, who was in a wheelchair and was a friend of my mother. Nigel went to Liverpool College so he had a long day and he spent a lot of time assisting his mother. He never complained. I knew that I was witnessing real human goodness and compassion and I wasn't surprised when he went into the ministry. He became the Bishop of Manchester and was a campaigner against violent video games. I suspect he would have seen all video games as a waste of time as there is so much to do in the real world.

CHAPTER 8

Lost Empires

Just prior to rock'n'roll in the mid-1950s, the mainstay of the provincial theatre was the variety show. These two-hour performances featured singers, comedians, jugglers, trick cyclists, magicians, animal acts and ventriloquists. There was Leslie Welch, the Memory Man, who would answer any question about sport. Some sceptical audience members wondered why he performed next to a table covered with a large cloth: could there possibly be somebody underneath it with reference books? No matter, he was always well received until he got to Liverpool, that is.

An audience member asked him, "Where can you find a Wembley cup winner's medal, an England cricket cap and a Wimbledon cup all in the same place?" Leslie Welch scratched his head and the man who might (or might not be) under the table had no idea. "I'm sorry," said Leslie Welch, "I don't know. Where can you find a Wembley cup winner's medal, an England cricket cap and a Wimbledon cup all in the same place?" The wag replied, "The pawn shop in Lodge Lane."

When rock'n'roll came along in the mid-1950s, the first acts – Tommy Steele, Terry Dene, Russ Hamilton, Marty Wilde – played on these touring shows which meant that teenagers had to endure endless variety until they got what they wanted. I saw

Sandy Powell say his catchphrase, "Can you hear me, mother?" and I appreciate now that I was watching history. Similarly, the older patrons didn't want teenage music.

Larry Parnes and Arthur Howes were the first promoters to realise that this new music should be packaged in its own shows. Larry Parnes cut out the middleman by signing the artists and putting them on tour together in exciting packages for theatres around the UK: Brian Epstein learnt from his example.

And then there were pantomimes. The first rock'n'roll star I saw was Tommy Steele in *Goldilocks and the Three Bears* at the Royal Court in January 1958. To this day, I can picture him singing 'Butterfingers' to a sorrowful Baby Bear. Tommy made his entrance from the rafters holding balloons and wearing a safety harness. My friend's mother loved his fresh-faced look and exclaimed, "But he's so clean!" Rock'n'roll singers, even Tommy Steele, were considered the great unwashed.

We missed, by a couple of days, an infamous matinee where students from Liverpool University shouted out the wrong responses. Tommy Steele, to his immense credit, told the students that they were spoiling it for the kids. They still wouldn't shut up and the performance was cancelled with patrons being given tickets for another date. Tommy wrote to the students' newspaper saying that if this was how students behaved, he was very glad that he hadn't gone to university.

The following year I went with a friend from Rydal, Barry C Noton - only 13 but dressed like a city gent – and we saw *Mother Goose* with Vince Eager in the Scala in Southport. I don't think Vince had much to do with the plot but he had a ten-minute rock'n'roll sequence, which was magic. With shades of the Royal Court, Barry C Noton insisted on calling "Yes" when the answer was "No", and vice versa.

For some years there had been a ban on American musicians playing in the UK. The Musicians' Union, believing it was doing its best for its members, said that the American performers could not play here as we had perfectly good acts of our own. This was nonsense. We hadn't acts as good as Louis Armstrong and Duke Ellington and probably never would have if the UK musicians couldn't experience the real thing. Nat 'King' Cole came here with Nat identifying himself as 'a juggler', although he did precious little juggling.

The ruling was relaxed in the early 1950s after the clarinettist Sidney Beçhet came to London and played with Humphrey Lyttelton's band. He stood and played in the auditorium while the band was on stage, so he wasn't technically breaking the rules. The ruling was relaxed in 1956 and Louis Armstrong toured with his band and amongst other places, played on a revolving stage at Liverpool Stadium, which was managed by Johnny Best, father of Pete.

However, the Musicians' Union didn't go overboard in its endorsement of American performers. They could only come here if a comparable UK act could tour America, which might be difficult to arrange. Which acts would the Americans want to see?

There were plans to bring US package shows *in toto* to the UK but mostly it was single acts who would be topping a UK variety bill such as Freddie Bell and the Bellboys touring with Tommy Steele and the Steelmen.

I saw Bobby Darin, Clyde McPhatter and Duane Eddy on an awesome show at the Liverpool Empire in 1960. Bobby Darin was jeered for being too cabaret but he did sing Ray Charles' 'I Got a Woman' and played drums. He was a brilliant showman, fully capable of dealing with hecklers, though one remark revealed his arrogance: "I'm earning $5,000 a week – how about you, buddy?" Duane Eddy and his Rebels played 'Peter Gunn' as the curtains were being raised, so we heard this throbbing music before we saw it. That doesn't sound a big deal but I can assure you it was. Clyde McPhatter was a real treat: he had no UK successes but he had a magnificent voice.

Billy Fury knew something about stagecraft or rather, Jack Good had coached him well. He had a solitary spot on his face for the eerie 'Wondrous Place', which got girls screaming. The song, a cover of a Jimmy Jones record although it was radically changed, was a love ballad but in later years it came to represent Liverpool. It was not a big hit, loitering at the bottom of the Top 30, but judging by the way it's viewed in Liverpool today, you would think it was up there with 'Halfway to Paradise' and 'Jealousy'. Poor Tony Orlando, who toured with Bobby Vee, was booed in Liverpool for singing 'Halfway to Paradise', but he had every right to do so as our local lad Billy Fury had copied his record.

Then there was Peter Jay of the Jaywalkers with flashing lights on his drum-kit and Joe Brown playing his guitar behind his head. He later told me he regretted this as it had given him a bad back. Marty Wilde knew how to be dramatic with 'Tomorrow's Clown' and 'Jezebel'. The Shadows did their funny little dance steps to 'F.B.I.'.

The concept of two houses was great as it meant that a pre-teen like me could go to early evening performances and not have to worry about getting home late. Parents wanted their children home early because of school in the morning. I had two drawbacks. One, I was on pocket money and couldn't afford all the records and shows I wanted. Two, I was at boarding school most of the year and so wasn't around when the Gene Vincent and Eddie Cochran package came to Liverpool. I only saw Eddie Cochran on TV but I saw Gene Vincent live a few times and loved his manic look: who was he singing to as he stared into the heavens?

There was another drawback to live shows. If they were on Sundays, they had to comply with the licensing agreed with the Lord's Day Observance Society. This sounds arcane if not stupid, and it came to a head in 1962 when Chubby Checker appeared at the Liverpool Empire. He'd sung a couple of songs when Neil Brooks the manager stepped out. "Mr Checker, you have been warned. You must not dance on stage on Sunday." Chubby did as he was told so I reckon I am one of the few who saw a non-twisting performance by the Twist King.

In the holidays, I made up for lost time and went to almost anything that was available and cheap. I went to a free cookery show sponsored by Danish Bacon at the Liverpool Empire with Fanny and Johnnie Craddock and the drummer Eric Delaney. He had lights in his drums and he leapt out from the back of the stage onto his kit and was a very vibrant performer. Sadly, it wasn't the day when he missed his footing and the drums came tumbling down around him.

Fanny and Johnnie were TV chefs and they came out between the acts and scolded us for not shouting that the sausage rolls were ready. "Oh, you naughty people," said Fanny, "You didn't tell us that the time was up!" I'm sure it was deliberate when Johnnie said, "If you follow these instructions, you'll have doughnuts just like Fanny's."

It was during 1956 to 1960 that I built up my lifelong love for American rock'n'roll, folk and country music. By and large, I preferred American films too but I came to loathe the Americanisation of the UK – I know this sounds paradoxical. I disliked chewing gum and hated bubble gum. I have never eaten a Big Mac and never will. There is a McDonald's close to where I live and it has a sign 'Drive-thru'. Drive past, in my estimation.

CHAPTER 9

Holly Days

The show I am sorry I missed above all others was the appearance of Buddy Holly and the Crickets at the Philharmonic Hall on 20 March 1958. I determined, once I was interviewing musicians, that I would find out all I could about it.

Released in the UK at the start of 1958, the cover photograph of *The Chirping Crickets* LP was simply four boys with two guitars, but it said so much.

"We saw the cover of *The Chirping Crickets* and we really liked the look of the Stratocasters," Bruce Welch of the Shadows told me. "We'd also seen a photograph of Ricky Nelson with his guitarist. We couldn't see the top of his guitar but we thought it was also a Fender Strat, although it turned out to be a Telecaster. There were Board of Trade regulations which meant that you couldn't buy American instruments here, not even in Denmark Street, and we sent away for one for Hank. It was flamingo pink, gold-plated and maple-coated. It looked like something from out of space."

Rock journalist John Tobler: "I clearly remember my first sight of a copy of *The Chirping Crickets*, although it was a ludicrous title for what is one of the finest albums ever released. What strikes me now is how immensely direct it is. 'That'll Be the Day' begins with an irresistible guitar riff which is a major reason for me writing about music rather than playing it. After many unsuccessful attempts to play that riff, it became clear that listening to music was a far less stressful way of enjoying music. The LP included 'Oh Boy!', an exclamation of innocent teenage lust and an early example of bubblegum, which Mud proved with their revival in 1975."

Scriptwriter Mark Kelly: "Buddy Holly looked like a nervous office clerk, fronting a band which was only booked for weddings. I loved that hiccup in his voice. Those simple, catchy melodies, quirky, varied arrangements, and lyrics which somehow, mysteriously, always worked."

In March 1958, the British impresarios, Lew and Leslie Grade, wanted to present the Crickets on a UK tour. There were 25 venues, usually in cinemas or municipal halls. After management and agency fees, Holly would get $1,500 a week and Jerry Allison and Joe Mauldin $750 each. Holly told *Melody Maker* that they had two managers and an agent to support, a caustic quip if ever there was one.

The Crickets had been performing on rock'n'roll package shows in the US, and variety shows were new to them. They topped the bill and were supported by a handsome British singer, Gary Miller, who had had Top 20 hits with 'The Yellow Rose of Texas', 'Robin Hood' and 'The Garden of Eden'. The Tanner Sisters were a popular radio act, and the compère, Des O'Connor, had made a name for himself on Billy Butlin's holiday camps.

Johnnie Hamp was one of the tour organisers: "Des O'Connor was a very good compère. On Sunday night, he couldn't tell jokes because of the regulations of the Lord's Day Observance Society. You couldn't laugh on Sundays! Des could introduce the acts and he would whistle 'Swanee River' instead. The audience loved it as he turned into a joke."

A publicity event was arranged in Wardour Street, Soho. The Crickets were photographed dancing with teenagers for the love comic, *Valentine,* and posing for the national papers with England cricketers, Godfrey Evans and Denis Compton. The combination of entertainment and sport for a news story was unusual in 1958.

After shopping in Oxford Street, the Crickets performed their first UK shows at the Trocadero in Elephant and Castle on Saturday 1 March 1958. There were 1,500 at the first house and 3,000 at the second. The top ticket price was 10/6d (52p). The Crickets were intrigued to see Teddy Boys with long hair, crepes and drapes in the audience as the fashion was unknown in America.

The Crickets appeared on the 100th edition of Val Parnell's ITV show, *Sunday Night at the London Palladium* with Bob Hope topping the bill. They rehearsed in the morning, did the early show at the Gaumont State Theatre, Kilburn, appeared on the Palladium, and rushed back for the second show.

Writing in *Disc*, the TV producer Jack Good wrote, "Their appearance on *Sunday Night at the London Palladium* was a disaster comparable only with Napoleon's retreat from Moscow. They had one mike through which Buddy Holly despairingly bawled three numbers in quick succession to a horde of sedentary cold suet puddings at an ever-increasing tempo (longing, no doubt, to be away from it all). Then, without a word, they were off."

Going to Nottingham, the touring party ran into a snowstorm, and the Crickets couldn't abide the continual rain, sleet and snow. Joe B Mauldin: "All the hotels had a small heater on the wall that you had to put a sixpence in, and we were running out of sixpences. By the time we got some more, the room had gotten cold again, so we usually stayed downstairs by the fireplace."

Des O'Connor: "We travelled together on the bus and I

shared a room with Buddy a couple of times. I was the only one who could drag him out of bed. He was a devil to wake up and the only time he wasn't smiling was in the mornings. One day I woke him up by pulling his legs, and sounding like Deputy Dawg, he drawled, 'Don't do that, Des, I'm tall enough.'"

A jazz authority and biographer of J.B. Priestley, Peter Holdsworth, reviewed the concert for *Bradford Telegraph And Argus*. He wrote, "Unless they had previously read the lyrics or heard them sung by an articulate vocalist, I would have defied anyone in the audience to tell me what 70 percent of the words were which issued from the lips of this foot-stamping, knee-falling musician. Where on earth is show business heading?"

"I met Buddy Holly and the Crickets over a cup of tea when they played in Britain," said Lonnie Donegan. "He was the first person to bring a solid guitar into the country and because of the Musicians' Union it was very rare to see an American singer with his own band. I'd never seen a drummer like Jerry Allison before. He was all over his kit. It was great Texas drumming."

When the tour played Ritz Theatre, Wigan, they stayed at the Grand Hotel, and Buddy invited the receptionist, Barbara Bullough, to the show. He dedicated 'Everyday' to her and took her home in a taxi to Shevington.

He wanted her to come on tour but she couldn't and heck, this was 1958.

After a trip to Hull, the touring party was back in the north-west the following day, 20 March 1958, for the concert at the Philharmonic Hall, Liverpool that I missed.

Beatles' biographer Mark Lewisohn: "The various members of the Beatles didn't see Buddy Holly when he came to Liverpool as it was the opening night of the Morgue skiffle cellar in Oakhill Park and the Quarry Men were either playing that night or wanted to go along. Considering what Holly fans they were, it's surprising that they did that, but theatre tickets cost money."

It is also surprising because the Philharmonic Hall is on Hope Street and only 100 yards away from both the art college (where John Lennon was) and Liverpool Institute (where Paul and George were).

John was rarely interested in seeing other performers – he preferred hearing records – and maybe he had talked Paul and George out of it. We don't know, but it is odd.

The Philharmonic Hall staged classical concerts and as it was under council ownership, they were reluctant to book hit parade artists. On this occasion, the venue was hired by the music shop, Rushworth and Dreaper, which also booked the Paul Anka tour for the previous night.

The reviewer for *Liverpool Echo* was an old-stager, George Harrison, who was soon to use his name as a meal ticket around the world. Just before Buddy Holly started to play, there was a loss of power to his amplifier. George Harrison wrote, "Harassed men dashed in from all directions, pushing electric plugs into plugholes all over the place, but not a bleep came from the guitar. The three Americans solemnly trooped off stage and back to their dressing-room. The long gap was filled by a 'hot' band, but the fear was that the top of the bill act would not go on. The road manager, Wally Stewart, unscrewed the bulb from a ceiling light and after running an extension lead to the guitar, it worked."

Everyone remembers the concert as though it were yesterday. Jim Newcombe: "I was only 16 when I saw Buddy Holly in March. I went with Geoff Taggart to the second house and we were in the first rows of the circle. We were queuing outside as the first house was in progress. We could hear the music through the walls but not clearly, and everyone was buzzing, talking about Buddy

Holly and his songs. Des O'Connor told a few good jokes but as the show progressed, everybody wanted to see Buddy."

The second house became so animated that Jerry Allison threw his sticks into the audience and Buddy Holly played his guitar over his head. UK concert goers had never seen a Fender Strat before, let alone one played that way, and wannabe musicians like Mike Pender were blinded by the light. "I saw Buddy Holly at the Liverpool Philharmonic and from that night onwards, everything I learned, everything I played was based on Holly. Groups now have banks of amplifiers and speakers all over the place, and most times they still don't get the sound they want. Holly came on stage with just a double-bass, drums and one amplifier. A lot of people have tried to imitate him but nobody's ever got close."

Dave Williams: "I was in my last year at school and I went to the second house. Buddy had a long lead and he was on his knees, on his back, everything, he really went to town. The audience participation pushed him on as he got a great reaction. Jerry Allison was a loud drummer too. We put up with the rest of the show as we knew Buddy was coming. Some people may have come for Gary Miller but not many."

Gerry Standard: "Des O'Connor said, with a wave of the hand, 'Ladies and gentlemen, Buddy Holly and the Crickets.' The group ran on stage - Jerry to the drums, Joe to the double-bass and Buddy to the centre. They began with 'Oh Boy!' and Buddy said, 'It's great to be in Liverpool but who wants to hear me talking. Let's get on with the music.' They also did 'Ready Teddy', 'Rip It Up', 'Everyday', 'Not Fade Away' and 'That'll Be the Day'. They took three curtain calls and then did 'That'll Be the Day' again."

Mike Pender: "I can remember going away thinking that this is what I want to do for a living. I was in my first job at Ray's

Tugs, one of the Merseyside shipping companies. It was a magical night. Holly had his Fender Strat with just the three of them on stage. The audience was on its feet, and it was fantastic."

The final interview with Keith Goodwin of the *NME* was very upbeat. They had loved meeting the fans and Buddy had enjoyed the polite way they queued for autographs. Buddy gave his acoustic guitar to Des O'Connor and everybody parted in good humour.

Record producer Stuart Colman: "Buddy Holly's future as a timeless icon was assured, not by his death but by coming to Britain in 1958. He was the archetypal rock'n'roller. His image would be recast time and time again - from Hank Marvin to Elvis Costello – and he would have been proud of what he had inspired."

This highly successful tour can be contrasted with Jerry Lee Lewis' a month later. He came over with his bride, Myra, who was only 13. Such marriages were legal in Louisiana, but the whole country was outraged – parents and rock'n'roll fans alike – and questions were asked in Parliament as to why he was even allowed in the UK. Jerry Lee performed three shows and returned home, but he was resilient and made an impressive comeback. This event had the potential to derail rock'n'roll completely and critics used his marriage as an indication that the music itself was untenable. Fortunately, the music was stronger than that.

Although I missed Buddy live in Liverpool, I have written three books about him, the most recent being *Learning The Game*. I curse being away at boarding school for many reasons but most of all, I regret having to miss Buddy Holly."

CHAPTER 10

Days In The Life: 1961-1963

Merchant Taylors' School on Liverpool Road, Crosby, looks very grand – a large, impressive, greystone building with a clock tower. In the early 60s it was a top-end grammar school which behaved like a public school. Indeed, Rydal played Merchants at rugby and cricket. It was a hybrid known as a direct grant school.

A huge sports field in front of the school meant that the public could watch cricket or rugby by looking over the fence. They could enter the grounds and stand alongside the playing area. There is now protective netting, but it struck me as potentially dangerous as a batsman could hit a six and hit a Ribble bus or a pedestrian, but maybe batsmen back then were warned against such macho behaviour.

I know without checking that the school was founded in 1620 by a merchant taylor called John Harrison, who worked in London but was born in Crosby. In assemblies, there would be prayers for him and if his fate hadn't been determined by then, it never would be. The school had a motto – in Latin of course – but along the lines of "Big trees grow from little acorns". There was a school song, but I can't remember it so it did nothing for me.

In September 1961 I joined Merchant Taylors' in the sixth

form S1, the form teacher being Donald Temple-Roberts. I was taking Maths and Further Maths but not Physics as my lessons had been so messed up by the absentee Fisher. Further Maths, a separate subject, was taught by the very precise Cliff Hamer. He said exactly what he wanted to say and no more and dressed immaculately: a very pleasant guy but with something of the automaton about him.

Instead of physics, I opted for Religious Instruction, which was moving away from Christianity towards multiculturalism. It was taught by Ralph Rolls who later had a senior role with the BBC and wrote books on religious topics.

What surprises me now is that I got hooked on religion. Mr Temple-Roberts went to our church, St Nicholas, Blundellsands, and I applied to be a Sunday school teacher. I was soon taking the collection and reading the odd lesson as a layman (as a young boy, I rather liked that term). I joined the English Church Historical Society, organised at the Bluecoat Chambers by Mrs Temple-Roberts and even gave a talk on Albert Schweitzer, who was my hero at the time.

I went to a lecture, *Being a Christian in an Affluent Society* at Merchant Taylors' girls school but I might have gone just to see the girls' premises. But maybe not as I also went to discussions on the Vatican Council and was enthralled by the Bishop of Woolwich's controversial book, *Honest to God*, contentious in that he thought that God was not up there in the sky.

Indeed, following *Honest to God*, Ralph Rolls asked me to help with a survey of the image of God amongst the students. It was intrusive to ask students what they thought of God, but they could fill in the form anonymously. However, most masters would recognize the handwriting.

Part of my obsession with God was down to my friendship

with Colin Oxenforth, who attended MTS and lived close by in Grosvenor Avenue. His ambition was to be a minister and indeed he was to have a parish in Toxteth for many years. He was gaining experience in his final years at MTS as he would accost parents in the street and ask them whether their children went to Sunday School. If someone said no, then he would recommend St Faith's. I'm surprised he was never thumped.

The school also made the A-level for General Studies mandatory. This was to broaden your mind and covered sociology, culture and the humanities. It had good intentions, but it wasn't a subject for which you could revise. We spent several lessons with Chris Price reading and analysing Willis Hall's play, *The Long and the Short and the Tall*, a wartime drama which raised ethical issues, but was this the best way to raise them? I never saw a syllabus but overall General Studies stressed the distinctions between facts and opinions and the importance of collecting information to back your arguments.

It did broaden our horizons. On Mr Price's recommendation I went to the left-wing Merseyside Unity Theatre in William Brown Street in March 1962 to see Arnold Wesker's *Roots* trilogy – that is *Chicken Soup with Barley*, *Roots* and *I'm Talking about Jerusalem*. These were dramas about growing up in a Jewish Communist family in the East End of London in the 1930s. Wesker himself attended the third play and addressed the audience. I shook his hand. He told me that his own name was an anagram of Ronald, but I can't remember anything else he said.

An unconventional teacher, R C Shepard, known as Yogi, would recommend us to read poetry, notably Dylan Thomas. Yogi read a strange story about a lad who had replaced his dead partner's heart with a clock, but I couldn't tell you what it was about.

From my viewpoint, Yogi gets brownie points for recommending the French songwriter, Jacques Brel.

The entire Sixth Form went off on Thursday afternoon for army drills and training as part of the Combined Cadets Force. Fortunately, the organisers had overlooked that I had joined the sixth form and as nobody ever asked where I was, I made myself scarce. There you are: I'd succeeded better than all of them with my skill at camouflage. The Lieutenant-Colonel was Lt-Col Tom Gribble. He too taught mathematics and he brought in his OBE which he passed round for inspection. The nearest I got to the CCF was holding his OBE.

Also in the Sixth Form, Arthur Johnson was the first politically-motivated boy that I knew. He sat down with a placard in the very busy South Road in Waterloo to protest against the Bomb. He stopped traffic and had to be removed by police. The event made national news and the headmaster, T J P York, was furious. He expelled Arthur for bringing the school into disrepute and he was found guilty of criminal behaviour and fined £25. Arthur was the nephew of the Liverpool actor, John Gregson. At the time, he was working with James Robertson Justice, who wrote to Arthur and said that he would be proud to pay his fine. You could argue that Arthur Johnson was making a more valuable contribution to our future than the whole of the CCF.

I didn't get involved in many political events myself but I did attend an anti-Polaris march in Liverpool in 1968. There were only four of us in the Crosby contingent, including a man in shorts who looked very cold. We were singing "We won't live in a Polaris submarine". The message was right, but it didn't scan.

I was involved in the obligatory cricket, athletics and rugby at MTS with little enthusiasm, mostly on the playing fields in Endbutt Lane. I joined the school chess team but I wasn't much good. I knew how to play but I lacked concentration; it seemed pointless – I'd rather read a book or do homework. I did take part in a public speaking competition. I was asked for my subject and I foolishly said "Nothing", which went down in the programme. It was a neat idea but I didn't have the skill to carry it off.

CHAPTER 11

Merseyside Hitmakers

What I like best about my old diaries are the references to records of the day. I had bought 'Emotions' and the EP *This Is Brenda* (Brenda Lee – no quarrel with that), 'I Cannot Find a True Love' (Cliff Richard - odd), 'Linda Lu' (Johnny Kidd - excellent) and 'What'd I Say' (Jerry Lee Lewis – clearly, the controversy over his child bride didn't bother me). I had thought about buying Billy Fury's 'Don't Worry' but had heard the B-side, 'Talkin' in My Sleep', and commented 'hopeless'.

On 13 January 1962, I bought the Everly Brothers' 'Crying in the Rain' and Andrew Doble and I were so impressed that we were playing it continuously until 11pm. We were right – it is one of the best records ever made.

We went to a dance at the Jive Hive (St Luke's Hall, Crosby) which was organised by Andrew's brother, Peter. He had been Merchant Taylors' head boy and had arranged this for the Young Liberals. Peter drew the raffle and when one of the committee won the main prize, everyone shouted "Fix! Fix! Fix!"

I have fond memories of a dance at St Faith's in Crosby with three local bands - the Flintstones, the Black Velvets and the Phantoms. The lead singer of the Black Velvets was a small guy who stood on a box to perform.

A beat cruise on the Royal Iris with Faron's Flamingos and

Lee Curtis was great fun, and it was known as the fish'n'chip boat.

I organised trips to see Brenda Lee and Tony Sheridan (Liverpool Odeon), Gene Vincent and Jet Harris (Southport Odeon) and Gerry and the Pacemakers and Louise Cordet (Southport Odeon). The role that cinemas played in promoting live beat music has never been appreciated.

My sometime tennis partner, Jenny Johns, was my second cousin and for some reason, she took me to see her grandparents, my Great-Aunt Ethel (who resembled Queen Mary) and Great-Uncle Cecil.

Uncle Cecil was wonderfully eccentric – he kept old newspapers in the basement and he would go on a train, reading a newspaper that was 20 years old and commenting as though it were today's. Each year he would label an empty bottle and would say, "This is a bottle of 1923 air." Just think how valuable his crazy collection would be for meteorologists today.

My father invited me to lunch at Reece's Grill Room. I was 17 years old and he said, "Spen, do you know how babies are made?" I was tempted to say, "No, please tell me", but I could sense his embarrassment and said, "That's okay. I think I know what's going on." He must have been relieved to hear that. Much as my father would have liked it to have stopped, the Swingin' Sixties was on its way.

When I was 18 on February 1, 1963, I had a party at Mersey Road with the guests being Mike Finlay, Peter Sutch, Andrew Doble, Barry, Brian, Colin Oxenforth, John Roberts, John J, Nick, Jenny Johns, Daphne Makinson, Sue Ashton, Dawn Flood, Margaret, Marion Roocroft, Beth Fisher, Jenny Morgan and Wendy Murphy. Unfortunately, I didn't list all the surnames and there's no way I can complete it today.

There's a note not to call Daphne Makinson on Tuesday nights – she would be washing her hair.

John Roberts' father had died a couple of years earlier, drowning in a Liverpool dock, possibly suicide and if it was an accident, what was he doing there? Then, only three weeks after my party, John crashed his scooter. He wasn't wearing a helmet and had brain damage. It was difficult for him to communicate but he tried hard and desperately wanted girlfriends.

The Roberts family moved to a ground floor flat, probably because it would make life easier. When John's mother and sister went out one evening, John was allowed to have some friends round. Somebody brought along a girl from Hillside who was game for anything. The door to the bedroom would open every 20 minutes and one young male left and another went in. John sat outside the door hoping that he would be called, but he wasn't. When John's mother returned, she saw the devastation in the bedroom and found John completely distraught. Even those of us who had had nothing to do with it were branded as guilty because we hadn't stopped it, so John was cut off from all his friends.

This poor girl hadn't got a lift back to Hillside and Peter Sutch volunteered to take her. I was in the back of the car too and she looked wrecked. "Good party?" I asked and she said, "I'll be aching in the morning."

Not that I was completely innocent. My parents paid an annual subscription of £10 for access to a wild park in Blundellsands, known as the key park. It had woodland paths, nooks and crannies, tennis courts and a play area for children. However, as night fell, it had other uses…

It was far better and more romantic than the back wall of the Regent.

I was 18 and wanting to impress Ginny Walker who worked

as a nanny at St Nicholas' vicarage. I asked her if she would like to see the Beatles – possibly the best chat-up line ever. They were appearing in Southport and naturally she said, "Yes!!". She was a popular girl: six boys had given her 'Ginny Come Lately' by Brian Hyland for her birthday or for Christmas. I was the only one to give her 'Ginny in the Mirror' by Del Shannon. She said her previous boyfriend was David Noble (a churchwarden): she called him David Ignoble so I knew I must be on my best behaviour.

The Beatles were in Southport for six nights, taking over the Odeon Cinema with their stage show. from Monday to Saturday 26-31 August 1963. It was a Brian Epstein presentation featuring four NEMS acts.

Ginny and I travelled the 12 miles from Crosby to Southport on the commuter train and I felt the tension rising (not just a euphemism) as so many passengers were going to the Odeon too.

We had good seats, five rows from the back, in the stalls. The compëre was Bob Bain, born in Scotland but with an American accent. The opening act was Gary and Lee who performed Johnny Kidd's 'I'll Never Get over You' and 'Twistin' to the Locomotion'. I can't even find them on Google. Brian Epstein nursed high hopes for Tommy Quickly, who had a lively personality and could dance, but was too showbiz. He sang his single 'Heaven Only Knows', Buddy Holly's 'Everyday' and Lennon and McCartney's 'Tip of my Tongue', the worst song they ever wrote. Scaffold parodied it as 'Tip of my Thingy'. (Scaffold also did 'All You Need is Plod', which suggests that Mike McCartney wasn't above having a little dig at his brother.) No matter, the girls screamed for Tommy Quickly, perhaps exercising their lungs for the Beatles. Tommy Wallis played a xylophone on wheels while wearing roller skates. His partner Beryl wore a swimsuit and also glided around on skates. No one paid any attention to them, poor souls, and the girls were screaming for the Beatles. Tommy and Beryl came from the dying days of Variety and maybe if they'd swapped their skates for American skateboards, they'd have done all right.

Gerry and the Pacemakers closed the first half. They opened with a Beatles' favourite 'Some Other Guy' and followed it with their first B-side, 'Away from You' which Gerry had written to his future wife Pauline when he was in Hamburg. This was followed by Chuck Berry's 'Sweet Little Sixteen' and a very good version of the cheeky 'How Do You Do It', written by Mitch Murray and their first Number 1: this really brought out the screams. A forceful version of Arthur Alexander's 'Shot of Rhythm and Blues' was well received and then came Nat 'King Cole's 'Pretend', although they were following Carl Mann's arrangement.

I would have been pompous at the time, if not insufferable, by maintaining that the American originals were better than the Merseybeat covers. I now appreciate that the Liverpool cover versions have charms of their own.

Gerry and the Pacemakers performed 'You'll Never Walk Alone' from *Carousel*, an inspired choice for their third single. They ended their set with their second Number 1, also from Mitch Murray, 'I Like It'. According to my notes, I enjoyed them more than the Beatles, which surprises me now but it must be true.

In the 1980s, I got to know Freddie Marsden, their drummer and Gerry's brother, as he had a driving school and used our corner for reversing.

Gerry and the Pacemakers was the first act to go to Number 1 with their first three records (Frankie Goes To Hollywood, the second.) Freddie Marsden was convinced it would have been four if they had released 'Pretend' as a single.

Gerry's own song, 'I'm the One', was not quite strong enough and couldn't shift the Searchers' 'Needles and Pins'. I'm with Fred.

The Fourmost opened the second half with a B-side 'Just In Case' and they moved into Doris Day territory with 'Everybody Loves a Lover', although the arrangement followed the Shirelles. Their hit single, 'Hello Little Girl' (again, Lennon and McCartney) was well received and Brian O'Hara did amusing impressions while singing 'September in the Rain' including Donald Duck and Frankie Valli. They were a cabaret act masquerading as a beat group.

The screaming was at fever pitch for the Beatles. I remember Ginny pounding my arms as George opened the set with 'Roll Over Beethoven'. The pounding continued for 'Thank You Girl', 'Chains', 'A Taste of Honey' and 'She Loves You'. All the girls were screaming and it was like a monkey house. John took the lead for 'Baby It's You' and then it was 'From Me To You', Ringo's offering 'Boys', Paul's 'I Saw Her Standing There' and the closer, John's raucous 'Twist and Shout'. I would have preferred the Beatles without the screaming, but I was with a girl who was loving it, so I have mixed feelings about that.

When we returned to the vicarage, the Very Reverend Basil Howell (what did his splendid title mean?) was asking about the Beatles and trying to understand the phenomenon. It must have worked out well as I saw Ginny on Thursday, Friday, Saturday and Sunday too. I even took her to the key park – and to the opening of an Oxfam Gift Shop. (I really knew how to treat a girl.) Then she went to America as a nanny and I never saw her again.

I was on the site of that very Odeon recently. It is now Sainsbury's and some customers may have wondered who was this crazy loon smiling in the aisles. They didn't realise I was thinking back to 1963 and my then girlfriend Ginny Walker and the Beatles. I think of the Beatles every day, but Ginny, well, I'd hadn't thought of her in years.

I originally wrote my memories of the Southport Beatles concert for *The Beatles 1963; A Year in the Life*, compiled brilliantly by Dafydd Rees for Omnibus in 2022. I know books are good when I think, "Grrr, why didn't I think of that?"

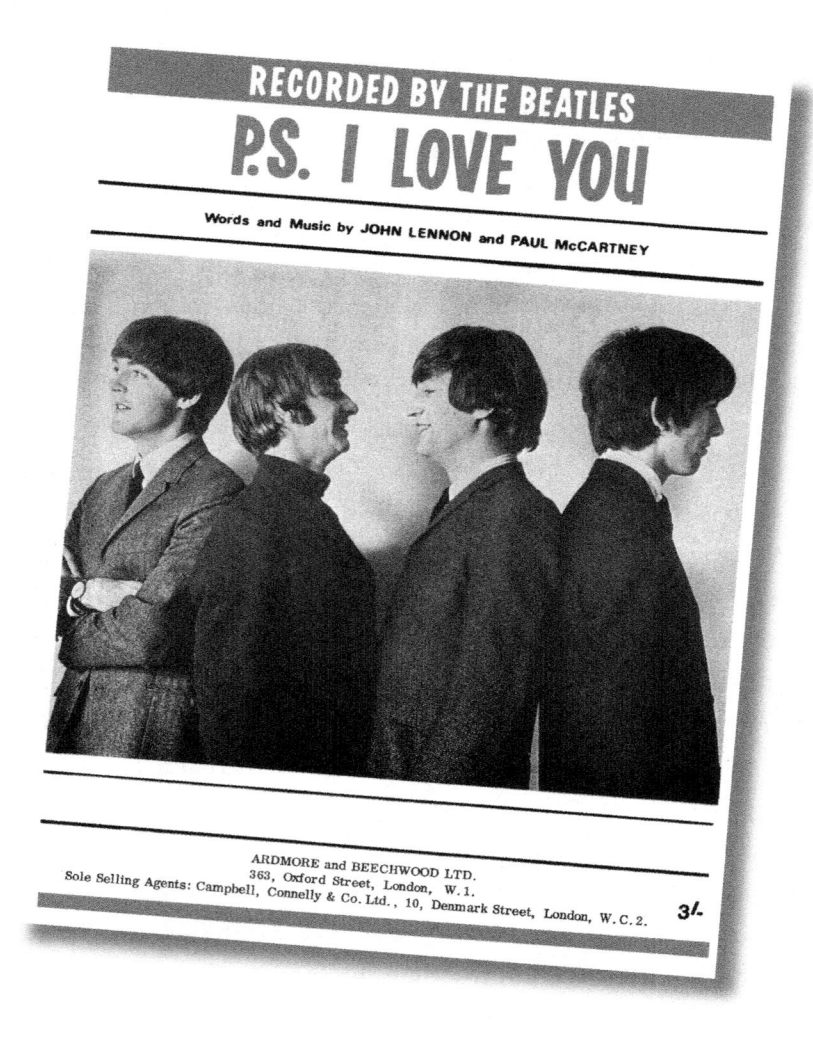

SPENCER LEIGH

CHAPTER 12

The Greatest Package Show

Unquestionably, the most exciting show I've seen featured the Everly Brothers, Little Richard, Bo Diddley and the Rolling Stones, all on the same UK package show in 1963. It was a long way from perfect (as you'll discover) but it was endlessly entertaining and often comes to mind. Was I really there? Yes, I was and I still have the notes I made as an 18-year-old.

On Sunday 13 October 1963 the tour played the Odeon in London Road, Liverpool, and I went to the first house with Andrew Doble.

The show began with the Flintstones playing the Mar-Keys' instrumental, 'Last Night', and then Mickie Most was given a ridiculous five songs and I was thinking, "Is this guy ever going to finish?" There was 'Kansas City', 'I'll Never Get Over You', 'The Feminine Look' (his new single and his best moment for what it's worth), 'It Doesn't Matter Anymore' and 'Johnny B. Goode', which he played by dropping to his knees. It was a thankless task as the entire audience wanted him to shift so we could see the stars.

It was only three songs for the Rolling Stones, They performed two Chuck Berry numbers, 'I'm Talkin' 'Bout You' and 'Come On', which had been their first single and a Top 30 hit. Taking a chance in Liverpool, they finished with Lennon and McCartney's

'I Wanna Be Your Man', which would be their second single, out in a fortnight. Sounded like a hit to me and considering they are rising stars, why did they only get eight minutes?

There was a long, pounding introduction to 'Lucille' from the Flintstones and we wondered where Little Richard was. He came screaming down the aisle, jumped on the stage and joined them for the vocal, following it in quick succession with 'Long Tall Sally', 'Tutti Frutti', 'Whole Lotta Shakin' Goin' On', and 'Rip It Up', but he could have been singing anything. It was total mayhem and total excitement.

Little Richard's showmanship was remarkable and at one stage he clenched the top of a chair with his teeth, held it aloft and then did a wild rockin' dance around the front of the stage. He stripped to his underpants, threw his clothes to the audience, put on a dressing-gown and closed with 'Hound Dog'. He'd been on stage for half an hour. We were exhausted just from watching Little Richard. Time for an interval.

After the interval, the German band, the Rattles sang 'Mashed Potatoes', an American dance number known in Liverpool through the Undertakers. It was a long way to come just to sing "Mashed potatoes, yeah". Then Julie Grant did Tony Hatch's 'Count On Me', another Lennon and McCartney song 'Bad To Me', a decent 'Will You Love Me Tomorrow' and her new single, 'Don't Ever Let Me Down'.

Bo Diddley with the Duchess on bass guitar and Jerome shaking his maracas created a relentless beat on a song about himself, 'Bo Diddley'. They followed it with 'Baby' (my title at the time – I don't know what this was) and 'Road Runner'. The sound of 'Road Runner' reverberated around the theatre and was the highlight of the show. Bo finished with more self-praise in 'Hey, Bo Diddley'.

Hardly pausing for breath and starting way too fast, the Everly Brothers opened with 'Bird Dog' and 'Wake Up Little Susie'. Were they fed up with these songs or did they have a train to catch at Lime Street Station? They slowed down for 'Cathy's Clown', 'All I Have To Do Is Dream' and 'So Sad', which was taken way too slow. It was back to speed with 'Claudette', 'Bye Bye Love' and 'Be Bop A Lula'. The Everly Brothers were good but they'd misjudged their tempos, the only perfect tempo coming on Jimmy Reed's 'Baby, What You Want Me To Do'. That song's title should have given them a clue: treat your songs with respect for a start. The Everly Brothers were disappointing when they could so easily have been great.

That's it – 600 words on the Everly Brothers tour written in 1963, but that evening kept coming back to me and around 2013, I decided to tell the story of the tour for the rock'n'roll magazine, *Now Dig This*. The five-part feature *We Used To Have Good Times Together* was published the following year and ran to 22,000 words. As I want to comment about research and writing in *80 at 80,* this is as good a place as any.

What attracted me was the fact that the tour could be told from different perspectives – star names, supporting musicians, crew, promoters and audience members. How did the Everlys, Bo Diddley and Little Richard get on with each other and how did they relate to the other performers and musicians?

This tour was taking place when the British beat movement was coming to the fore, especially the Beatles and others from Liverpool. How would that affect ticket sales? And why were they touring through the Odeon cinema chain?

These stalwarts of American rock'n'roll were touring with the new kids on the block, the Rolling Stones. They were known around London and had had a minor hit with 'Come On'? How would they fare on their first national tour? The bill was a mix of old and new, and yet the new was so influenced by those old acts. Did tensions erupt?

In 1962 the Everly Brothers had come to the UK to tour with Frank Ifield, but Don Everly fell ill and Phil continued on his own. Actually, Don had taken an overdose but this was not revealed to the press. How could their new promoter Don Arden ensure that the Everlys would honour their commitments? What was the relationship between the brothers like?

Was it difficult for Julie Grant as the only girl on the tour?

What was the experience of the Hamburg band, the Rattles? The Second World War ended in 1945 but there was bomb damage around the UK, and cinemas showed war films.

Nobody had written a book about the tour so there were numerous angles to explore and so much interplay between the characters that I was sure that the feature, if researched right, would cover new ground.

I recently asked my friend Andrew Doble for his recollections of that evening in Liverpool: "The Everly Brothers were disappointing as they could easily have been much better, but Little Richard more than fulfilled my expectations. His suit was soon covered in sweat and he took it off and came back in a fluffy white bathrobe. It was all part of the show and he was an absolutely great showman.

Like Little Richard, Bo Diddley was exciting and had pizzazz but all the time I was wondering if the Duchess was his sister or his mistress. I saw the Rolling Stones and I thought they would never make it. They seemed limp compared to the other acts and I was deeply unimpressed. However, Mickie Most was the bottom of the bill by a very long way."

The Southport crime writer Ron Ellis had also been at the

show: "The Everly Brothers were very efficient as though a Sgt Major had told them to get on with it and they had brushed their hair forward to give themselves a Beatle look. Little Richard was very good and still doing rock'n'roll and it never occurred to me that he might be gay. Bo Diddley was great: he didn't move much but his body swung as he played and he had a weird-looking guitar. Mickie Most was okay as he had a good personality and moved about. I remember him more than the Flintstones and Julie Grant, who just stood still."

Once you've been writing for a while, you have your own archive and so there's a bank of interviews to draw upon. I had spoken to the Rattles for my *Beatles In Hamburg* book, I had interviewed Mickie Most, Bill Wyman and Bo Diddley for local radio. I spoke to Bill Wyman when he formed the Rhythm Kings. He had a proviso that only half the questions could be about the Stones, which was fair enough. He wanted to promote his new band and with such members as Georgie Fame, Albert Lee, Gary Brooker and Beverley Skeete, it was a brilliant outfit. He told me he envied George Hamilton for having a song on most Beatle albums - Bill had only managed two on Rolling Stones' albums as Mick and Keith had it sewn up – most people think, "Poor George".

I got in touch with fan clubs and made contacts over the internet. I traced Julie Grant, who was 17 in 1963, and found her most helpful, telling me that she had her mother on tour as chaperone. "I wasn't happy about that, but she probably saved my life. I never got into the drugs scene." Similarly, Bo Diddley called the Duchess his sister as he felt it would be easier to protect her.

Mickie Most said, 'I had to earn my keep and as I could play guitar and sing a bit, I thought I would go on this tour and use it as an opportunity to look at groups around the country," and as a result discovered the Animals in Newcastle and recorded 'The House of the Rising Sun' with them.

I consulted the British Library, the British Newspaper Archive, the BBC Written Archives and the Theatre Museum. My friend John Firminger has an archive of old music papers.

I'm always tempted to write my features in the present tense because then your characters can't know what will happen next. It's a valid approach but the results can look like affectation.

When you've got a draft, rewrite it – almost every sentence will undergo some change. Avoid repetition as people don't want to be told the same thing twice, but that is difficult when writing about the repetitive nature of touring. Look out for typos and discrepancies but almost certainly you won't spot them all.

During my research, I uncovered a few things which answer some of those questions I posed about the tour earlier:

When the Everlys arrived at London Airport, they were asked about the new British music and they assumed the reporters were talking about the Dallas Boys and Matt Monro.

And the reason for Don and Phil's speedy delivery of some of their numbers? Tom Paley from the bluegrass group, the New Lost City Ramblers, told me that a lot of bluegrass musicians wanted to play songs as fast as they can. "Don and Phil came from Kentucky and so it's possible that they had picked up this trait. Did they come off stage and say, 'That was good. We knocked another four seconds off 'Cathy's Clown' tonight.'"

Although the Everly Brothers loved Little Richard's music, they were antagonised by the way he would overrun and act like the bill topper. Richard wound up Bo Diddley and they would argue as to which of them was going on first. If Bo got on before Richard, he would add a couple of numbers to his set.

Keith Richards said, "Our first proper tour was with the Everly

Brothers, Bo Diddley and Little Richard. What an education – it was rock'n'roll university. You want to know anything about rock'n'roll – well, the best teachers are there."

The Rolling Stones were paid £40 a night but it was only in Liverpool they learnt that Brian Jones was getting extra as 'the leader' of the group. They never trusted him again.

The Rattles weren't paid anywhere near what the Stones were getting. The promoter clearly didn't rate them. Steve Ellis of Love Affair says, "Don Arden was like a caricature of Edward G Robinson", so you get the picture.

The owner of the Star-Club in Hamburg, Manfred Weissleder, had been telling Don Arden of the popularity of beat group the Rattles at his venue. Weissleder managed them and wanted to see how they would perform in the UK. They came over for a combined daily allowance of £5. They had to find their own accommodation or sleep on the bus.

A dramatic and highly entertaining film could be made about this October 1963 tour by the Everly Brothers, Little Richard and Bo Diddley. The tensions between all the performers make for entertainment and you would have great music too.

Little Richard at the Star-Club, Hamburg

CHAPTER 13

Days In The Life: 1963-1964

I was never impressed with Careers Masters. I always felt if they were any good, they wouldn't be Careers Masters, but Merchant Taylors' did show us what was available. We went to St Helen's Glass where Lady Pilkington herself welcomed us and shook our hands. We saw how glass was manufactured and how a job at the factory could be a job for life.

Norman Graham, an actuary at Royal Insurance, told us about the opportunities in life assurance: people would always need cover and so there was job security. He said actuaries were so important that they had been exempted from national service. Conscription had just been abolished but this was good news if the Government were to bring it back. The work, he said, was strictly mathematical but if you were that way inclined, it was very rewarding.

That sounded ideal. I told the Careers Master I was interested. I don't know if I was the only one, but I went on my own to meet the head of the Royal's life operations, Mr J M Beattie, in Liverpool.

Royal Insurance had its head office at an impressive Victorian building on the corner of North John Street. The organisation had long outgrown its premises and the life and pensions operations were in Derby House and Sefton House respectively, both offices being in the three-sided building surrounding Exchange Flags, the fourth side being the Town Hall.

Mr Beattie's first words to me were "Put your mackintosh in my wardrobe" and I was impressed that somebody should have a wardrobe in their office. He said that actuaries undertook statistical work for life assurance companies and it was one of the smallest professions in the world. There were 1,200 members of the Institute, which was based in Staple Inn in London, a building featured in Charles Dickens' *The Mystery of Edwin Drood*.

In *The Apartment* (1960), Jack Lemmon plays an insurance clerk who is nominated for promotion, but the company officials think it a fiddle: "The last time anyone was put in line for prometon, he was found to be using the machine in the actuarial department to calculate betting systems."

I was shown round the office and met a couple of students, who were warm and friendly. I had been told that actuaries were impersonal and lacking in social skills, the joke being that accountants were "actuaries with personality". I didn't have that impression at all.

One of the older actuaries, Henry Elderton told me that when he says he deals with compound interest and mortality rates, people say "How very morbid" but then if he says, "I never meet these people", they say "How very impersonal."

My dad had been made redundant and so it wasn't practicable to go to university. I applied to join the Royal and I never regretted it. I passed the medical (as we were given free life assurance benefits) and I started my employment on Monday 2 September 1963.

I would get study leave for the examinations, which was three half-days a week. However, I also had to work alternate Saturday mornings. I would get the grand sum of £425 a year. Over £8 a week: it sounded like a fortune! My first pay day was one of the most exciting days of my life even though it coincided with Ginny Walker, my girlfriend back then, going to America.

However, I was on trial. I had to pass the preliminary examination in November before I could take the actuarial examinations. It sounds a bind but there was nothing new I needed to learn. I wasn't given any study leave until I passed so I was working fulltime in the office which was a good discipline for me.

I was involved in calculating individual surrender values for life assurance policies and working full-time helped me to get to grips with office politics. Some students were more concerned about their examinations than day-to-day office work, which led to frosty relationships, but overall, it was a friendly place. I was sure I had made the right choice.

You had to sign in every morning and if you were late, you had to give your excuse. I remember someone giving "Fog" as his excuse and somebody else added, "in his brain". Everything appeared to be good-natured and it was certainly a happy workforce.

The actuarial department was part of a large Head Office life administration team and my first job was getting to know everyone and what they did. We could have a subsidised lunch in the old Liverpool, London & Globe building next to the Town Hall for 10d (4p). Through this I got to know people in marine, household and car insurance and I formed a theory about their effectiveness from the speed at which they ordered their food, though I never shared this thought with anyone.

In the administrative areas, I met old hands who had come to the Royal after war service. They had done their bit for the country and now were determined to do as little as possible, which was fair enough. There wasn't the discipline to bring them into line. Indeed, some years later I had to manage someone who had been a fighter pilot during the war. As I told him what to do, I wondered, "What is this guy really thinking?"

The elderly Ronnie Hill handled staff policies. He had a mound of work on his desk and if somebody asked him to hurry something along, he would find it in the pile…and put it on the bottom.

When the actuarial examinations took place, Bert Wilson would supervise the candidates and the individual answer papers had to be tied together with string. In the run up to the examination, he would spend a whole day cutting string into the designated length. He would have a 'liquid lunch' and he would fall asleep when he returned. It was my job to nudge him awake at 3pm so that he could go to the tea-room. All this sounds fanciful and from another age, but it's true. In 2022, the Bill Nighy film, *Living*, showed exactly what office life was like in a London office in the early 1960s.

But there was one little difference in Liverpool – the Cavern. The club was seven minutes' walk from the office and they held lunchtime beat sessions. I never went to one, but you could always tell the girls who had been as Eau de Cavern was far stronger than Chanel No. 5.

Productivity cannot have been high as we used heavy barrel calculators. There were metal levers for each number, and you could add, subtract, multiply or divide by turning the handle. Division was awkward but heck, the whole thing was bad. One student claimed he was faster with a slide rule but I think he was showing-off.

However, I saw first-hand how brilliant Norman Graham was at mental arithmetic. You might be going to multiply 356 by 292 and he would have the answer before you'd touched the calculator.

He told me that in 1955 they didn't allow logarithms in actuarial examinations, so he gave himself practice in mental arithmetic by doing surrender value calculations in his head for two months and by the end of it, he was as quick and as accurate as a barrel calculator. How impressive is that? Nobody liked to play bridge with him as he would quickly determine who held what. He had missed his calling as he could have made a fortune in Vegas.

I thought the barrel calculators were unbreakable, but a student called David managed to damage one. Indeed, he broke so many things that we wondered if he was doing it deliberately. He said to his manager, "I've broken something else. Can you ever forgive me?" The lad got involved in a church youth film of *The Passion* and wanted to play Jesus. However, the world was not ready for a 16-stone Jesus and they cast him as Judas instead.

I did some work on Quotations. We were involved with film companies who would take out short-term life assurance cover on, say, Roger Moore in case he died while a film was being made. One of our policies had been on Elizabeth Taylor when she was making *Cleopatra*.

After a year on the Life side, I moved over to Pensions in Sefton House, which was a bigger operation run by Jimmy Kettlewell, a very social chief actuary, and Hugo Johnson, his assistant, a big man who padded his way around the floor and would suddenly be standing beside you.

I worked directly for Peter Cardus who had been a student for many years and seemed happy about it, a bit like Kennth More in the *Doctor* films. The Royal was happy too as they could pay him a student's salary when he was effectively a qualified actuary.

He was dating one of the secretaries in the office, Carolyn Swift. They might hold hands in the workplace, but they wouldn't kiss until they got to the lifts.

The admin manager in Pensions was Willie Walpole and when I came into work in a bright blue shirt, he said, "That shirt would look better on the beach. Don't wear it again."

Robin Mason was a manager who would often take other people's ideas and parade them as his own. He worked his staff hard and was proud when his employees were on anti-depressants. One of them was slagging him off in the toilets when a voice came from inside a cubicle, "I heard that!"

I sometimes travelled with him on the Southport line. If a person put down his newspaper, Robin would say, "Have you finished with that?" and more often than not, it would be given to him. His favourite pastime was walking up and down Lord Street in Southport, looking for the best interest rates from building societies. He kept a note of every penny he spent and he had housekeeping books going back to the 1940s. I have never met anyone before or since who was so miserly but maybe his approach was good for keeping the Royal's business in order. There would be no *ex gratia* payments from him. I did enjoy his company but for all the wrong reasons.

There was one actuarial student who had never failed an examination in his life. He was mortified to think he might come unstuck with the actuarial ones. It was too much to take and he decided to do away with himself, but thankfully failed. The other students didn't know why he was in hospital, and someone took him a copy of *You Only Live Twice*. The lad gave up the actuarial examinations and a psychiatrist told him that he should take a job for a year in which he wouldn't have to think too much. A few months later I met him in Lime Street Station where he was working as a porter. He said, with a grin, "There's no pressure now. If someone asks me where their train is, I just pick a platform from 1 to 8."

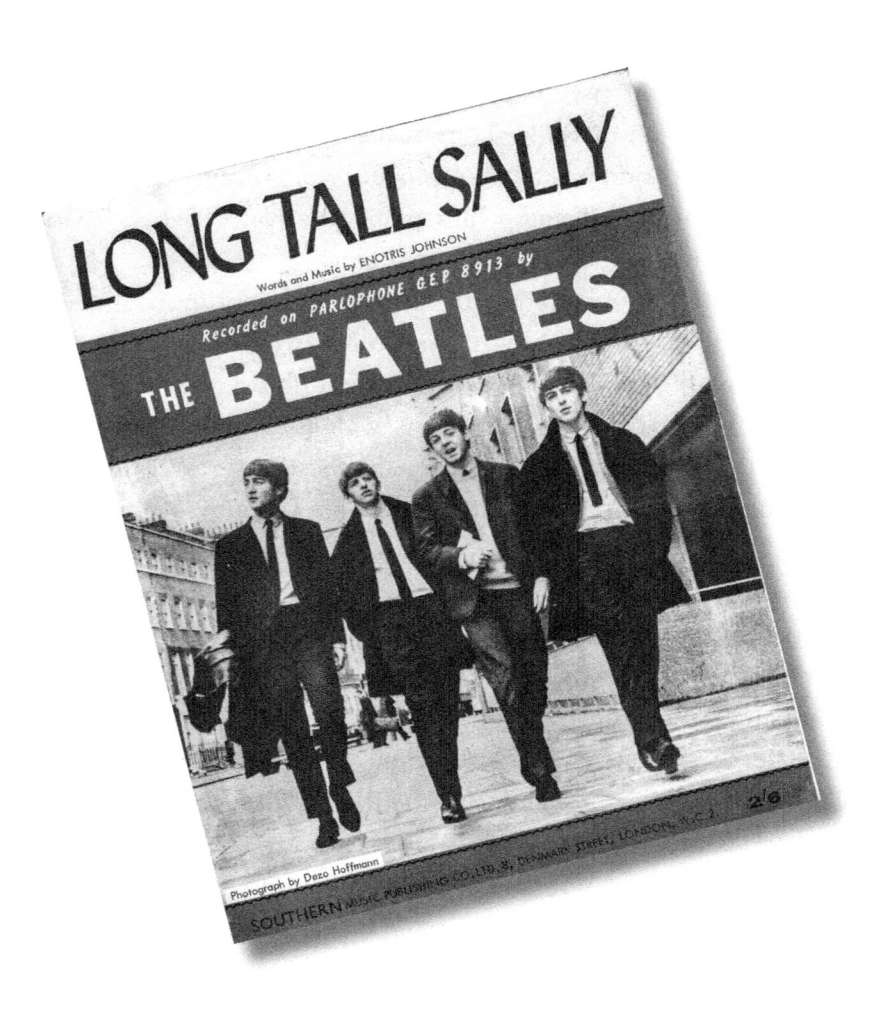

CHAPTER 14

Honey, Just Allow Me One More Chance

On Saturday 1 May 1965, Bob Dylan crossed the Pennines to appear at the Odeon in Liverpool. Cup Final day, as it happens. The Odeon, around the corner from the Empire, showed films but there was the occasional stage show and I saw Brook Benton, Timi Yuro and Dion on a wonderful package in October 1963. Dylan checked into the Adelphi Hotel and was taken by their Cheshire cheese.

Only a few weeks earlier, I had gone to a poorly-attended Tamla-Motown package at the Empire Theatre with Stevie Wonder, the Supremes, the Four Tops and Martha and the Vandellas, so within a month, I saw Stevie Wonder, Diana Ross and Bob Dylan. I had no trouble in purchasing Dylan tickets – the *NME* said when tickets would be on sale and I walked across town in my lunch-hour: there wasn't a queue.

I bought two tickets, one for myself and one for my girlfriend, Diana. I wasn't sure that Diana would like it. She'd heard me play Bob Dylan's albums, especially *The Times They Are A-Changin'*, and she didn't care for him. She hated his voice, his songs, his stark instrumentation – in fact, the whole enchilada. I told her that he would be different in person and she would love him. I realise how naive I was – you shouldn't browbeat your tastes onto other people.

We went into Liverpool on the Ribble bus, got off at the terminus in Skelhorne Street and walked down Lime Street towards London Road. As we turned the corner we saw above the entrance: "The Sound of Music, 2.30" on top and "Bob Dylan, 7.30" underneath as though Dylan wasn't providing the sound of music.

The plush curtains were shut and in front of them on a small stage, a platform really, were two microphones, one head-high, one waist-high, a stool and a table with harmonicas, a carafe and a glass. Minimalistic but strangely exciting. If the show had been at the Empire, the curtains would have covered the stage, but this was great – the anticipation of knowing that my hero was about to stand there and play his songs. If there was a programme, I wouldn't have bought one – in my arrogance, I would have told Diana that I knew it all already: I was insufferable and I'm embarrassed to write this but it's true.

The place was full and Dylan did two sets, but everything didn't go to plan. Dylan started with 'The Times They Are A-Changin", or at least I think he did, as his vocal mic wasn't working. A technician sorted it out while Dylan stood around. Surely this man who was so good with words could have said something through the other mic. As it turned out, he didn't say a word to us all night. When the technician got it working, there was a huge cheer, and Dylan started on his rallying song, opening with a quick burst on the harmonica. It was followed by the beautifully sensitive 'To Ramona'. He was singing his lyrics much clearer than on record as if he wanted to get his words across to a UK audience.

The lengthy and complex 'Gates Of Eden' was next but he lightened the mood with the humorous 'If You Gotta Go, Go Now', which we'd never heard before. He played up the absurdity in the seven-minute 'It's Alright, Mama (I'm Only Bleeding)' but I'd noticed Diana had stopped clapping – did she ever start? The wonderfully lyrical 'Love Minus Zero / No Limit' was next and he closed the first half with 'Mr Tambourine Man'. "Don't worry," I told Diana, "The second half will be better." I don't remember anything else about the interval except that it was awkward.

The funniest moment of the night occurred in the opening song from the second set, 'Talking World War III Blues'. He changed a line so that when he turned on the radio, it was no longer Rock-a-day Johnny but "Donovan (pause, laugher from audience), whoever Donovan is (more laughter)". He changed the line, "I think Abraham Lincoln said that" to "I think Robert Frost said that". A friend told me that he said, "I think T S Eliot said that" in Newcastle so he was testing variations.

'With God On Our Side' was chilling and that line about Judas Iscariot is the most surprising, the most thoughtful, the most provocative line ever written in a popular song. It was followed by the cheerful mysteriousness of 'She Belongs to Me' and the bitterness of 'It Ain't Me, Babe'.

There was the tragedy of 'The Lonesome Death of Hattie Carroll', a protest song in which he named names. Dylan had a coughing fit when he started 'All I Really Want to Do' and after drinking water, he started again, almost yodelling the title line. Everything about Dylan was anti-showbiz so why did he close with 'It's All Over Now, Baby Blue'? But it was all over now, baby blue, as there was no encore. You knew an artist wasn't coming back when the National Anthem started. I'd been hoping for 'Subterranean Homesick Blues' as it was in the Top 20 and even though he recorded it with rock musicians, surely he had composed it acoustically. Not to worry, the concert had been great, superlative even.

Somebody said, "I don't how he remembers all those words" to which the reply was "I don't know how he wrote them." Amen to that.

There was a wonderful feeling on Lime Street as Liverpool had beaten Leeds at Wembley and had therefore won both the League and the Cup. The supporters coming off the London trains or out of the pubs were as happy as we were. Did Bob Dylan think Liverpool was always as happy as this? Did he appreciate that Liverpool had won the Cup?

I'd love to add that Diana was converted but she complained that I had wasted two hours of her life. She finished with me there and then.

After the Liverpool show, Dylan was at the Blue Angel, owned by the Beatles' first manager, Allan Williams and he met up with Merseyside personalities including Roger McGough and Mike McGear (Paul's brother) from Scaffold.

Roger McGough told me, "I was at the Blue Angel and Allan Williams said, 'Bob Dylan is coming' and a buzz went around. He introduced us and I had a group of girls called the Poppies at the time, whom I was thinking of managing with a friend called Clive Goodwin. We all went on his invitation to the Adelphi. Bob Dylan sat in the corner talking. We were talking about Liverpool and this, that and the other. I was a bit in awe of him and I found him to be very nice."

There is a rider to this story, as Diana and I got back together and, in 1966, we were again having a threesome with Bob Dylan. I told her it would be different this time as he had a band, indeed The Band, with him, but she thought him even worse than before. It really was all over with Diana after that.

CHAPTER 15

Days In The Life: 1965-1966

I always enjoyed working at Royal Life. I never woke up with dread for what I would have to do that day. Work could be repetitive, but it needs to be. You'd go mad if you had to do something stimulating every day.

It was good to talk to the senior actuaries in the 1960s as you learnt how to look at problems and come to decisions. Not that they all thought alike by any means.

When J M Beattie retired, his successor Tony Baker was urbane and knowledgeable, but he was regularly visiting hospital for a new knee or a new hip. He called himself the world's first bionic actuary.

Harry Elderton was affable and charming with a wallet bulging with £5 notes, which he said was "the benefit of being an actuary". He was full of good advice although he once ran adrift himself. He had feigned sickness as he wanted to go to Old Trafford, but he was snapped by a photographer and had to explain himself once it was printed in *Lancashire Life*.

Donald Patton was brusque and opinionated and had come from London after Royal Insurance had taken over the much smaller Law, Union & Rock. He wouldn't allow his wife to have a refrigerator as "the North was cold enough already".

Shortly after I'd started, he decided to sack an actuarial

student. He told me to come into his room "so that you will see how to sack somebody.". It was horrific. Not only was this poor chap sacked but he was humiliated. Patton told him, "Look at Leigh, I could light a match on his forehead. With you, it would sink in like putty." Rather than being flattered, I felt my time would come if I stepped out of line.

Patton had moved to Liverpool with another LUR actuary, the mild-mannered Richard Tidy. I suspect that Tidy had been bullied for years, and even though Tidy was an actuary himself, he was treated appallingly by Patton, who would come out of his office and shout, "Tidy, do this!" Tidy received a Christmas card from one of the girls who signed it "With love". Instead of thanking her, Tidy told her that it was most inappropriate. These were very different times, very different people.

On the whole, the LUR staff were eccentric, which made me wonder about that office's recruitment policy. You easily pick them out in a line-up. Talking of which, I was walking by the police station in Dale Street one lunch-hour and invited to join a line-up. It was unnerving as this poor lady made her way down the line and I hoped I wasn't going to be selected.

The most pernickety LUR actuary was John Hobbs, a keen athlete who always believed that he was right. He had protruding ears which he attributed to a superabundance of brain pushing his ears out. He was obsessed with being first in the queue and indeed, every morning when he arrived from Bebington on the train, he had to be the first through the barrier at Liverpool.

I reported to him for three years in the mid-60s and it was exhausting. He had to be right no matter what, which meant finding fault with everybody else's work.

All the typing went to a pool. Even if it was a simple letter for him to sign, "Thank you for letting us see this document", it might have to be retyped as "We thank you for letting us see this document", or vice versa.

John Hobbs didn't so much *do* work as create it. I described him as the 'most pernickety actuary': he would have changed it to 'pernicketiest'.

Hobbs put his passion into his garden. He won prizes - he had to win prizes – in the Royal's horticultural show and, astonishingly, he sold his vegetables to his wife. He used that money to buy more seeds, so the housekeeping money was going round in circles.

On the other hand, I worked for an actuary with the splendid name of Crosby Barnes and his attitude was, If I can live with what has just been typed, we can send it out. Excessively intelligent and urbane, he ran Scheme Rearrangements, but he didn't want to rearrange them at all if it were possible, so he was probably the wrong man for the job.

Everything took its time. Photocopiers were a novelty, and you couldn't just go to the photocopier and use it. You might, after all, break it. No, you had to put your request for a photocopy in the out-tray and, if it was before 2pm, you would get it back that afternoon. A photocopying clerk did all the work. The GPO had cheaper rates for telephone calls after 1pm, so we were encouraged to ring branches and clients in the afternoon. Hence, photocopies in the morning, phone calls in the afternoon!

The girls wore green overalls during the 1960s. Some girls came from more affluent homes than others and so might wear better clothes. The green overall was seen as a great leveller, but really it converted them all from office workers to factory workers.

There was no need to go to an optician if you worked alongside LUR staff. Their entrance qualification might have been the ability to write The Lord's Prayer on the back of a postage stamp.

Mr Bates and Mr Wilkinson had worked together for years, always addressing each other formally and being critical of each other. Most people thought Mr Bates was a hard worker but he wasn't. He didn't like missing *Test Match Special* and he had a transistor radio in his pocket with a wire running up his sleeve. He would put in the earpiece and hold his left hand to his ear as he worked. Even on the hottest day of the year when we had permission to remove our jackets (yes!), Mr Bates was still there with the earpiece up his jacket sleeve.

Mr Wilkinson was four foot eight and a very dapper little guy who had great difficulty in finding shops that sold clothes to fit him. He was thorough and precise. In the toilets, there were large, frosted windows which you could unlatch at the top using a pole and then they swivelled in the middle. They could be dangerous and certainly were for Mr Wilkinson. The office was on the fourth floor and he fell out and was killed.

There had been nobody else in the toilets and so there were no witnesses, but it was said that, rather than use the pole, he had stood on the windowsill to reach the latch and fallen out. That is possible but unlikely. Who would take the trouble to unlatch a window in a toilet anyway, especially when it required some agility on Mr Wilkinson's part? I'm inclined to think it was deliberate as he had been diagnosed with cancer.

The Coroner for obvious reasons gave him the benefit of the doubt. No warnings were put on the windows, nor any changes made to them, which suggest that it was deliberate,

There is nothing much to report regarding office romances. I occasionally went out with a girl from the office but nothing serious.

A few students did marry girls from the office but I preferred to keep things separate.

I returned from lunch one day, did the first item on my desk and looked at the next item in the pile. Under a few sheets of paper, another student Paul had put nude photographs of his girlfriend. He laughed when I was surprised and I said, "How did you get Boots to print them?" Come to think of it, there was a girl in the Liverpool branch who posed for *Penthouse* but I never met her or saw her photographs.

You could get away with doing very little work and some students avoided going to the study room. Alan Wilkinson never went there, or rather he did but only to deposit a message, "Gone to library". I doubt if he knew where the library was.

Bill Hudson was a good student but he would nap in the afternoon. When asked why, he said, "If the Royal only pays me one half of what I'm worth, I'm only going to work half a day." As far as I know, no manager ever questioned this.

In December 1966, Elsie Law, the manager of the Odeon Cinema in Crosby, was short of a Father Christmas for the Saturday morning programme and asked me if I would step in. The Father Christmas from the previous year got into deep water when children asked him about his Cuban heels.. As I had some wellingtons, I agreed to do it.

When I walked into the foyer, a horde of children followed me to the stage, all anxious to get a good look at me or at least, see what I had on my feet. My first job was to present prizes in a fancy dress competition. The winner was a little boy with a cardboard clock on his chest and wings on his back: he had come as 'Time flies'. I suspect his parents had worked that out.

I thought the children would think "Well, there's a Father Christmas at Blacklers and another at T J Hughes, so he can't be here as well", but fortunately children don't think like that — at least they didn't back then - and the trick of playing Father Christmas is to believe that you are, indeed, Father Christmas.

One small girl said her mummy was outside and would I say hello to her sister in a pram. Imagine you're a baby. You see a man with a long and filthy white beard. What do you do? So did this baby.

I got away with it, just about. I was still Father Christmas at the end of the day, which got me free cinema tickets. I was lucky that nobody tugged at my beard.

CHAPTER 16

Timon My Hands

This story is an expanded version of an article published in Roger Eagle's north-west magazine, *The Last Trumpet*, in October 1975. It's a tale I'd rather not relate. I wish the facts were different. It's about how one hell of a talented guy, Timon, has been messed about by almost everybody he's been with. That you may never have heard of Timon is certainly not his fault. The blame lies with some of the most respected and revered names in the music industry. Read on and find out.

Timon is Steven Murray, a Formby lad, who started performing during the Bob Dylan/Donovan era. He sang their songs and he played the Peppermint Lounge regularly and the Cavern occasionally. He had a distinctive voice and could play harmonica and guitar. He didn't do anything too adventurous but then he was only 15 or 16. Those who remember him mention his proud father who turned up at every gig: a chemist by day and roadie by night.

When I met Timon, I asked him if he would like to write some songs for an amateur revue in Crosby called *Bless This Scouse*. To his surprise, he found that composing came naturally and I'm still very fond of 'In Out of the Rain', a jaunty song about a girl who hears him singing Paul Simon's 'I Am a Rock'. He followed the revue with a successful one-man show in Crosby and then another at the Crane Theatre in Liverpool. We publicised that he would be singing the full 11-minute version of 'Desolation Row', a good way, we thought, of generating publicity, even if there were a lot of words to remember for Timon.

Record companies were bombarded with press cuttings. It took a while but Cyril Stapleton, the 50s bandleader and part of Pye's management team, invited us down to London (I was a sort of honorary PR man.) "I don't understand this song." he said as Timon recorded his demos, "What does 'I am a rock' mean?"

Stapleton placed him with Jerry Martin, a Canadian trying to make it here as a producer. There's not much wrong with 'The Bitter Thoughts of Little Jane' and 'Rambling Boy' which formed Timon's first single in January 1968. Unfortunately, Jerry was given the chop just before the record was released and as Pye would look idiots if his final work was a hit, it was given a low profile.

The Noel Gay Organisation considered paying Radio Caroline £200 for two weeks' intensive plugging, but they doubted its effectiveness as 'Neon Rainbow' by the Box Tops had had this treatment and hadn't sold. Left to its own devices, the single surfaced once on *The Tony Blackburn Show*, and Timon was offered a spot on the TV show, *First-Timers*, on which Timon chose to sing a new song, 'Something New Everyday'.

Brian, the local sales rep, told me that NEMS had taken six copies, Rushworth's two and Beaver Radio one. Nine copies for sale in Whitechapel then. Brian had done okay on the Wirral and shifted 75 copies in total.

After Jerry Martin, Timon was assigned to Tony Macaulay, Pye's new wonder boy with hits for the Foundations and Long John Baldry. Macaulay was disinterested but who can blame him as he had enough on his plate. At the session for 'You'd Better Not

Say You Love Me Now', he had overlooked the orchestration for the bridge and so a 15 minute break was called and Timon was asked to write a third verse in its place. The results were okay but Pye decided against its release and arranged a further session with Frank Barber and Cyril Stapleton, which put Timon's songs into waltz-time. The additional cost was substantial but still Pye didn't release a second single.

Cyril Stapleton was more interested in his next signing - Prince Charles' dustman. The papers reported that he had woken up the Prince so why not put him on record? It was to counteract the success of the Singing Postman with EMI.

Brian Hutch from the Noel Gay Organisation introduced Timon to Peter Asher of Peter and Gordon who liked his songs and put him up for the night in London after taking him to the Speakeasy. He wanted him for Apple but it depended on the Beatles. John Lennon had gone to see Brigitte Bardot (having whittled down the number of Beatles who could go!) and Paul was in Scotland.

Being musicians themselves, the Beatles were determined that Apple would be different from other labels. They wanted to avoid the usual hassles. Paul McCartney told Timon that nothing like his Pye troubles could happen here. After meeting McCartney, Timon went to Hyde Park where he wrote 'I Am Not Important', still one of his best songs. It has the memorable line, "I'll climb into your suitcase and we can move as one."

Apple was besieged with tapes from young hopefuls. I can vouch for this as I saw them piled high in Peter Asher's office. "Are you going to play them all?" I asked. "How can I?" he replied. As far as I know, no one was signed because of these tapes. Apple's most successful signing, Mary Hopkin, had won the ITV talent competition, *Opportunity Knocks*.

Asher was already working with James Taylor who could be seen wandering around with a pen and a yellow legal pad. He was trying to complete the songs for his first album. I said, "Haven't you got any old ones you can use?" He said, "Man, I haven't written 12 songs in my life."

Timon even received a postcard saying, "Great to have you with us" and signed by all four Beatles. Timon said everyone but the Beatles was pretty well broke at Apple. Jackie Lomax was given George Harrison's session money because they thought George had forgotten about it.

McCartney gave Timon a demo of 'Miss Pringle' a Herman's Hermits-slanted song they had been sent. Timon persuaded him that he would be more comfortable with his own material and a session took place with some heavy talent (McCartney's piano, Taylor's guitar, Mike Vickers' arrangements).

The word Apple did have some mystical quality as I went backstage at the Empire Theatre in Liverpool to meet Johnny Cash and hand him one of Timon's songs, 'Morgan the Sailor'. Nothing came of it.

Timon's Apple session was on 13 August 1968 and was produced by Peter Asher. 'And Now She Says She's Young', a marvellous song about a bored society lady, and the atmospheric 'Who Needs A King?' marked Timon's best studio work to date. The results were not as good as they should have been as Asher didn't know where to stop and the brass riffs on 'Something New Every Day' sounded inappropriate.

Unfortunately, George Harrison didn't care for the results, so a single wasn't released. I don't know if there was a knock-on effect, but after Paul McCartney and Jane Asher split up, it was goodbye to Peter Asher, James Taylor and Timon, who didn't have an Apple single to his name.

Timon spent a few months chasing up dead ends and gigging around the London area, and then the BBC DJ David Symonds introduced him to the Moody Blues. They were starting up their own record label, Threshold, and they told Timon they would record him and learn from Apple's mistakes.

When he appeared with the Moody Blues on a UK concert tour, the programme notes, somewhat optimistically (and written by me), promised a forthcoming album. Justin Hayward produced his single 'And Now She Says She Young' and 'I'm just a Travelling Man'. The A-side featured Timon with the Moody Blues and was more austere than the version at Apple. 'I'm just a Travelling Man' featured just Timon and Justin Hayward on guitars and was an excellent performance of a happy-go-lucky song. Despite being featured by Bob Harris, the single didn't take off and Timon had difficulty in getting them together for another session. The band's keyboard player, Mike Pinder, was busy building a fountain in his hall. So, it was goodbye from Threshold.

Then followed a brief encounter with Muff Winwood at Island – again no single – and Timon's management became a story in its own right. They got him few gigs and even fewer auditions. As I wrote in 1975: His Threshold single was in 1970, and we are still waiting for a follow-up. It's a shame because he has written some of his best songs over the last year and I particularly like 'The Eye in the Pond': "And I thought we were alone and come undone, Now someone's come and told me there's an eye in the pond." Another excellent song was 'The Ghost of Sister Ruth' – intriguing titles, good words and strong melodies.

Far from being disillusioned, Timon remains optimistic. He could have written 'Prince of Wonderland' about himself. He may not have made much money in the last few years (often supplementing his income by busking) but he has no intention of giving up. I hope he strikes a winner but only time and Timon will tell.

When Timon does make it, he thinks reporters will say "Where have you been?" and he'll reply, "Under your nose."

*****

So, that's what I wrote in 1975 and I was sorry that his career hadn't taken off. Now in 2024, Timon is still performing but as Tymon Dogg. I'm still sorry and frustrated about his lack of exposure. To complete the story, here's an update on what I'd written all those decades ago.

In 1971 Timon and John Mellor became flatmates in Palmers Green, London, calling their squat Vomit Heights. This changed Timon's life as John Mellor became Joe Strummer and Timon often worked with him. He sang his own song 'Lose This Skin' on the Clash's album, *Sandanista!* and he became part of Joe's other band, the Mescaleros. He played violin, usually holding it against his ribs, and he acquired several exotic instruments in his worldwide travels.

By 1973 Timon was fed up with people calling him Tim On, so he changed it to Tymon. When a landlady asked him his surname, he said "Dogg", and realised that Tymon Dogg sounded good.

Between 1975 to 1978 he had a unique look – half long hair, half bald with half a moustache. The half-moustache never caught on, but you never know…

He had some songs recorded by Ellen Foley in the late 70s, but not enough artists have recorded his songs. Then he explored the calmer New Age music in the Frugivores with his first wife Helen Cherry.

During 2009 Tymon appeared live on my *On The Beat*

programme during Beatle week and greatly impressed the German artist, Klaus Voormann. The following year he married Susan De Muth, and they have set some of William Blake's poems to music. In 2015 he again appeared in *On The Beat* and met Mike Badger, originally from the La's, who booked him for his monthly music night in Liverpool.

Tymon's career has lasted nearly 60 years. He has never had great success but he has always been true to himself. *The Irrepressible Tymon Dogg* is a collection of tracks from 1968 to 2009 and released on Cherry Red.

CHAPTER 17

Days In The Life, 1967

It was in the year 1966 that the Beatles moved completely away from their contemporaries with *Revolver,* which had shades of psychedelia ('Tomorrow Never Knows') but not too much. Although Gerry and the Pacemakers and the Searchers did try psychedelia, their hearts were not in it: they were lads who wanted to end the day with a pint and had no interest in what the Sandoz Laboratory was manufacturing. The Stones, on the other hand, were busted for drugs, which led to the editorial in *The Times*, '*Who Breaks a Butterfly on a Wheel?*' demanding the relaxation of penalties for their kind of offences and written by William Rees-Mogg, father of Jacob. Mick Jagger recalled reading it in his prison cell.

The good and great of psychedelia were at the Monterey International Pop Festival (a bizarre name but laced with irony). Over three days in June 1967, the hippies heard Janis Joplin, Jimi Hendrix, Jefferson Airplane and the Byrds. The UK was represented by the Who and Eric Burdon, a streetwise Newcastle lad who had gone hippie.

The Beatles developed their own stance on psychedelia. A glorious single from February 1967 combined Paul's hippie take on Penny Lane, seemingly relocated to Chelsea, and John Lennon's anguished memories in 'Strawberry Fields Forever', which foreshadowed his first solo LP in 1970. When the 45rpm was featured on BBC-TV's *Juke Box Jury*, the chairman David Jacobs said that he had no idea what 'Strawberry Fields Forever' was about - him and the rest of the UK, come to that, but unlike David Jacobs, we found it compelling and intriguing.

The 45 sounded like those friendly Beatles experimenting as opposed to confrontational and more demanding records from Captain Beefheart and the Mothers of Invention. Looking back, that is one of the Beatles' strengths: whether music, film or fashion, they made their changes in a self-deprecating way and not forcefully.

The year 1967 is synonymous with the Summer of Love, but even though I was 22, the Summer of Love passed me by. I bought some of the music including Scott McKenzie's glorious anthem, 'San Francisco', and I had some tie-dye jeans (£2 in C&A), but otherwise there is little to report. I did visit London's King's Road and Carnaby Street but hardly anything was happening in Liverpool.

Actually, I was never very conscious of fashion although I liked to look decent. There was good, hard-wearing stuff in the Army & Navy Stores. They claimed to sell surplus clothing, which puzzled me. Had the services or at least the army and navy overstocked on everything? However, we did win the World Wars.

John Gorman of Scaffold owned a hippie boutique, Through the Looking Glass, and indeed, the only hippie-styled event I attended was a one-day festival at Formby Hall, headlined by Scaffold. I have a happy memory of talking to some girl and placing flowers between her toes. That's it, my total involvement with the Summer of Love.

There were a few local psychedelic bands – Zelda Plum comes to mind – but not many. I went to a poetry reading in the small Sandon Theatre in the Bluecoat Chambers and the guest poet was Pete Brown from London, who had been a prime mover in getting a scene started in Liverpool in the early 60s. Some of his lyrics had been accepted by a new band, Cream, and he read 'I Feel Free' and 'Wrapping Paper'. I was impressed. Pete was staying with Adrian Henri and they took too much of something. When Adrian awoke, he found a naked girl asleep downstairs and, on her back, Pete had written with a black felt marker, "Adrian, Gone back to London, Love, Pete."

Adrian's group, Liverpool Scene, had a weekly residency at O'Connor's Tavern in Leece Street. There were three components to the pub. Upstairs was the performance space where Liverpool Scene performed and, more than anything, a new song from a unique performer, Mike Hart, would set me up for the week. The sculptor Arthur Dooley might be around. I once read out a poem about Vietnam and he called out, "Which fucking side are you on?" Served me right for being pretentious.

Downstairs you might find shady businessmen cutting deals in complete disregard of the police station further up the road. Indeed, any undercover cop who wanted to increase his tally of arrests would only need to spend a couple of hours in O'Connor's,

Then there were members of the Royal Liverpool Philharmonic Orchestra as the Phil was only up the road, just past the police station.

The one I remember most is Andy Woodburn. He had played in a brass band attached to a Scottish mill and he had lost an eye in an accident. He wore a patch and he was a formidable figure, always arguing and spouting left-wing causes, a Jeremy Corbyn of the 60s. I learnt that he was argumentative in rehearsals but the management tolerated him because he was such a brilliant player. When the conductor Sir Charles Groves wanted a composition to be played for the third time, Andy snarled, "We're not fucking students!" and walked out.

The Beatles had a remarkable year in 1967 with that single, the hippie anthem 'All You Need Is Love' and 'Hello Goodbye', the LP *Sgt Pepper's Lonely Hearts Club Band* and the TV film *Magical Mystery Tour*, which was castigated at the time, but who can deny its soundtrack? There's the brilliant gibberish of 'I Am the Walrus' and an orthodox reflective ballad, 'The Fool on the Hill', which nevertheless had a unique string arrangement.

The life-changing event for the Beatles though was the death of their manager, Brian Epstein, over the August bank holiday in 1967. The Beatles did not know what to do next and considered recruiting Dr Beeching who was responsible for axing UK train services and closing so many stations in a mad economy drive. Surely the fact that the Beatles were even considering Dr Beeching is proof positive that they were taking things that they shouldn't have done.

CHAPTER 18

Strange Days Indeed

Happenings started with the American *avant-garde* in the 1950s. I'd read how an audience had to crawl through tyres to gain entry and how sensibilities were challenged once they were inside. There had been the occasional Happening in Liverpool, emanating from Adrian Henri and the artistic community in Liverpool 8. When *Bomb* was held at the Cavern in 1965, the audience was covered with fake fall-out.

Yoko One was an *avant-garde* film-maker and her film of 365 bottoms (one for every day of the year) was being screened in London in 1967. One backside belonged to the TV presenter Michael Aspel, but the jazz singer and art critic George Melly declined, thinking the project too ridiculous.

It was announced that Yoko Ono would stage a Happening at the Bluecoat Chambers in Liverpool on 26 September 1967. I went with Andrew Doble and this is what happened.

The tickets had been reduced from 7/6d to 6/- (37p to 30p). About 400 of us were kept waiting 20 minutes before being allowed into the auditorium, but that could have been Yoko's plan– she wanted us to get to know each other.

Here are my notes from the time:

Number 1. Pig Piece

Loud wailing over the speakers is interspersed with sexual

grunting and panting. A large white box is placed on stage. Enter Yoko Ono in a white Japanese-styled outfit. She goes inside the box. Five minutes later, she comes out of the box and walks off. The audience is noisy and restless but having fun. This will be a unique evening.

Number 2. Torch Piece

A large black cloth is brought to the front of the stage and held upright. It contains five holes. From out of four of the holes come battery-powered torches on long, wooden, pliable sticks, On the fifth is a pair of knickers. The sticks reach into the audience and then retreat. They are replaced by long, thin balloons, also on sticks. A balloon bursts. The black cloth is taken away.

Number 3. Cleaning Piece

Yoko sweeps the stage while her husband Tony Cox asks the audience to create an 'Add Red' abstract. Adiran Henri sketches something in red. Paste is available to stick things onto a board. Someone adds a red shirt, and everybody cheers when a girl comes on stage in a red sweater. She keeps it on, but John Gorman has some red knickers.

Number 4. Fly Piece

Two large ladders and a piano stool are brought on stage. People are invited to fly. Tony Cox demonstrates by jumping from the piano stool to the floor, although that's hardly flying. An art student with a safety helmet climbs to the top of a ladder and jumps, Applause. Another audience member climbs the larger ladder and two-thirds of the way up, he jumps. Applause. Nobody else wants to try.

Number 5. Tuna Piece

Seven people at the front eating tuna sandwiches. They are joined by Tony Cox who offers large black bags to the audience. "Will anyone please try one? You can see out, but the audience can't see in. If you take off your clothes, be careful where you put them and put them back on before you come out." There is a double-bag which is given to a student couple with everyone urging them to get it on. The bag people remain on stage for the rest of the Happening.

Number 6. Wrapping Piece

Yoko bids us all goodnight as she won't be able to do so later. She breaks a white jug and says, "Collect a piece and we will meet to put it together in 10 years' time." She sits down. I go on stage for a piece of jug and Tony Cox hands me a bandage and says, "Wrap Yoko." I wrap her legs. I collect my piece of jug (and I still have it). Adrian is wrapping her head. My friend Andy joins in.

Number 7. Goodnight Piece.

One sign says 'Wrapping paper', another 'No.4'. (The repetition of 'No.4, No.4' is a precursor for 'Revolution 9' on the Beatles' *White Album*.)

Tony Cox operates a smoke machine to create fog. Yoko holds a microphone, and she is being wrapped like a mummy. John Gorman shouts, "You're wanted on the phone!"

The audience sings the National Anthem led by someone from a black bag who has put up an umbrella. Pantomime responses of "Oh yes, we are" and "On no, we're not" ensue. Andy is wrapping Yoko Ono and she says, "This is the end of the Happening. Continue it in your dreams." Yoko is carried off into the smoke.

The Happening lasted two hours. I have no idea what to make of it and indeed, I'd never seen anything like it before. It was possibly a study in audience reaction which is underlined by the camera crew filming us. No matter. I still have my piece of jug and so has Andy. Yoko never arranged that reunion but we haven't given up hope.

CHAPTER 19

Everybody Razzle Dazzle

I've been lucky enough to meet the artist Sir Peter Blake four times: he is a marvellous man with a positive personality. He made a name for himself with *Self-Portrait with Badges*, a prizewinner at the John Moores Exhibition at the Walker Art Gallery in 1961, That self-portrait defines him as he loves talking about rock'n'roll and the Beatles.

My main interview with him was in 1987 when he spoke at length about his sleeve for *Sgt Pepper's Lonely Hearts Club Band*. That interview has appeared all over the place but has a permanent home, as it were, in my book, *Love Me Do to Love Me Don't* (McNidder and Grace, 2016).

When I met Sir Peter at the opening of Blakes Restaurant at the Hard Days Night Hotel in North John Street, Liverpool, also 2016, I told him I had been speaking to Dion. Dion said: "I met John Lennon and Ringo Starr when they first came to New York. I met them on 57th Street in Manhattan as they were popping in and out of clothing stores. John told me that he loved 'Ruby Baby' and they used to play it when they were honing their skills in Hamburg. When it came to *Sgt Pepper*, they took my photograph from the cover of 'Ruby Baby' and they put it on *Sgt Pepper* and I thought, 'Ah, that must be because John likes 'Ruby Baby' (laughs) – I don't really know but I would like to think that is so."

I told Dion that I was meeting Sir Peter and I would ask him: "Oh dear, I do hope he isn't going to be disappointed. I was a Dion and the Belmonts fan and it was me who chose him rather than one of the Beatles. The system we used was that we had the four Beatles, myself, my then wife Jann Haworth whom I did the cover with, and Robert Fraser all making lists. We selected the names from the lists. Dion was on my list. I thought Dion had a wonderful voice and of course, 'The Wanderer' is a great song."

Peter continued, "There are only two musicians in that montage behind the Beatles – Dion and Bob Dylan. Bob Dylan was probably John's choice. John chose Jesus as a joke as he had got into terrible trouble for saying that the Beatles were bigger than Jesus. Jesus didn't go in and Ghandi didn't go in because it was too delicate politically, and Hitler wasn't a good idea. They were all jokes by John really."

"And there is Albert Stubbins!" I said, wanting to know who had suggested the Liverpool footballer.

Peter Blake: "John definitely chose him! His dad was a great fan and John told me that he didn't really know who Albert Stubbins was. He'd heard his dad talk about him and he loved his name."

Peter's involvement in Liverpool goes far beyond his work with The Beatles. This is what I wrote for *Record Collector* in August 2016.

Now 83, Sir Peter Blake is still working immensely hard and his brightly repainted Mersey ferry, *Snowdrop*, has become one of Liverpool's leading tourist attractions. It was based on the First World War idea that strikingly painted ships might confuse the enemy – and apparently it worked!

In view of the ferry's success, Liverpool Biennial has announced a new limited edition silkscreen *Dazzle*, which will help fund its educational programme. It features a part of his design for the ferry and links back to his early Pop Art paintings from the early 60s. There are 150 signed and numbered copies available for £720 each.

Sir Peter launched the silkscreen at Blakes Restaurant, which is named in his honour and is a part of the Hard Days Night Hotel. He has many connections to the city, not least in winning a prize in the John Moores exhibition in 1961. He knew the Beatles through the 60s and designed the much-imitated sleeve for *Sgt Pepper's Lonely Hearts Club Band.*

"I don't mind the parodies at all," says Sir Peter, "and I do parodies myself in a way as I love to make crowds. I did a special one for my 80th birthday and one for Liverpool's 800th birthday in 2007. I have just completed a crowd collage for 25 chefs who are each cooking dinner for 10 people on 25 different tables."

In the past Sir Peter has created album sleeves for Eric Clapton, the Who and Paul Weller. "My latest one is for Norman Watt-Roy of the Blockheads and I was very glad to do one for Brian Wilson. The album, *Gettin In Over My Head*, didn't get much distribution but I was very pleased with it. I would have loved to have done *Pet Sounds*. I like to think I could have done a great cover for that album."

CHAPTER 20

Days In The Life: 1968-1970

In 1967 the Government permitted the BBC to open local radio stations. Not before time and if there had been local radio in 1963, imagine the wealth of local history that would have come from Liverpool.

The first stations to open were in Leicester and Sheffield with BBC Radio Merseyside being the third, opening on 22 November 1967 from offices in Sir Thomas Street. The opening programme on BBC Radio Merseyside featured invited guests from the Cavern aboard the Royal Iris and I was on during the day with some thoughts on disc-jockeys. No idea what I said but I was paid £3. Hope my thoughts were worth it. The Royal Iris was going to be a floating casino but that idea has long been abandoned and now it is rusting in a berth on the Thames.

A week later, I was invited onto the early morning programme to review the newspapers. I was waiting in the corridor to be called and then told I wasn't needed because somebody would talk about trout-fishing instead. Later, I was asked to say something about Leonard Cohen and to bring along one of his records as I was lecturing about him somewhere. Hence, I might have been the first person to play Leonard Cohen on BBC Radio Merseyside, certainly on a breakfast show.

Once I was on straight after Dennis Waterman, so I spoke to

a star, reviewed the newspapers and then went to work at Royal Life, and all before 9am.

In February 1968 I was moved from Pensions and brought back to the Life department, working on policy surrenders. By and large, it was straightforward work but there was a huge PR problem.

Millions of people took out endowment policies with life offices as investments, often to cover mortgages. The policies provided life assurance cover should you die early but with an investment component to repay your mortgage at the end of the term, hopefully with a tidy bit extra if bonus rates had been good.

The trouble occurred when policies were terminated early. There was no surrender value in the first two years and it was relatively small in the immediate years after that – it could be eight years before you would even see the return of your premiums.

There was a good industry wide reason for this, namely, the commission that had been paid to insurance brokers or banks who had sold the policies on our behalf. They received the bulk of their commission upfront. When clients complained of a measly surrender value, we were not allowed to say, "Well, the broker has £800 of your money" or whatever. We looked like crooks – indeed, I remember one letter addressed to "Those Robbers and Crooks at Royal Insurance".

Time and again, I would explain to unfortunate clients why the values were low but it was with one hand tied behind my back. It was a PR disaster. I would have favoured Royal Life finding a different way of remunerating brokers, but we were bound by industry-wide regulations. Nowadays, policyholders have to be told how much commission the agent would receive.

Still, apart from that, I was enjoying the work and the friendship in the office. There was a very good-natured actuarial student, Janet Ferry, who had come from a village in Wales, graduated from Aberystwyth University and knew no one in Liverpool. We went out a few times as friends and she was at our house once when Dad asked her to sign the Visitors' Book. Some of the girls in the department were keen that we should be a couple and wrote notes on the back of dinner tickets, allegedly in my handwriting, to her.

What they didn't know was that I was already dating someone in the office, Dorothy Chandler, who worked on the same floor but in an administration area. She lived in Maghull and had been Miss Maghull in 1965. She nursed ambitions to be a novelist and her short stories were good, although she was doing nothing with them. I lent her books and she returned *The Heart of the Matter* by Graham Greene with the last page torn out as she couldn't stand the ending.

We went to John Lennon's *In His Own Write* at Liverpool Playhouse which was twinned with *Black Comedy*, a play entirely in the dark: a stage production of a radio play if you like. We went to a few parties and once to the Lake District but nothing very thrilling. I remember bringing her home and my father brought out that wretched Visitors' Book and one of the recent entries was from Janet Ferry.

I'm not including a list of girlfriends here but I can appreciate why nothing lasted very long. Almost invariably, these hapless girls went where I wanted to go. I didn't say, "Where would you like to go?" I'm still inclined to be that way today – and Anne is the same way with her interests, so in a way we're right for each other and everything works out fine.

In November 1968 two famed novelty records were in the charts at the same time – 'I'm the Urban Spaceman' by the Bonzo Dog Doo-Dah Band and 'Lily the Pink' by Scaffold. They did a short, inspired tour together and they agreed that whoever was highest in the charts could top the bill. I saw them at the Philharmonic Hall with a girl called Shirley Telfer and I'd never seen anyone laugh so much, so my suggestion that we went to the concert was, for once, correct.

As well as individual sets, they combined forces for several items including the opener, a mock church-chant called 'A Long Strong Black Pudding'. One of Roger Ruskin Spear's explosions dislodged dirt from the ceiling and the Phil had to pay dry cleaning bills. In a similar incident, Black Sabbath played so loud at Liverpool Stadium that it unsettled rust on the overhead girders.

Some months later when Scaffold were No.1 with 'Lily the Pink', I met Roger McGough upstairs on the L3 to Crosby. It seemed amazing that someone who was No.1 was on a Ribble bus but he was visiting his mother. Roger had a choice of black spectacles with clear lenses, black spectacles with tinted lenses, and contact lenses, and he would decide what was best for a TV appearance, a concert, an evening out or visiting his mum. Decisions, decisions, decisions.

Another gifted observer of Liverpool life was John Cornelius. I'd known John during the 1960s. He lived close to me in Crosby but as his father imported reptiles, I was never keen to visit his home. He moved to Liverpool 8 in the mid-60s and was involved with its cultural scene – John could paint, write songs and perform. He was very influenced by Mike Hart and that cruel streak in Arty's songs came into his. I remember a tirade against a girl, Ruth, who had let him down. Because of childhood polio, he walked with a limp and was self-conscious, but he had a good sense of humour.

He wrote and illustrated a very good book, *Liverpool 8,* which was published by Liverpool University and I met up with him when it was reprinted in 2002. He'd been a teacher but he had his problems: he sued for wrongful dismissal and had been awarded £35,000.

He and his wife Pam, who taught history, moved to Hastings, where he wrote for the local paper and told stories about growing up with exotic (and often dangerous) animals for a nature magazine. His disability worsened with the years and after a breakdown, he was forcibly placed in a nursing home. He died in 2019 but was writing until the end.

Around this time, the comedian Norman Wisdom filmed *What's Good for the Goose?* in Southport. The mayor and councillors were delighted but they didn't know that Norman was changing his image and that it was a sex comedy with Sally Geeson, partly shot nude in Ainsdale Sandhills. Norman played a staid bank executive who was transformed into a hippie in Southport of all places. It opened at Southport Odeon in 1969 with the mayor and councillors in attendance. The mayor walked out, telling the press, "Southport is not full of loose women". That could be a reason why Southport never recovered its tourist boom.

Maybe I wasn't a big spender as every six months I would tot up how much I was worth, or at least what was in my various savings accounts. In April 1969, around the time of my tax return, it was £558, and six months later it was £689. In December 1969, I had a salary increase which took me from £895 to £1,140. I was doing okay: I'd got half of the actuarial exams and it was too late to stop now. I wanted to qualify but the exams were hard.

Some of the students were delightfully eccentric, none more so than the woolly-hatted Malcolm who devoted himself to acquiring old pennies of collectable years. Decimalisation was on its way and all these coins would become obsolete.

Malcolm would take £10 to the Bank of England in Castle Street and receive 2,400 pennies. He would check the dates: 2,350 might be returned but 50 were okay. Then he would request another £10 of pennies and so on. "Guess how many 1947 pennies I've got?" he would say, a real conversation stopper.

This was a daily ritual. The Bank of England, which had better things to do, told him that they couldn't deal with him anymore and another bank gave him back the pennies from a previous visit. He went through thousands of pennies in a ten-week spell and kept £100 of them. His parents brought up a van to take him and his coins home. Did he have the last laugh and is he now sitting on a fortune?

When I went over to the Globe building for lunch, there was someone who worked there who would say, "Are you one of the actuarial students? Well, my advice to you is to be human." But it wasn't just the actuarial students who were eccentric. I went to lunch with a group of people on the general insurance side, one of whom was Brian Hallows.

Brian Hallows gave his wife a monthly allowance for housekeeping but if he was out with the boys one night, he would deduct the cost of a night's meal from that money. He didn't think much of the company's lunches and he moaned about the poor meals he got at home. He sent his long-suffering wife to night-school but it turned out the cookery class was taught by the Royal chef.

Brian was a gambler and had the notion that racehorse owners were not philanthropists and so if a horse was last, there was a reasonable chance that it would be placed in the next race. One day he was going to place a bet after lunch as by applying this theory, there was a horse that might make him £140. It did, indeed, come first but unfortunately for him, he had been called away to an urgent job and he never had the chance to place his bet.

There was a postal strike in 1969 and naturally the Royal wanted its mail to get through. They delegated certain staff to spend their days on intercity trains. For example, someone from Birmingham would catch the Liverpool train each morning with the mail for Head Office. When the train stopped at Wolverhampton, he would wave his pink *Financial Times* so that someone on the platform could recognise him and give him Wolverhampton's mail for Head Office. At Liverpool, he would meet someone from Head Office and he would swap his mail for the mail going to the branches, and so on. I never heard of this system breaking down so it worked well. I did find myself on the Liverpool to Manchester run once and was amused at other people on the train who seemed to be doing something similar for other offices and there were a few pink *Financial Times* around. The trains were comfortable and it was a pleasant way to spend the day.

Talking of which, there was a sale for the belongings of the Great Train Robbers which raised £16,000 for the insurance companies. You could buy a pair of trainers belonging to a train robber for £15.

I was still doing a few poetry readings and 'Bless this Scouse' was picked up by Jacqui and Bridie and often performed by them even at the Philharmonic Hall. They did record it for a live album, *Liverpool Echoes* for the *Liverpool Echo*, but it didn't make it on to one of their official albums because there was a clause banning parodies from the publishers of 'Bless This House', which had been written in 1927.

During the year, I also got to know the *Punch* and *Private Eye* cartoonist, Bill Tidy, who lived nearby in Birkdale. I invited him onto a couple of local shows where he could draw rapidly and amusingly in front of an audience, which was very impressive. I wrote about him in the Royal Staff Bulletin which led to him getting a couple of commissions from the Royal. Today, *The Bulletin* seems like 100 years ago. There are pictures of a branch manager's conference and everyone is a middle-aged white gent.

During the 1970 election campaign, I went to an election meeting in Crosby with the standing Conservative MP, R Graham Page, who refused to be on the same platform as the Labour candidate, Peter Caswell. Mr Page told us how reliable he had been as Crosby's MP. He said, "I have stood up for Crosby and asked over 200 questions in the House." Someone shouted out, "You ignorant bastard!"

CHAPTER 21

Are You Paying For Scarborough Fair?

My brother Chris and I loved the Dustin Hoffman film, *The Graduate*. Indeed, for many years, Chris could quote the screenplay line by line, a neat party-piece. I never heard his full, 100-minute version but I believe he could do it. This is a shortened version of what I wrote about *The Graduate* in *Simon & Garfunkel: Together Alone*, published by McNidder & Grace in 2016.

In the early 60s, Mike Nichols and Elaine May had a popular satirical comedy act in the States. There was a marvellous single 'A Little More Gauze' where a doctor refuses to continue with an operation unless the nurse goes on a date with him.

After a while Mike Nichols found success directing plays on Broadway. His first time out as a film director was with the volatile Elizabeth Taylor and Richard Burton in *Who's Afraid of Virginia Woolf?*, which would have been a challenge for anybody. It was an artistic and commercial success and his second film, *The Graduate*, was about a young man's initiation into adulthood.

Mike Nichols loved Simon and Garfunkel's album, *Parsley, Sage, Rosemary and Thyme*. It was music that his central character, Ben, would enjoy. He gave Simon and Garfunkel the novel, *The Graduate*, by Charles Webb, on which the script by Buck Henry would be based.

Paul Simon dismissed the book as "bad Salinger" and added, "I didn't like anything about the film at first. I was only impressed with Mike Nichols who asked us to do it."

However, that was enough to persuade Simon to write the score. He told *Melody Maker* in 1971, "We had nothing to lose and we didn't think that we had much to gain either. We weren't paid an enormous amount. We didn't think it was a big job. Dustin Hoffman was unknown."

Thirty-year-old Dustin Hoffman looked too old for the graduate, but he is so convincing as the shy Benjamin Braddock who has no idea what do with his life.

Benjamin is told that the future is in plastics. He is seduced by the wife of his father's business partner, Mrs Robinson (Anne Bancroft, wife of Mel Brooks) and then falls for her daughter, Elaine (Katharine Ross). When Elaine finds out what has happened, she ditches Benjamin and marries someone vacuous on the rebound. Benjamin arrives too late to stop the wedding but fights off the congregation with the cross from the altar. Elaine leaves the church with him and they board a bus and look at each other and realise what they have done. End of story.

The social satire holds good and the film has many comic scenes, especially when Benjamin is getting a hotel room for himself and Mrs Robinson. He encounters Buck Henry as a niggling receptionist. It could be argued that Ben was taking advantage of the seriously distressed and alcoholic Mrs Robinson. Later on, Mrs Robinson claims that she was raped and although she wasn't, Benjamin's behaviour could be questioned.

Simon and Garfunkel saw the rushes and were commissioned to record the soundtrack. The production team placed 'Scarborough Fair' and other songs into the film for the time being, and the intention was to replace them. The music worked so well that there was no need for new material. As so often happens, accident become innovation. Paul Simon: "Nobody had ever thought of taking old music and putting it on a soundtrack before."

Simon had the riff for 'Mrs Robinson' but he was singing 'Mrs Roosevelt' to it. Mike Nichols said, "Don't be ridiculous. We're making a movie here. It has to be 'Mrs Robinson'." 'Mrs Robinson' is the only new song by Simon and Garfunkel in the film and even that is not complete. There are two short passages, one of which opens with a magnificent chord when Dustin Hoffman crosses a bridge. The song was completed and recorded after the film had been made.

The Graduate had its finger on the pulse of modern America. Its themes included lack of communication, insincerity and the inanity of cocktail chatter. Mike Nichols could not have found more appropriate music for these topics already featured in Simon's work.

The combination of music and story was perfect and the film drew huge audiences and rave reviews. The new head of Columbia Records, Clive Davis, insisted on a soundtrack album. Paul Simon said no, the songs were on existing albums. Davis disagreed: the film was going to be massive and there had to be a souvenir album. He agreed to put their name in small print on the cover to avoid it looking like a new Simon and Garfunkel album.

Davis had a brainwave for the new album, *Bookends*: put in a poster and charge $1 extra. It worked well but both Simon and Garfunkel thought this a hard-nosed business strategy. In his book Davis says, "I didn't detect any gratitude for my efforts to make Paul and Artie superstars."

When the souvenir album from *The Graduate* was released, it topped the album charts, although much of the LP is incidental music written by Dave Grusin. This was not a record for Simon and Garfunkel fans but more for those who wanted a keepsake from the film. There isn't even a picture of the duo on the cover unless you think that is Art Garfunkel's leg on display. That famous picture was parodied for the film, *Percy*, which had music from the Kinks.

Nevertheless, the soundtrack album topped the US album chart for nine weeks, being replaced by Simon and Garfunkel's next album *Bookends*, and it remained on the listings for a year. In the UK, *The Graduate* made No. 3 and stayed on the charts for over 70 weeks.

When 'Scarborough Fair/Canticle' was released belatedly as a US single, it made No 11. It should have gone higher but it was already on two hit albums. The song was credited to Paul Simon and Art Garfunkel and published by Lorna Music, which is fair enough as it was way out of copyright, but should Martin Carthy have been credited for his arrangement? Martin Carthy had one of the UK's Rottweilers, the manager and promoter Jeff Kruger, fight his cause.

Jeff Kruger told me, and this is a man who never had self-doubts: he was always right, "'Scarborough Fair' was an old British song and there had been a relatively new recording by Martin Carthy, and we published that song and that recording. My partner Hal Shaper said that Simon and Garfunkel were coming to the office and I played them Martin's recording. They were going to record it and I was very pleased because I was sure they would make it a worldwide hit. When they released it, they listed it as their arrangement of a traditional song and claimed the copyright. They put it in *The Graduate*, which was going to open with a Royal Film Show the following week. I said I would put out an injunction to stop the release of the record and the film until my rights were acknowledged. United Artists must have spoken to Simon and Garfunkel as their manager sent me a first-class air ticket to New York. Simon and Garfunkel were okay at the meeting but their lawyer called me every insulting thing it was possible to call me. After an hour or so, I said to them, 'You may believe the rubbish that your lawyers are telling you but the bottom line is this: unlike America, your celebrity will not protect you. When you go into the witness box, the first question my QC will ask is, "Do you normally steal songs from poor British writers?" That is the reality of it. You heard the song in my office, you got the music from my publishing firm, and you stole it. There are two possible solutions: you acknowledge us as the publisher and pay us the royalties or I will sell you the copyright', and it was the latter that they did. We lifted the injunction and I walked out with a lot of money for my publishing company, and the hatred of that lawyer who stopped me getting UK tours with a lot of major artists, but you have to protect what you believe to be right."

In turn, Martin Carthy had seen the song in Ewan MacColl and Peggy Seeger's book, *The Singing Island*, so who really knows who deserves the money? Still, Martin Carthy paid off his mortgage. Martin Carthy: "It was never my song. It was there for anybody to do. The only thing I resented is that Paul Simon implied he had written it when he had taken enormous pains to learn it. I wrote the words down for him and his way of promoting the song wasn't entirely honourable, but it's tough bananas, isn't it? It's ridiculous to suggest that had it not been for Paul Simon, I would have had a hit with 'Scarborough Fair'. I wouldn't have had a hit because, leaving aside the question of whether people would have bought my version, I wouldn't allow Fontana to issue a single of it. I don't believe that my version would have made me

$20m or whatever or that I would have got to do the music for *The Graduate*."

Simon and Garfunkel developed 'Mrs Robinson' into a complete song. It was very catchy, featuring very rhythmic guitars and congas, and less complex than most of Simon's work, being a two-chord tune. The lyrics, largely in blank verse, were outstanding. Simon was proud of them, telling *Melody Maker* in 1971: "'Mrs Robinson' was the first time that Jesus was mentioned in a popular song. Nobody had said 'Jesus' before. People thought it was a word that you wouldn't say in pop music. On the radio they wouldn't play it; they'd find it blasphemous."

The song has its serious moments and there is the much-quoted line "Where have you gone, Joe DiMaggio?", a reference to the baseball star who married Marilyn Monroe. Said Paul Simon, "It's an interesting line for a song that has nothing to do with Joe DiMaggio." Joe DiMaggio did ask Paul Simon, "What does that song mean? I haven't disappeared. I'm doing ads for Mr Coffee." It is, I think, a reflection on lost youth, time moving on and a lack of new heroes.

There was tough competition for the Record of the Year at the Grammys – 'Mrs Robinson' (Simon and Garfunkel), 'Hey Jude' (Beatles), 'Harper Valley PTA' (Jeannie C Riley), 'Honey' (Bobby Goldsboro) and 'Wichita Lineman' (Glen Campbell) – all five being familiar oldies today. My personal preference would be for 'Wichita Lineman', which is a highly unusual Jimmy Webb composition, but the voters went for 'Mrs Robinson'. Simon was surprised; he had been certain he would lose to 'Hey Jude'.

CHAPTER 22

Almost Liverpool 8

Those who saw Mike Hart perform will testify to his brilliance, unless they saw him on a bad night which unfortunately was quite often.

His 1969 album, *Mike Hart Bleeds* on John Peel's Dandelion label, remains an eccentric, defiant record by someone prepared to argue his corner: 'Aberfan' berates celebrities for crying publicly at the tragedy; 'Shelter Song' criticises the Church for not housing the homeless in their huge cathedrals; and 'Almost Liverpool 8' is a diatribe at the latest girl to leave in his extensive list of hopeless relationships.

The album was the antithesis of easy listening and his career was equally edgy: there can be few artists who have consistently sabotaged their own careers.

Michael William Hart was born in Bebington on the Wirral on 4 December 1943 and educated at Birkenhead School, which means he was a bright lad.

Its current prospectus states that it provides "a caring and structured environment where pupils grow in self-confidence". Mike Hart was not a model pupil.

When Mike's parents migrated to Australia, he stayed behind and in 1962 he formed a rhythm and blues band, the Roadrunners, which had residencies at Hope Hall (now the Everyman Theatre) and the Cavern. Roger McGough claims that they performed 'Twist and Shout' and 'Money' better than the Beatles. "Arty, the wild man in front," he remembers, "was very popular with the ladies. He was weird looking, but he was very charismatic, a Jaggeresque thing."

In 1963 George Harrison told some Liverpool musicians that he had seen the Rolling Stones "who are almost as good as the Roadrunners." Their *tour de force* was Bobby 'Blue' Bland's 'Cry Cry Cry' which Hart would perform passionately; his eyes tight shut as if reliving past ordeals.

Mike McCartney recalls, "I can see Mike Hart now with his big lips and his eyes closed going (sings) 'Cry, cry, cry'. It was one of my favourite songs and he always gave it the welly in terms of soul. Whenever he sang that, you were crying."

The Roadrunners turned down a management offer from Giorgio Gomelsky and a recording contract with Fontana. If Hart said no, that was it and although there is little of the Roadrunners on tape, there is a live set from the Star-Club in Hamburg and an EP for Liverpool University's Panto Week, recorded at the Cavern's short-lived studio.

After travelling with the band to York, Arty refused to play and said it was all over. No arguments, no recriminations – he just left.

Instead, Mike joined a unique music and poetry collective called Liverpool Scene with Adrian Henri, Andy Roberts, Mike Evans, Percy Jones and Brian Dodson. Their first single was his witty, rasping song, 'Son Son' (1968), in which everyone is too preoccupied to answer a child's questions. At a guess, it was inspired by Jermey Taylor's 'Ag Pleez, Daddy' in the South African revue, *Wait A Minim*.

The Liverpool poet and GP, Sidney Hoddes, recalled, "I love

'Son Son' as the mother can't hear her son because she isn't listening. Her mind is on the shopping list. It's very funny but the humour makes the point that you can't grow up without being inquisitive. The kid in the song will resolve that when he grows up – he's going to tell his kids everything."

"It was exposure to the poets that changed him and he found out how to express himself," says Andy Roberts, "but he wouldn't tolerate things going wrong. He would throw his old Framus cello guitar against the wall if he'd had a bad gig. It was a third division guitar from the era of the dance bands." That battered guitar was in an even worse state than Willie Nelson's.

In 1968 the key track of their first album, *Amazing Adventures of Liverpool Scene* was Hart's bitter-sweet 'Gliders and Parks', where he hopes a girl will honour a date in Coronation Park, Crosby. He doesn't think it will happen. Then unexpectedly, she arrives and the song is over, a rare Hart composition with a positive ending, although a drunken row isn't far away. The song opens with the words, "Saturday, got a Ribble bus", an example of how Hart chronicled daily life.

Another girl, this time from Belgium, appears on the cover of the aptly-titled *Mike Hart Bleeds* (1970). Hart dripped his own blood on her photograph and snubbed his cigarette out on her face, writing the liner note as if he were in an asylum. She is probably the subject of 'Arty's Wife', although he never married. Mike Evans from Liverpool Scene recalls, "Arty's Wife is a wonderfully rambling, Dylanesque thing, and it is typical Mike Hart. His affairs were always doomed and would end in terrible bust-ups."

"It is a brilliant title with a brilliant cover," says Roger McGough of the album, "and I loved his heart-wrenching voice, but he lacked confidence and would back away from opportunities. He couldn't believe that people admired him. He didn't trust that response and maybe that is where the pain and the soul came from."

John Cornelius "I would place Mike Hart on the same pedestal as Bob Dylan and John Lennon. He was that good. He let himself down in the way that he conducted himself but he was the genuine article, a Woody Guthrie who led a rolling stone lifestyle."

The Liverpool Scene lived as a bohemian collective at 64 Canning Street, itself the subject of Andy Roberts' song '64'. One of Hart's long-suffering girlfriends, Jude Kelly, says, "His life was his guitar, his lyrics and his performance. He wasn't even remotely interested in being at home doing things. He was a very chaotic and deeply creative man. He felt he was a poet and a musician and that's all he should do with his life. The rest of it didn't count."

Maybe that's just as well. Mike Evans on Mike Hart's home improvements: "On one occasion Mike decided to paint his whole room pink. He painted the ceilings, the floors, the furniture, everything. There were even pink footsteps from the front door upstairs to his room."

Although Liverpool Scene were bohemians, there had to be some discipline and Hart was too wayward to last beyond the first album. He returned to Liverpool and formed a duo with Jude Kelly, who later became the artistic director of the Southbank Centre. "I was 17 and doing my A-levels," she recalls, "and he was a lot older than me with a malfunctioning lifestyle. I could never have introduced him to my parents and I didn't know what to do with somebody who drank so much."

Although young, Jude Kelly appreciated his commitment. Jude Kelly: "It was that whole territory of celebrating the local that you later associate with the Smiths and Billy Bragg. He wasn't talking about the status of Liverpool. He was singing about the ordinariness of things."

Mike Hart would call the Anglican Cathedral, the largest unoccupied building in Liverpool. Sidney Hoddes: "He was left wing in the days when being left wing meant something. 'Shelter Song' was about people who suffered with poor housing and he had a simplistic solution of using St George's Hall and the cathedrals to create accommodation. It is brilliantly done and that song has a great verse about a landlord showing a couple around a tatty flat."

Jude Kelly: "'Shelter Song' was very moving and Mike himself was very near to being somebody who was dispossessed. He had a real empathy for the outsider and a wonderful voice as well, very powerful, not a folk voice at all."

Mike Hart moved to Edinburgh in 1971 and worked with actors around its fringe festival. This led to a second Dandelion album, *Basher, Chalky, Pongo And Me* (1972), which combined jokes and sketches with strident songs, including one about a brief affair with the playwright Nell Dunn, 'Nell's Song'. I heard him perform the song only a few days after their relationship had ended..

Although many thought of Hart as the Liverpool Dylan, his songs were too raw to find a larger audience. Mark Kelly, then a schoolboy who became a writer for Jo Brand and other well-known comics, was fascinated. "I was struck by his honesty, but I now realise it was double-edged. I think he was very influenced by the Theatre of Cruelty. You can admire his integrity, but the songs are cruel. In 'Bitchin' on a Train', his girl goes off with the lighting man from Principal Edwards Magic Theatre and the lyric is very specific and very true."

The songs might have been shattering to his girlfriends if they heard them. I would be thinking, "I hope she's not in the audience." In 'Bitchin' on a Train', Hart wonders why he ever slept with the girl, *"Was it the ale or was it the sex or was it just nothing at all?"* and he remembers her chasing Adrian Henri, *"After you'd told me and I'd told him, You said you wouldn't lay him."* Extraordinary stuff – singing your diary, indeed.

Arty's health deteriorated with the constant drinking and he lost his memory. He spent his later years in a nursing home in Edinburgh, where, ironically, he was cared for better than at any other time since childhood. He died on 22 June 2016.

Even though Mike's legacy is small, it is amazing how many times I come back to his songs. There are about 10 songs that are classics but that's enough. There are also a few unissued songs on the net like 'Nita Nicholson', a specific song about another ill-fated relationship.

In the mid-70s I booked him for a folk evening at the brand-new Crosby Civic Hall. The previous occupant of his dressing-room had been the operatic legend, Victoria de los Angeles. I gave him the room and when I went to see that he was all right, I found him peeing in the sink.

What you've just read is based on my CD notes for the reissue of *Mike Hart Bleeds* (2008) on Cherry Red and my obituary for *The Guardian*. If you haven't heard this guy, please check him out.

CHAPTER 23

Days In The Life: 1971

Royal Insurance owned many buildings in Liverpool city centre and the company was growing so fast that it was getting out of hand. Although I worked officially in Head Office, I only set foot in the historic Head Office building in North John Street a couple of times a year and that was usually when I needed some large cheque to be countersigned.

Some of the company's old buildings were put to good use as Albert Finney filmed *Gumshoe* around Queen's Arcade on Dale Street.

In the spring of 1971, plans were announced for a new Royal Insurance head office in Old Hall Street. The site was going to be shared with the *Liverpool Daily Post and Echo* whose current offices in Victoria Street were the worse for wear. There were major innovations in the printing industry, so this was the ideal time for a new move, although planning and construction would take some years.

Britain's currency was changing in 1971 by going decimal and I was given a one-off job as Decimalisation Officer. Fortunately, there was a large team involved so I didn't have to do it on my own! Every insurance company was experiencing the same problems so it was more an exchange of ideas than offices acting competitively.

The day of reckoning was 15 February 1971 when everything would go live and there was apprehension as that day approached. Especially for me as I could be out of a job by lunchtime! All was well and there were few complaints from policyholders, largely because we had taken the decision to round down rather than up so that nobody could say we were trying to extract more money from them. After all this excitement, I went back to calculating surrender values on life assurance policies.

The poetry events on Merseyside were often organised by Harold Hikins, the librarian at Spellow library and a left-wing firebrand. He had a very good poem about the different factions in Vietnam which he read at every reading and planned to do so until the fighting finished.

He encouraged everybody to write poems and he said, "Poetry is like speech; it is verbal communication. Everybody can write a poem." He was very talkative, very left-wing and had a very overgrown garden. Everybody looked to Harold Hikins for advice, and I remember Henry Graham fancying Olga Benjamin and saying to Harold, "Is she married?" When Harold said, "Yes", Henry said, "Happily?"

Harold organised evenings for the Merseyside Poetry Circus which included Matt Simpson, Sidney Hoddes, Mark Kelly, Malcolm Barnes, Brian Wake, Peggy Poole and Dave Calder. They provided a complete evening's entertainment, perhaps for organisations which couldn't afford the better-known Mersey poets.

Harold could be contentious and there was a poetry and blues evening I'd organised in Crosby Central Library where he was on first because he had to go elsewhere. The audience had not been attuned as to what they might expect. He looked like a friendly librarian with Willie Nelson eyes, but his poems could contain expletives. This was one such night and it led to people walking out before he had read more than a few lines.

At the next meeting of the Crosby Arts Association, Councillor Peat said to me, "I heard you had some trouble at your poetry reading."

Me: "Just a little – the first poet used four-letter words."

Councillor Peat: "He'll regret it in 20 years' time."

Me: "I doubt it. He's 51 years old and the librarian at Spellow Library."

Councillor Peat: "Pathetic. He's trying to be with it."

Geoffrey Peat was impressed when my 'Bless This Scouse' won a prize in a *Liverpool Echo* competition. This was because the poem mentioned Blackler's, a store in the city centre where he had been chief electrician. One of his recruits had been a young George Harrison. He gave George some advice, "Always carry a screwdriver in your top pocket", which was no doubt useful as the Beatles moved equipment from one venue to another.

In May 1971, our London Life Centre had a campaign for new business, which went very well. They were overwhelmed with work and time could be saved if they could process the work in London rather than sending it to Liverpool.

I was asked to go to London so that this business could be streamlined locally. If I went to London for a couple of months, the company would set me up at the four-star Harrington Hall Hotel by Buckingham Palace and I could do whatever I liked in the evening on Royal expenses. I could stay the weekends if I wanted, again on expenses.

In my view, it didn't need to be an expensive hotel – Toc H would suit me fine – largely because I would rather use the allowance on other things. However, Tony Baker said, "Nonsense, you've got a bath at home so you should have one here. You're doing us a favour, so make the best of it." So, I had a room with all mod cons and knew my expenses would not be challenged.

This sounded very attractive and if I did it well, it would do me no harm in Head Office. When I got to London, I found the troubles were nowhere near as bad as had been reported. The staff thought they were being overworked, but they didn't know what overwork was. When I looked at the signing-in book, I saw one employee had been late 170 times in a year. I said nothing but felt that the real issues hadn't been identified.

The staff lacked motivation. There was one lady who relied on Mars bars to get her through the day. She had her first Mars bar at 10, the next at 11.30, lunch at one with another Mars bar, yet another at 2.30, and her fifth and final Mars bar at 4pm as she made plans to go home.

One manager, Peter Weedon, had lost the plot. Because of building work, his office was being moved and his new office would be where toilets had been. There was no way he was going to work in a toilet and his main aim was to have the building plans reversed.

By the end of a couple of days and not even working flat out, I had made a decent start on the backlog and would have it cleared within a fortnight. Then I'd have a very pleasant couple of weeks, dealing with the new work as it was coming in, and that is indeed what happened.

Everybody was very nice, and I was seen as heroic. The sales force was delighted that their clients' work was being processed speedily. They took me out to meet clients – I rarely met policyholders in Liverpool – and I had a great time. I was taken to Simpson's in the Strand for lunch, which had a marvellous carvery and was where Dickens used to eat.

I had an even greater time in the evening as I went to one

West End show after another, again on Royal expenses. I went to the controversial sex comedy devised by Kenneth Tynan, *Oh! Calcutta!,* largely because it had a sketch about a masturbation club, *Four in Hand,* written by John Lennon, which reminded me of Rydal. One of the actors was Tony Booth from Liverpool and famed as the leftie son in *Till Death Us Do Part.* I later told Cherie Blair that I had seen her father in *Oh! Calcutta!* She'd been studying in London at the time but was too embarrassed to go: "You've seen more of my father than I have!"

I caught Jack Good's production of *Othello,* now called *Catch My Soul,* with Lance LeGault, Marsha Hunt, Lon Satton and Dana Gillespie. P J Proby had been in the cast but was having an operation on his knees. Othello had a knife in one hand and a guitar in the other.

Big Bad Mouse was a farce with Jimmy Edwards and Eric Skyes, a feeble script enlivened by ad-libs (or ad-fibs as they probably faked spontaneity). I was in the bar when the bell rang for the end of the interval. Jimmy Edwards shouted out, "Don't hurry! They can't start 'til I get on stage!"

I walked to the Nashville Rooms one night. It was normally a country music venue and Kathy Kirby was getting a poor reception. She wanted to slow things down with a ballad, 'Someone to Watch Over Me', but the crowd was restless and noisy until someone shouted, "Shut up!" The room went quiet and Kathy Kirby said, "Thank you", and got the response, "No, not them, you!"

I saw Timon while I was in London. He had left the Moody Blues' label, Threshold, after one single, really because the Moody Blues were concentrating on their careers and although they liked having a record label, they didn't want to spend time on it, just like the Beatles. Timon said, "The talk of the Moody

Blues being an underground group is rubbish. They want all they can get, and they know that to be really big, you have to appeal to everyone."

Timon had had a BBC Radio 1 session with Bob Harris. He had also witnessed an argument between Lionel Bart and one of the Hollies. Lionel Bart took his wig off and said to Timon, "Here, hold this!" before getting into the fight.

When I came back to Liverpool after what was little more than a paid holiday, I was called "one of our most flexible employees" by Donald Patton and indeed given a decent pay rise for what I'd done. So, everybody was happy.

CHAPTER 24

Wrongly Accused

This is the strangest incident in my life and the most unexpected. A jobbing actor and writer, Ray Dunbobbin, had written for *Z-Cars* and played Mr Boswell in *The Liver Birds*. He wrote and produced a twice-weekly soap for BBC Radio Merseyside called *45 Darby Terrace*, but I was only doing odd bits and pieces for the station and had never come across him.

Someone in Crosby told me that he was preparing a revue for the English-Speaking Union and would I like to help. I went to a couple of meetings late in 1970 where they were rehearsing sketches.

Ray Dunboddin was tetchy and awkward but he was pleasant enough with me. All the potential cast was older than me but I thought I might submit a couple of sketches. They would be looking at potential material and trying it out in the new year.

In January 1971 a Panda car called at my home and a policeman asked me to visit a particular station next Saturday night at 7pm. I wondered what it was about and the next day, I rang the station and spoke to the detective in question. "I can't tell you over the phone," he said.

"But what am I supposed to have done?"

"You may have done nothing" he said in a voice implying I had done everything.

"I can't have this hanging over me. Can't I come today?"

At first, he said it wasn't possible and then agreed to let me come later in the day,

I was led to a room where three detectives were waiting for me. The one I'd spoken to was looking at files. He didn't acknowledge my entry.

Silence.

Eventually he spoke. "I believe you know a Mr Raymond Dunbobbin."

"Yes, I've met him a few times but always in the company of others. I haven't really had any conversations with him."

"Really? Since last September he has received 241 anonymous telephone calls. We think you made them."

"That's ridiculous!"

"We not only think you've made them. We *know* you made them. Listen to this."

The detective switched on a tape-recorder. "*...and when it comes to the ending, boyo, it's going to be something very beautiful. The ending's coming very soon. You've been a very silly little boyo.*".

"It's a good recording," said the detective, "and Mr Dunbobbin thinks that voice is yours."

"Well, it isn't. It's a bit similar but I don't call people 'silly little boyos'. If I'm not going to change my voice, what's the point of changing my vocabulary?"

"Well, that's just you being clever."

"This is absurd. You seem to have made your mind up that it's me, but why should I do it? What motive have I got for giving someone I hardly know 241 telephone calls?"

"We usually find that the guilty person will tell us."

Another detective spoke up. "Can we ask you a few questions. If you're innocent, you won't mind."

"All right, but if you were me and you were innocent, would you get a solicitor at this stage?"

"*If you were me and you were innocent.* Do you mean that you are not innocent?"

"You're twisting everything I say."

"Look," said the lead detective, "you've caused us a lot of trouble." He waved an enormous file at me. "There are the details of the phone calls you've made."

"If I made them."

Then it got even crazier. "We think you're part of a conspiracy and we have to find the other members. We will interview your family, your friends and the people in your office."

"You're wasting your time as they'll all say I don't make anonymous phone calls but the whole thing is going to be very embarrassing for me."

"Of course it is, but if you say you've done it, we can adjust the evidence to make it look like the work of one man. You can say you did it under pressure and you'll get off with a fine. Otherwise, it's a conspiracy charge and that could be five years."

I wondered how many innocent people would give in because they feared the intrusions and the potential sentences.

"No," I said, "I didn't do it and I'm not going to say I did. I'd get a fine and what would happen next? The next time somebody makes a complaint about anonymous phone calls, you'd be round to see me."

"Okay, here's an ultimatum. You've got until Monday to tell us you did it. If you don't, you'll be sorry. You'll cause us more work and we won't be giving you another chance like this."

I did contact a solicitor who spoke with the detectives and it was agreed that I would do a voice test that would be studied by an expert at Sheffield University. The police asked me to read the exact transcript of one of the threatening calls. I said that this was biased, which it was, and it was agreed that I would read the threatening passages followed by my normal speech. The learned professor heard the tapes and said, "It's not him.".

I had to pay the solicitor's fee, I never got an apology from the police, nor from Ray Dunbobbin. I certainly wasn't going to call him and ask if it was ever resolved. In 1998 Ray Dunbobbin died at the age of 67 from a heart attack: had all this paranoia affected his health?

CHAPTER 25

Days In The Life: 1971-1974

When I joined Royal Insurance in 1963, we had noisy barrel calculators. You set the levers for the first number you wanted to multiply and if that was to be multiplied by 39 say, you turned the handle three times in one position and then nine in another. All the calculations were checked and then they were reviewed to ensure they looked about right before the calculations were sent to clients. It was a long process, but it didn't go wrong. I can't recall any instances where someone had been paid way over or under the odds.

The machines were noisy, but we had fun with them. If someone sang out "And I'm feeling…", everybody else would go "thump, thump" on the machines and we would then all go "Glad all over!" It was a fun way to end the day.

Around 1971, electronic calculators had been invented for office use. They would greatly reduce the workload, but how fast were they and were their answers always right?

Donald Patton wanted to test them before placing an order and I was given a pile of calculations with a barrel calculator while somebody else used an electronic one. It was a curious experiment as it was in my interest to lose, but of course the electronic calculator was going to be faster and just as accurate, provided that the right figures had been inserted. The order for calculators was placed, but what would have happened if I had beaten the machine? The Royal might still be in the Dark Ages.

The Royal didn't throw the old barrel calculators away. They were offered to staff at £5 each with the proceeds going to charity so maybe some people have them today – a museum relic as any calculation can be done nowadays on a smartphone in seconds.

Despite calculators, barrel or electronic, we all had a good feel for how numbers worked and very roughly, the size of the answers. The other day I was in the Coop and I was asked to pay £12.13. I handed over a £20 note and the assistant went to the tray to give me my change, £7.87. I quickly said, "Hang on a sec. Here's 13p" and that really confused him. What do children learn in school about numbers? Has numeracy vanished because everything can be calculated on a phone?

When I was involved in inter-office meetings in London, I usually stayed at the President Hotel. This was often called the pop stars' hotel as a lot of groups stayed there: the Beatles and the Searchers were there in their heyday. It was reasonably cheap with a good breakfast when the pop stars would usually not be around. However, my reason for staying was because it catered to American clients, hence the name. The IRA's bombing campaign was under way but I assumed that they would have to be crazy to bomb a hotel catering to Americans. Whether this was a sensible thought, I've no idea but it did mean that I slept soundly.

In Liverpool, we did have several incidents where we had to assemble on Exchange Flags behind the Town Hall because of a bomb scare, sometimes as regularly as once a week. One of the senior managers, David Parry, who later ran Royal Life's operations, refused to go if he knew it was a drill, but this sent out the wrong message to staff and might have led to casualties in a real incident. I was surprised it was allowed but David Parry was a law unto himself and in many ways as preening and ridiculous as Donald Trump.

There was one actuary, Dave Bagshaw, who had too much to drink the previous night. He came into the office about 11am but because of his hangover, he hadn't realised that everybody was standing in Derby Square because the building had been evacuated. Somehow, he strolled into the office and saw nobody there. "Oh," he thought, "It must be Saturday and I must have slept through Friday'' and he went home.

Another staff member in marine insurance came into work with a ticking clock in his briefcase which he put into his locker. Someone reported the sound and the whole building had to be evacuated. As he was leaving, he thought he'd get his briefcase. He went into the locker room to find that the fire brigade was sandbagging it.

I saw the American singer/songwriter Tim Hardin strung out on heroin at the Liner Hotel in Liverpool, though we didn't know that at the time. His performance got more wayward as the set progressed. Instead of his guitar and his hit songs ('If I Were a Carpenter', 'Reason to Believe'), he played the piano and sang the blues. If we wanted to hear the other songs, "You can go home and play the records." As people left, he said, rather pitifully, "I knew you'd do this. I knew you'd walk out." "It's not you, Tim," said someone, "It's late. They've going for the last buses." Tim Hardin put his hands up: "Man, they do this at matinées."

In 1974 I saw both Leon Russell and Neil Young at the Liverpool Empire. Neil Young opened with the opening cut from his new album, *On the Beach*, and then performed the rest of it. Everyone was calling out for 'Heart of Gold' and 'After the Goldrush'. He took his applause which was good but not great and returned for an encore. He said, "Thank you. I'd now like to do a song that you've heard before" and the audience cheered. He then performed the opening song from *On the Beach*. That was a good joke but impolite. The audience had paid good money to hear his successes.

Although I'd written several articles, I'd never written a book and once the actuarial examinations were over in May 1973, I thought I'd write one on Paul Simon in the evenings and at weekends. A local company, Raven Books, run by a friendly but argumentative couple, Sue Place and Ben Coker, were prepared to publish it. I had a deadline and so I got writing. I planned to write 10,000 words a week and finish it in six weeks. In retrospect, unfortunately, it seems that I was focused on writing 60,000 words rather than ensuring those 60,000 words were the right ones.

I had loved Simon and Garfunkel from the start and had amassed press cuttings and this would be the first book about them. The book reads like one long review, but some people like it. The only people I interviewed were Wally Whyton of the Vipers who had worked with Simon in London folk clubs and Paul Simon's UK publisher, Alan Paramor. The fact that the book was only priced at 60p was no excuse; you should always do the best you can. What's worse, I followed the *NME* which had said Paul Simon was related to Carly Simon without checking whether this was right.

However, because there were so few rock books around, it got decent reviews and sold 5,000 copies. I'm fond of the book and the text is at least better than its garish cover.

CHAPTER 26

Viva Las Vegas

I lived in Mersey Road in Crosby and I would walk to the train station by going down Kenilworth Road. Every time I passed a certain house - a perfectly normal suburban home with a neatly kept front garden, I would think, "How few people know what is behind those curtains."

Two sisters lived in the house, both around 40 years old, Maria and Gladys Davies who had decent nine-to-five jobs. If you spoke to them, you would think that they were perfectly decent citizens, paying their taxes, keeping their home tidy and seeing their friends. Just like anybody else.

All this is perfectly true, but with one major difference. Maria and Gladys were devoted to Elvis Presley. They collected records and memorabilia from around the world, communicated with fans and most of all, saw him in Las Vegas.

Here's the rest of what I wrote back in 1976, which is adapted from my book, *Presley Nation*.

The sisters made three trips to Vegas and saw 36 shows, which surely is no stranger than following a football team. "I don't really think about the cost. I think of it as buying a slice of happiness," said Maria, "Everything's different with each Elvis show. He never did anything the same." Elvis' father, Vernon Presley gave them a black suede waistcoat with fringes that had been worn by Elvis. Elvis was generating so much income that the Presleys could afford to give such things away.

"Oh, I thought I wouldn't live through it," said Maria about seeing him for the first time, "I got so excited and I was afraid of fainting. I took a deep breath in the way that guardsmen do. My heart was pounding and my head was banging. I just thought I wouldn't live."

Elvis loved communicating with fans and he would kiss them and distribute around 30 scarves in each performance. His guitarist Charlie Hodge would hand them to him one by one in rapid succession and fans would crowd to the front, hoping to catch Presley's eye. I'd rather have preferred another couple of songs but this created fan fever.

Having special clothes made for you wasn't confined to Elvis. Another Brit, Rex Martin, ran the *Worldwide Elvis News Service* which had 32 pages in a busy month. Prior to attending the shows, he had a jacket made with large inside pockets in which he concealed cameras and cassette recorders. Although he would keep the cassettes rolling, he would only run the camera for a few seconds at a time.

He photographed girls that Elvis was kissing as selling copies would repay his costs. When he got carried away by Elvis' leg movements in 'Fever', his camera was seized and confiscated. The following day Rex bought smaller equipment, but Tom Diskin had had him tailed and that night he was frisked and barred from the show.

In 1974 Rex found it easier to bask in the anonymity of 20,000 people in an arena and he saw 20 shows in 11 different venues which meant covering 4,500 miles in two weeks. He was still filming but he didn't offer anything for sale. Indeed, the most poignant item he had for sale was a copy of a telephone call with

Colonel Parker. He created a healthy and harmless underground and showed how Elvis is endowed with a special mystique.

By tipping the maître d', Maria and Gladys were able to sit up front. Maria was impressed by the gold belt that Elvis was wearing, given to him by The International Hotel. Maria Davies: "Elvis loved to embarrass people. He'd been given this very large gold belt and the fan club had asked me to read the inscription. He always came down to the front row and when he did, I grabbed hold of his scarf and said, 'Elvis, what's on your belt?' He didn't hear me the first time – 'Huh?' he said - and so I repeated it. This time a mischievous smile came over his face. He thrust his hips right into my face to allow me to read the inscription, saying at the same time, 'You gotta lotta nerve there, baby!' Well, the whole show room erupted with laughter as they'd not heard my question, only Elvis' reply. It was so funny. Even Gladys thought I'd had a brainstorm and asked him to take his clothes off."

Elvis had been lucky as he got through his first season in Las Vegas with few vocal problems. Working in such intense, dry heat can be hard and many singers suffered from 'Las Vegas throat'. Living in air conditioning 24/7 is hardly good for your throat. Even such a hardened Vegas pro as Frank Sinatra had trouble with his throat, although, in his case, it was lubricated with bourbon. Tom Jones had a machine that made steam (no, not a kettle) and he avoided the problems.

Maria was right when she said that every Elvis show was different as he will talk about anything on his mind.

Elvis on Jerry Hopkins' biography: "The only thing that guy got right was my name." He hated his family being called white trash as they were poor through lack of opportunity, not laziness. What's more, his mother was not an alcoholic.

Elvis on appearing on the Steve Allen Show in 1956: "I didn't move a muscle the whole song. The collar was so stiff, I'd have cut my throat if I had."

"When I did *G I Blues* I blocked a kick the wrong way and there I was with this big fat hand. Nothing they could do about it. They tried to put make-up on it, nothing. You can see it on the back of the album."

"Those of you of the Caucasian race...well, we are, aren't we...it was on my draft card...Caucasian...I didn't know what it meant...Thought they were going to circumcise me."

"I was in the dining room at Paramount studios, just came out of Memphis, and there was Moses. Charlton Heston. He was doing *The Ten Commandments*. I'd like to ask him what state of mind he had to get in for that part. He'd just talked to God and here he was in the canteen."

"I don't do karate to break bricks or boards. How many times does a brick come out and attack you?"

"Ladies and gentlemen, I just want to say one thing. They don't give you anything if you're strung out. Last week I was made an 8th degree black belt in karate and it carries the title, Master of the Art. I couldn't face my father, Priscilla, my baby, my friends, nobody, if I were strung out and if I ever catch anybody in this hotel, bellboy, room service, maître d' telling anybody that I'm strung out, then I'll pull his goddamn tongue out by the roots." This last part was yelled and as if to prove it, he coughed and spluttered on stage. "Sorry, but if it comes up, its's gotta go, you know. It's not cool on stage, but I can't help it."

On Priscilla. "Most of the stuff you read about me is junk. We're the very best of friends and we always have been. Our divorce came about not because of another man, not because of another woman, but because of the circumstances involving my career. I was travelling too much. I was gone too long."

Or there could be new lyrics to old songs, all of which is very Dean Martin.

"*Love me tender, love me true, all my dreams fulfil,*
For my darling, I love you because you're on the pill."

"*Do you gaze at your bald head and wish you had hair.*"

"*Captain Smith poked his Pocahontus.*"

Maria: "People think that we make up for shortcomings in our own lives by following Elvis, but my own life is much fuller because of Elvis. Whenever I meet a fan, I meet a friend. If I didn't do it, I'd probably be like 99% of the population, vegetating in front of the TV."

CHAPTER 27

Days In The Life: 1974

During Covid, I walked around Ainsdale and I've kept it up ever since. Outside of the winter months, the pine woods are enticing, and I might end up walking along the beach towards the road taking me back to Ainsdale village. Unfortunately, the buildings around that entrance are mostly derelict. The Marina was once a tourist hotspot; the Sands pub is run-down and neglected; Toad Hall, once a highly popular dance venue, has been closed for decades and for some daft reason the well-known mural artist Paul Curtis has painted a huge natterjack toad around two sides of the building. It signified that something was happening, but it only underlined that nothing was happening. Even worse, the Marina and Toad Hall are next to Pontins, the providers of cheap holidays and specialist weekends for many years. It is owned by Britannia Hotels, whose dismal reputation is second to none. They shut the site in January 2024 and now it is deserted.

In 2001 I went to interview Lonnie Donegan before his show at Pontins. He was late and I saw the band arrive. Lonnie took one look at his accommodation and booked a room at the Scarisbrick Hotel in Southport.

Lonnie, who never spent money unnecessarily, determined that the star's quarters were so bad that he had to book elsewhere. His band were surprised but Lonnie's generosity didn't extend to his musicians who made do with bog standard accommodation with the emphasis on bog.

All in all, the area is a disgrace and even though sewage might be pumped into the bay, the large beach does attract tourists. The sea is so far out that when Phil King was appointed Southport's Tourism Officer in the 1970s, Ken Dodd said, "Here's your first job. Find the sea."

Back in 1973, the area was a hot spot. The Sands was a popular pub and Toad Hall a thriving night-club in the pre-*Saturday Night Fever* era with a stuffed gorilla and a suit of armour in the vestibule. In December 1973 the big dance hits were 'My Coo-Ca-Choo' (Alvin Stardust), 'Merry Xmas Everybody' (Slade), 'I Wish It Could Be Christmas Everyday' (Wizzard), 'Dyna-mite' (Mud), 'Caroline '(Status Quo) and, I hate to say it, 'I Love You Love Me Love' (Gary Glitter).

My brother Chris was going out with Linda Wolstenholme, who worked at NatWest, and they suggested a foursome with me, the elder brother, and Anne the elder sister.

Anne, who was born in 1942, had worked in Southport Library since she was 15. She was an ideal librarian, reading a lot of books herself and at the time, overseeing the Music Library, which was mostly classical albums that ticket holders could borrow. There was rock and folk too which was a way to familiarise yourself with certain albums without buying them.

Anne and Lynda were the daughters of Granville and Lilian Wolstenholme and they lived two miles from the town centre. Granville also ran his coal delivery business there. His own father had started the business and lived in the house next door.

Granville Wolstenholme was a brilliant name for a coalman and he expected to be the last coalman in Southport. 1974 could be a busy year as the Prime Minister Edward Heath was introducing the Three Day Week. Collecting coal from the yard, putting the sacks on the wagon and delivering it was hard physical work.

Offices were only allowed electricity three days a week and the temperature could be no higher than 17 degrees. The barrel calculators had an unexpected revival as staff worked by windows in natural light. This was on top of disruption from the IRA, so a normal working day was a rarity.

Football under floodlights was seen as irresponsible. For the first time, the authorities allowed games on a Sunday which is now a norm.

The situation in the UK was so serious that Idi Amin, the President of Uganda, sent the UK a food parcel. Ted Heath was not amused and even though Amin was an appalling despot, that was one splendid joke.

Less funny was David Bowie's reaction to broken Britain. In 1976 he praised the Third Reich and gave the Hitler salute or something very like it to fans at Victoria Station. Most people assumed that Bowie hadn't thought through what he wanted to say, but Bowie was a wily cove, who knew how to generate the maximum publicity. He said, "I believe very strongly in fascism. Adolf Hitler was one of the first rock stars."

Having lived through both the three-day week and the Covid restrictions, I see parallels. Many workers enjoyed the three-day week and wanted it to continue. They were taking work home and preferred a full week with two days of home working. However, the hierarchy ensured that working practices were soon back to normal.

The friendship between my brother Chris and my girlfriend Anne's sister Lynda didn't last and I don't think we had another foursome. However, Anne and I kept seeing each other and we got engaged in January 1974 with a ring from David Robinson's on the day that we were going to see Jess Conrad in *Godspell*.

That sounds so bizarre – why did we celebrate by going to see Jess Conrad? Possibly they were press tickets as I might have been reviewing it for Radio Merseyside. I do recall that a few years later we were at the Liverpool Empire for another rock'n'roll musical, *Leave Him to Heaven,* where the rising rock star was played by Jess Conrad. A coachload in front of us left in the interval, but we had to stay as I'd arranged to interview JC after the show. When the audience was leaving, we were walking towards the stage door. Peter Grant of the *Liverpool Echo* said, "Spen, are you going to interview Jess Conrad?" "Yes," I replied. "Give him hell!" said Peter and walked on.

A far better production and the first stage play about the Beatles was *John Paul George Ringo…and Bert* by Willy Russell at Liverpool Everyman in May 1974. It was a tribute to the Merseybeat era and how the Beatles had been formed. Bert was someone who was nearly in the Beatles but not quite – and if you've lived as long as I have on Merseyside, you'll have met a few Berts.

There was a tremendous take of the Beatles' 'Twist And Shout' in the production and I wondered why I hadn't heard it before. Willy told me it had sounded so good because they had overdubbed another bass part on the original to make it really powerful. Most of the music was played live by the Scottish folk singer, Barbara Dickson and it was very clever to have the Beatles' songs reworked in that way and so distinctively too.

The show made it to the West End but George Harrison left at the interval. His feedback led to the Beatles putting a block on the play going to Broadway. The Beatles could block Willy Russell's play in the US as legislation was different to the UK.

Paul told Willy that he was sorry and that it was no reflection on his writing, but the Beatles didn't want a play about them on Broadway. It's an early example of the Beatles controlling their legacy.

Later on, McCartney told Willy that he had to do that and to make amends, would he write a film script for Wings? Willy went to Scotland to watch them rehearse and sent in a script. He thought that Macca decided against it as it called for 'proper acting'. However, the plot in a roundabout way fed into *Give My Regards To Broad Street* in 1984.

Finding a house and obtaining a mortgage were ridiculously easy. Andrew Davies had recently qualified as an actuary, and he and his wife both wanted to move to London. They were in a new build at Westway in Hightown, a small but growing town between Crosby and Formby. Anne and I went to see it and it was fine. It was open plan downstairs with the lounge, dining room and kitchen: there was a long narrow hall, a wooden staircase and three bedrooms upstairs. It was close to Hightown Station and as we didn't have a car, this was ideal for us going to work, albeit in different directions. We agreed £6,000. I paid a 10% deposit and we were on the Royal's staff mortgage scheme. I only wish it could be so straightforward for everyone.

Those months before our marriage in July 1974 were hectic. I had been determined to get the final two papers in the actuarial exams in May as not being fully qualified was holding me back. That became my priority and I qualified a few weeks before our wedding.

Anne had to determine where to put her horses. She had only meant to buy one but the mare, unknown to her, was pregnant and so Anne had two horses. There was stabling in Virgins Lane, Little Crosby, and Anne developed a lasting friendship with the

Gilbertson family who owned it. There was the use of a horse box so she could participate in some shows.

Both families were glad to have a wedding in the family at last. We got married in St Paul's in Scarisbrick Road, Southport, the connection with the Wolstenholme family being that Granville delivered the church's coal. It was quite a big wedding as there were many cousins and partners.

Hightown was a pleasant place to live though not much happened there, Les Braid of the Swinging Blue Jeans lived round the corner; and the greengrocer was a former beauty queen. From time to time, the cast of *Z-Cars* could be seen in the Hightown Hotel. All in all, we enjoyed living in Hightown but it was time to move on down the line, literally as Ainsdale was another stop on the way to Southport.

CHAPTER 28

John Stonehouse: My Part In His Downfall

I've been watching the first part of the ITV series *Stonehouse* starring Matthew McFayden as the arrogant MP who faked his own death by leaving his clothes on a beach in Miami in 1974.

At that time, I worked for Royal Life at its head office in Derby House and a few weeks earlier, John Stonehouse had taken out a life assurance policy with us.

My boss Cliff Jaggers was a marvellous actuary who looked and behaved like a character from Dickens. He read *The Guardian* not because it confirmed his views but because it challenged them. He read about John Stonehouse's disappearance and said to me, "Find out who sold him that policy."

I went back half an hour later. "He wasn't sold the policy," I said, "He went into a branch and bought it." "Then he's alive!" declared Jaggers, "Nobody buys life assurance – they are sold it. Ring some other companies and find out if they've also got cover on him."

Within a couple of hours, I'd found out that he had taken out several policies with other life offices and his life was assured for over £1m. A missing person would normally be pronounced dead after seven years and then any life assurance proceeds would be payable. Jaggers said, "We are never going to pay this. Contact the police and tell them he's alive."

I enjoyed meeting the detectives and John Stonehouse was found a few weeks later. He'd gone to Australia but acted suspiciously. Somebody thought he was Lord Lucan and he was arrested. Then the whole story came out.

Cliff Jaggers was the happiest I'd ever seen him and he should have had a little cameo in that series.

CHAPTER 29

Days In The Life: 1975-1979

Royal Insurance had premises all round Liverpool 1 – two head offices (Royal and Globe), departments in Derby House and Sefton House, and more besides. Since the early 1970s, there had been a desire to build a Head Office from scratch on the waterfront and so a huge site was developed in Old Hall Street. Royal Insurance's new head office was opened in 1976. We shared the site with the *Liverpool Daily Post & Echo* who worked from an adjacent building.

It was not before time, but whoever approved its appearance got it wrong. Another life insurance company, Royal Liver, has the most iconic building on Merseyside with its famed Liver Birds. Our brown sandstone boxes jutted out higgledy-piggledy on every side and from every level. Even before it opened, the building was called the Sandcastle. It looked like a tribute to a container port but maybe that had been the object all along.

Naturally, staff weren't allowed on the site while it was being constructed from 1972/5 but my manager Ken Macphail was in his fifties with white hair and wearing the smartest suits. He looked important and could blag his way into anywhere. He would go to the site in his lunch hour, be issued with a hard hat and receive a guided tour.

Together with its impressive 1,000 car parking spaces, the

building opened in 1976 and the staff moved there in stages. The life department was there in 1977, mostly on the second floor. Despite its outward appearance, it was a splendid place to work, plus there was a gymnasium, a conference theatre, a library and a bar for nighttime use. There was a Royal Club with chess, bridge and whist divisions.

The first event I saw in its theatre was a one-off from Ken Dodd. He wrote many of his own jokes but he also collected them from other comics and writers. He would take a bundle of them and do an hour's stand-up where he could test reactions. Even if they were feeble jokes, you were royally entertained as his reaction to the reactions would always be funny.

The office departments were divided by screens rather than walls, open plan discussion areas and potted plants. Indeed, there were notices not to put out cigarettes in potted plants ("peat will burn"), although smoking was soon banned. Once, a member of security followed a couple suspected of smoking out of the premises, but when they found a corner shielded from the road, instead of lighting up they stripped for action: nothing like a quick one in the coffee break.

There was a union office for ASTMS but I can't remember much trouble in the Royal. There were threats of union action but usually everything was negotiated satisfactorily. There was one strike where a manager had to walk through a picket line that included his wife.

The Royal owned a wonderful building, Inglewood on the Wirral, which looked like a stately home. The plants in Head Office came from its gardens and once a year, department managers and their wives would be given an evening out with a party there.

As well as Royal Insurance, the Lord Lieutenant of Merseyside had his office on the ground floor of New Hall Place and in the 1980s Simon Weston ran his charity from the building. Simon had been severely injured in the Falklands War. Pretty well his whole body had been in flames, but he had survived and made a remarkable recovery, although just to see his face and his hands was shocking. I only spoke to him a few times, but he was a remarkable man who dismissed his injuries with a "worse things happen at sea" attitude. He raised thousands of pounds for charity, and I'm very glad to have met him as I saw remarkable compassion and perseverance.

I had done bits and pieces on BBC Radio Merseyside since it started, sometimes on the arts programme, *Close Up*. That was presented by Margaret Roberts, who would travel in by Merseyrail with something to sit on as she thought their standards of hygiene were appalling. There was also *Light and Local* with Eddie Hemmings and Reg Brooks, a daily news-based show, although the title suggested everything would be positive. These were good programmes and the station matched national broadcasting.

In 1972 I worked with a Merseyside poet, Nigel Walker on a fortnightly poetry series which ran for 14 episodes. I named it *No Holds Bard*, a ridiculous title for a radio show as that joke only works on paper. At that time poets were paid by the line and I remember Brian Patten writing out his best known poems but chopping up the lines so that they were twice as long and hence, he would get twice the payment. All that trouble for £2! The best episode was when we asked poets to write something for World War III, which was Adrian Henri's suggestion. It was broadcast on New Year's Eve, 1972, a sombre ending to the year and the programme never returned.

A commercial radio station, Radio City, was being set up in

Liverpool and its MD was Terry Smith, a happy, positive bloke from the Mercury Press Agency. Back in 1965 he had organised a *Pantomania* EP, produced by Peter Hepworth and Nigel Greenberg at the new Cavern Sound studio for Liverpool University's Rag Week. It featured the Roadrunners with Mike Hart and comedy from the students. 5,000 copies were pressed but there were 10 special copies with a bonus track, *My Husband and I*, a sketch about the Royal Family. Terry Smith did a press launch about these rogue copies which might be found in the stores and it was a good way to generate sales.

They should have pressed them all with the bonus track but this way they could claim it was a mistake if the University hierarchy complained. No one wanted to be sent down for a Rag Week prank.

In 1984 I was invited into Radio City by Terry's head of programming, Gillian Reynolds, again somebody I knew vaguely. Her husband was *Guardian* writer, Stanley Reynolds, who had written a hit novel, *Thirty Is a Dangerous Age, Cynthia*, made into a film with Dudley Moore and Suzy Kendall in 1968. He had planned to write a musical about Merseybeat with Bob Wooler but nothing came of it, probably because it was more fun just to discuss it at the Press Club over a drink.

Stan was TV critic for *The Guardian*, a job he enjoyed as he didn't have to leave the house or, indeed, his bed. He watched the programmes, filed his copy, and that was it. Unfortunately for him, *The Guardian* wanted to make changes: Nancy Banks-Smith would review TV and Stan would review drama in the north-west. He was in a continuous bad mood as he had to leave his house to reach the theatre, so theatre managers complained about poor reviews. One night at the Everyman, a character on stage said, "I'm just going for a drink", and Stan shouted, "Hang on, I'll join you!" Stan was asked to leave but never mind, he was a resourceful journalist and could still write a review.

Setting up a new radio station must have been difficult for Gilian Reynolds but it was probably nothing compared to living with such a cankerous and often drunken husband.

Gillian had an idea for *Popinion,* an appalling title for an opinionated programme about pop. There would be Mike Evans, the saxophonist from Liverpool Scene, Highly Inflammable and now Deaf School, who wanted to make it as a writer, and Barry Coleman who had a degree in philosophy and wrote about motorcycling for *The Guardian*. Each week we could chat about new releases and what we had seen, along with interviews.

We were broadcasting in the first week of the station – 26 October 1974 – but I contributed to a Radio City programme before that. John Gorman had a DJ show as P C Plod and he had wanted to play Adam Faith's 'What Do You Want'. Radio City didn't have a record library and the shops were closed. John was insistent that P C Plod must play 'What Do You Want', so he rang me in the early evening to see if I had it. A taxi was sent to Hightown to collect it for the programme.

Popinion would either be produced by Clive Burrows or John Henry. Clive had played saxophone for Alan Price and Zoot Money. It made me appreciate that everybody had a story and you just had to find it, a principle I later applied when writing the history of Merseybeat.

Usually though, the producer was John Henry, an awkward guy who enjoyed being awkward and he would go mad if anything went wrong. One week we were going to do something for Elvis' 40th birthday and I brought in Maria and Gladys Davies, who had seen him in Vegas. John thought I had invited just one guest and he went berserk – there's no other word for it – when two people arrived. In front of Maria and Gladys, he called me every name under the sun and asked what two people in Liverpool could tell him about Elvis anyway. It was so embarrassing. I said, "These are our guests and Mike and Barry knew they were coming. They will be good, trust me on that. Do this, and then I will walk out of here and leave you in peace." He said, "Well, I'm never going to work with someone so unprofessional again."

It was pathetic but I was right – they were good and so my last *Popinion* as far as I was concerned was fine. It continued for a few more weeks without me and then Mike moved to London.

If John Henry tried to get me banned from Radio City forever, it didn't work as I was invited onto the literary programme, *Bookshelf* and I was reviewing books once a fortnight for much of 1976. That had to stop when BBC Radio Merseyside gave me regular programmes. I did a series about comedy records, *Jollity Farm*, and one hour specials on Valentine's Day, classical rock, Christmas records, and a celebration of vinyl, *Don't Leave Your Records in the Sun*.

BBC Radio Merseyside's star DJ was Billy Butler. He had been on the panel of *Spin a Disc* on ITV's *Thank Your Lucky Stars* and was a regular DJ around Merseyside clubs, often at the Cavern. He had joined BBC Radio Merseyside when it opened and somehow broadcast daytime programmes while still holding down a job at the docks, although he soon became a full-time DJ.

In December 1978 he was leaving the station to join Radio City, which was a coup for them. The forthcoming Radio Merseyside programmes appeared in *Radio Times* and for his final Saturday morning, he had listed *When I'm Dead and Gone* by McGuinness Flint. During the week, he mentioned Radio City on air and the management suspended him. They asked me to present his one-hour show, *When I'm Dead and Gone*.

The first extended interview I broadcast was with Ron Goodwin, who was conducting film music with the Royal Liverpool Philharmonic Orchestra. His manager Laurie Bellew (ex-Crosby) asked me to write the notes for a double album of his EMI recordings. I say 'a double-album' as EMI had the bizarre marketing strategy of "Buy this album and get the second one free."

I was doing one-off shows at bank holidays from 1978 to 1981 and I interviewed Joan Armatrading, Rod McKuen and Frankie Valli. My oddest interview was with Marc Bolan at Southport Theatre early in 1977. I saw him as arranged in his dressing-room but he said, "You must see the show first and talk to me afterwards." When I went backstage afterwards, Marc, who was with his partner Gloria Jones, said, "Come to the hotel." He took my hand and said, "See what Bolanmania is like" and led me out through the fans to the coach. Some keen fans had worked out he would be at Royal Clifton Hotel and we got through them and went to his suite. "Phew"! said Marc Bolan, "Let's have a smoke"! The first person to offer me something illegal was Marc Bolan – how cool is that?

I'd written some profiles for *Blues & Soul* magazine including a series on Stevie Wonder. When the *Daily Mirror* published a book on Steve Wonder, supposedly written by Ray Fox-Cumming, whole paragraphs had been lifted from my work with no acknowledgement. I dropped him a line but heard nothing, not even an apology. He became a well-known journalist, notably writing for *The Observer,* but every time I saw his name, I grimaced. Still do, as you can tell.

In my life, I have met thousands of people but I've only met one Prime Minister – and he has only said one line to me, but what a line. A senior actuary at the Royal, Ken Percy, had asked me if I would like to go to Manchester with him as he had a spare ticket for a talk on the financial market given by the former Prime Minister, Harold Wilson. I jumped at the chance and Wilson gave a very impressive talk, full of experience and dry humour. After the event I went into the Gents and there too was Harold Wilson. He said to me, "You never stand next to Tony Benn in the Gents. If he sees anything big, he wants to nationalise it." I'm very fond of that joke as I told it to my dad and it is the only time that I really made him laugh.

CHAPTER 30

Music Games

I had taken part in pop quizzes on BBC Radio Merseyside and in March 1977 the station asked me if I would represent them in a Radio 2 quiz against other local stations. That was okay, but my win was no big achievement as the other stations hadn't selected candidates on merit. My victory meant that I would represent the UK in the European final in May.

Judging by the plane journey, it was a BBC junket to Norway for lower-order executives. The presenter was David Gell, a BBC veteran, who had been part of the reviewing panel for new singles in *Record Mirror*. His challenge to himself was always to complete the review before the record had finished playing.

There was a meal before the quiz at which I discovered that the smart money was on Sweden to win. Their guy knew a heck of a lot. My strategy was poor: almost Bazball. The questions in the rounds were for 10, 20 or 30 points and I decided it was better to establish a lead than play catch up. I did okay with the 30-point questions at first but I foolishly decided to continue in that vein and my luck ran out.

I didn't know the original name of Creedence Clearwater Revival (astonishingly the Golliwogs, but these were different times), nor could I remember where 'If My Friends Could See Me Now' came from – I owned the LP and could see Shirley

MacLaine's face but *Sweet Charity* eluded me. The quiz was mine for the asking – after all, everybody else was being asked questions in their second language. I lost by showing off. I came second and was annoyed with myself.

Whilst there, I strolled around Oslo and came to the Angry Sculptures, a park devoted to naked figures. I still can't believe that there is such a place but there we are.

Participating in the European quiz led to a very enjoyable spin-off. The BBC producer Mel House was also producing the afternoon show for 'Diddy' David Hamilton. They wanted to establish a daily *David Hamilton's Music Game*. The contestant would be asked five questions and would go on every weekday until he or she got one wrong. I was setting questions at £1 a time and each question included a snatch of music. You know, "What is the title of this instrumental hit by Duane Eddy?" and then there's a snatch of 'Peter Gunn'. The BBC's rule was that at least half the questions should pose no problems to listeners. I set them for five years, and ironically, I also set them for the national and international contests that followed the one in Oslo, although that junket finished in 1980.

Early in 1980 Raven Books published a collection of my interviews, *Stars In My Eyes*, which has endured okay as there are long interviews with Charles Azanvour, Burl Ives and the songwriter Mort Shuman, I spoke to Dr Hook at the Holiday Inn after a lively two-and-a-half-hour stage show at Liverpool Empire. Could a group really be that enthusiastic and what was that funny smell? Dr Hook performed wonderful songs, full of humour and insight and usually by Shel Silverstein.

A few days later a drugs cartel was busted at the Holiday Inn and one of the charges was "Supplying drugs to Dr Hook". The police must have been in the bar and wondering "When's this berk going to stop asking questions so we can see what they're up to?" Dr Hook could have been thinking the same thing.

The book ends with my most difficult interviewee, the country singer Don Williams. He was perfectly pleasant but he was a quiet Texan who didn't say much more than 'Yup' or 'Nope' and I was desperately trying to think of questions that he couldn't say 'Yup' or 'Nope' too. "How many hats have you got?" "I have two hats." It was desperate stuff, but you can sense my struggle.

After writing this section, I dreamt that I was compiling the greatest interviews of all-time and at No.1 was Pontius Pilate asking Jesus if he was the Messiah and Jesus replying, "Thou sayest". In my dream, I said that the response was pure Bob Dylan – and I could be right.

CHAPTER 31

North-West Country

Rock'n'roll was an American creation and although the first British attempts were clumsy and silly, they were not without charm and within a few years, we had got the hang of it and the music developed into the Beatles and the British beat scene where we conquered the world.

British blues was an anachronism as our performers lacked the authenticity and hardships of the first American performers, who often came from plantations and prison life. I once walked across London with Alexis Korner and he gave money to every beggar he saw – "Could have been me," he growled. Maybe this was how he made the blues contemporary and relevant to himself. However, John Mayall's Bluesbreakers and Eric Clapton found a way of making the music relevant to Brits in the 1960s.

In the 1950s, British country music was hard to find but record producers knew the songs were good and there were MOR versions of the Hank Williams songbook – 'Half As Much' from Lita Roza and 'Settin' the Woods on Fire' from Dennis Lotis: competent but hardly country. Eventually, Lonnie Donegan (from time to time), Johnny Duncan (actually from Tennessee) and Karl Denver had UK successes with country music performed more appropriately.

Hank Walters worked with his Dusty Road Ramblers

(established 1948) and they became one of Merseyside's top club bands. Hank himself was a mixture of Hank Williams, Jimmie Rodgers and Ken Dodd and I was the one who named him the Hillbilly Docker. When they appeared at the Cavern John Lennon told him, "I don't go much on your music, Hank, but lend us your hat."

The hard drinking, hard fighting Lee Brennan was also around and in 1975, he recorded a tribute album to Johnny Cash for Decca. However, because of his volatility, he was reduced to playing in a duo with his wife on drums. He reworked Joe Dolce's 'Shaddap You Face' as 'Shaddap You Gob'. When some extras were recruited for an apocalyptic film being shot in Liverpool, they were given rags to wear, but when the casting crew saw Lee Brennan, they said, "You're okay as you are. Just go to the set."

Phil Brady and the Ranchers were far more reliable and found work outside Merseyside, often recording sessions for the BBC, notably on Wally Whyton's *Country Meets Folk* in the late 1960s. Phil Brady could get as deep as Kris Kristofferson and his country version of 'Last Train to Clarksville' is superb, He also recorded the first and only single made at Cavern Sound, 'An American Sailor at the Cavern' (1965). There aren't many copies around as they were confiscated by the Official Receiver and no doubt became landfill.

In the 1960s the Merseybeat group, Sonny Webb and the Cascades were on the country side of rock'n'roll. They performed in the same venues as the beat bands but took their repertoire from George Jones ('White Lightnin'', 'Who Shot Sam?') and Hank Locklin ('Border of the Blues'). They recorded for Oriole and when the Merseybeat bubble burst, they went full country, renaming themselves the Hillsiders.

The Hillies made albums with Bobby Bare and George

Hamilton IV and became a favourite act on the chicken-in-a-basket circuit of the 1970s. That US breakthrough never came. Close but no cigar.

Kenny Johnson left the Hillsiders to form his own band, Northwind, and he became a fine songwriter and top presenter at BBC Radio Merseyside. He played his own records and promoted his own gigs but he never referred to himself by name (he always said "Yours truly") and maybe he thought nobody realised he was into self-promotion. He had an excellent singing voice and wrote good songs and although he and Northwind were on national tours and festivals, they never moved much beyond their fan base. Part of this was down to Kenny's personality as he could be belligerent and awkward with promoters and some stage announcements were borderline aggressive. I saw him with backing tapes at the Neptune Theatre and he was angry that my review referred to this, but my job was to write what I saw.

Joe Butler continued with the Hillsiders, who were a hard-working club act but they didn't have anyone to develop their interests. They made an album called *On The Road* and the front cover showed them in a boat. Duh!

A couple of days after I had broadcast an interview with Michael Clarke of the Byrds, I bumped into Joe in the street. He said, "That was a wonderful interview, Spen. You asked him why he had left the Byrds and he said, 'Because I hated all of them.' I have never heard anyone ever say that before. Well done!" I realised of course that what Clarke had said really resonated with him.

Also, Joe presented a weekly country show on Radio City. When Radio City decided to drop country music, the MD Terry Smith came into the studio to tell Joe that this would be his last programme. With great presence of mind, Joe said, "You're wrong there, Terry. Last week was my last show" and he picked up his records and left.

Around 1976 I was writing for the magazines, *Country Music Searchlight,* edited by a bank manager from the Wirral, Derek Wakefield, and *Country-Music Roundup,* edited by former footballer, Colin Kettle from Lincoln. Colin, bless him, really pushed British country music. After a couple of years, I moved over to *Country Music People* and I was with them for 40 years. I didn't so much leave country music as country music left me.

In 1977 I was very taken with Poacher, a country band from Warrington, who set the judges alight on ITV's *New Faces*. They had good people behind them – Dave Warwick and Tony Graham at Northern Promotions, Robert Kingston and his son Barry at R.K. Records…and the Vladimir Vodka factory! What follows is my sleeve note in June 1978 for Poacher's first album. I'm reprinting it because it never got a fair outing. The record company printed my text over a blue negative of the front cover and it became unreadable. They are being reprinted here because I'm determined that somebody's going to read them at last. I'm not saying that my notes would have made any difference, but it was indicative of the sloppiness of promoting Poacher. If all the parties had done things right, Poacher could have had the first UK country chart hits. The producer had found the right song for the first single, 'Darlin'', written by Oscar Blanderner, but it was covered by the Scottish rocker Frankie Miller and his raspy, Joe Cocker-styled version went into the Top 10.

In 1977 Tom Jones, then based in Vegas, had secured a US Country No.1 with 'Say You'll Stay Until Tomorrow'. Poacher made the charts as well but 'Darlin'' got no further than Number 86. Knowing a good song when he heard one, Tom Jones covered it and picked up the US country sales.

Poacher's album was simply called *Poacher* and the cover showed them by the biggest cartoon in the world, Bill Tidy's Vladimir Vodka mural. It was an indication of their sponsorship but it didn't get the message across that this was a new country band: it seemed more like a group of lads who liked vodka. Admittedly, they toured Warrington in a Wells Fargo stagecoach, but most people wondered what that was about.

Anyway, here at last is my sleeve note: it's over the top but then sleeve notes always are – you're telling the buyer, "Well done you for spending your hard-earned cash on this."

There's more to Warrington than a rugby league team and a vodka distillery. The Cheshire town now boasts the first country-rock band in Great Britain and the album shows what all the excitement is about. I am sure that Poacher's success on ITV's *New Faces* is only the beginning: Poacher could be to Warrington what the Beatles are to Merseyside. *(I told you it was over the top.)*

Poacher was formed early in 1977 by 27-year-old Tim Flaherty: "I'd played in local bands, but I'd always wanted to be in one that had a pedal steel and a banjo."

Steel guitarist Pete Allen and banjoist Pete Longbottom had country roots, but the other three members came from the rock world. Lead guitarist Adrian Hart and bass player Allan Crookes have been playing locally, while Sten Bennett had played drums for Barry Ryan.

After an appearance on BBC-TV's regional *We'll Call You*, Poacher won a *New Faces* heat with Mickie Most calling them "the best British country band" he'd ever heard. They let fly on the spirited 'My Uncle', a Gram Parsons and Chris Hillman song about draft-dodging where the uncle in question is Uncle Sam.

Considering Poacher had only been formed a few months earlier, the *New Faces* win was impressive. What's more, they won the All-Winners Final with a new British song, the happy-go-lucky 'Silver Dollar Hero'. Although they appeared carefree, considerable thought had gone into the arrangement. The three-part harmonies were spot on and the instrumental break switched from lead to steel to banjo in a few glorious seconds. "They're great," said Tony Hatch.

At a St Valentine's Day vodka party, Poacher entertained distillery staff and signed a contract with R K records. A very catchy first single, 'Darlin'', followed, which came close to making the national charts. In these days of throwaway B-sides, purchasers must have been delighted to find another gem on the back, their interpretation of the Outlaws' So Afraid'.

Turning fully professional meant a new steel player had to be found and Poacher were fortunate that one of Britain's top players, Pete Haywood was available. You can check out your own albums for his credits - I found him on a Mike Harding LP.

In concert, Poacher show the same exuberance and *joie de vivre* that Dr Hook and Lindisfarne have and you don't blink for fear of missing something. Although they sing well-known songs like 'Hot Rod Lincoln', 'You Ain't Goin' Nowhere' and 'I Still Miss Someone', they turn them inside out. 'Fire and Rain' is a moving song James Taylor wrote about the death of a friend but Poacher have come up with a new arrangement which enhances the material still further. Poacher they may be called and in a sense they are but they know how to take others' material and make it their own.

It's a very pleasant duty to tell you that every song I have written about is included in this, their debut album, *Poacher*. Furthermore, the album contains 12 tracks (instead of the customary 10) and they include notable new songs like 'One More Fool'. Poacher have spent many hours in the studio with their producer Barry Kingston perfecting their sound and I don't think you'll be disappointed.

Quite simply, I think Poacher are marvellous. I doubt if there's a duff song a or a duff note anywhere on this album, but you don't have to take my word for it. Put the album on and judge for yourself.

The album didn't sell the way that Poacher had hoped and Poacher lost a New Year Gala final to Patti Boulaye but they continued to work on the club circuit and play places like the Wooky Hollow in Liverpool.

Wooky Hollow was owned by Terry Phillips, once Mr Universe. When Neil Sedaka did his soundcheck, he sang some recent material. Terry Phillips said, "What's all this?" "My new songs," said Sedaka proudly. "You'd better be doing your hits tonight," said Phillips with a strong implication that there was 'or else' attached.

Poacher were a very nice and friendly bunch of lads. When Anne and I went on holiday to Lincoln, Anne injured her back after falling on the notorious Steep Hill. She had come off her horse, Ozzie, some months earlier and this made it worse. She had to go into Lincoln Hospital for traction. The nurses and patients were very impressed when Poacher sent her a beautiful bouquet.

When the steel player left, a new guitarist and keyboard player, Peter John Frampton, added some teen idol looks and wrote the excellent 'Buttermarket', prompted by Buttermarket Street in Warrington. It was a B-side but it should have been promoted as a top side.

The singles, whether for RK or Ritz, never seemed to be right: a patriotic flag-waver one minute ('England Forever'), a parody of Smokie the next ('Suzy Loves You No More') or a rewrite of 'Darlin'' ('You Are No Angel'). I've a demo of a decent song, 'Another Train, Another Town, Another Dream', written by Vincent Bibby, but I don't think it was ever released. They made albums which were designed to sell at gigs: *Along the Way* and *Alive and Gigging*.

I lost touch with Poacher except for Alan Crookes who joined Kenny Johnson's Northwind and became a popular producer on Merseyside for club acts.

However, when I hear the first Poacher album today, I still think it is a good 'un and I can't see why, with all the TV promotion from *New Faces*, they didn't make it. After all, they did have a few weeks' start on Frankie Miller. I still think 'Darlin'' is the best record by a British country band, although 'lonesome' and 'phone some' is an annoying rhyme. However, for some crazy reason, RK Records promoted it alongside another single – Stan Holden's inane 'Great Big Pickled Gherkin', one of the unfunniest records ever made. This is what I'm saying throughout this book – whether Timon, Gavin Stanley, Dean Johnson or Poacher, you need a promotional team that knows what it's doing.

CHAPTER 32

Days In The Life: 1980

For some years, I had been doing backstage interviews, 15 minutes before international stars like Glen Campbell or the Four Seasons went on stage. It was very pleasant but there was history on my doorstep that nobody was recording.

The first time I spoke at length to four members of the same group was with the Fourmost and I realised how the same events could be regarded differently – in particular, Brian O'Hara often had different takes from the rest of the group. I thought it would be good to follow this through and interview as many musicians I could find who were connected to Merseybeat. I had permission to make a 12-part documentary of one-hour programmes which BBC Radio Merseyside said could replace soccer in the summer of 1981. I hoped to have enough material for a book as well.

There was a growing interest in Merseybeat and the history of our music. Bob Wooler and Allan Williams had organised the first Liverpool Beatles' Convention at Mr Pickwick's in 1977 and, to their surprise, 300 people attended. Allan said there would be an interview with a real live Beatle and we all wondered who it could be, although we didn't really believe him. Some thought Paul McCartney would be coming but I doubted that, placing my money on Pete Best. The anticipation grew until the moment Allan Williams announced, "And now ladies and gentlemen, a real live Beatle, please welcome Tommy Moore." Who? We all applauded but most of us were thinking, who the hell is this?

Tommy Moore had been the drummer for the Silver Beatles when they backed Johnny Gentle for a week of dates in Scotland in May 1960. He didn't play with them again, largely because he had a decent job at Garston Bottle Works.

Considering that he had forgotten nearly every detail of that trip, he received a surprisingly good reception and tacky as it was, Liverpool's first Beatles Convention was deemed a success.

Despite the erratic behaviour of Williams and Wooler, they were both fond of each other, although you'd never guess it. Bob Wooler: "We are often put together at events, like a double-act. I told Allan, 'We strike people as has-beens and curiosities. They look at me and they can't believe I was a DJ all those years ago.' But put it this way - at least the has-been has been while the never-was never was.' Billy Butler called us Tweedledee and Tweedledum, and I said, 'Who's Tweedledee, Billy? I demand top billing.' Allan and I have a love-hate relationship but at times it is more like a loathe-hate relationship."

My first job in preparing a Merseybeat series was to write down the Merseybeat groups and their personnel. By and large, I needed groups who made records so that there would be something to play and I always asked if there were unissued tracks around. This was a masterstroke as I unearthed performances that no one had heard and they were featured in one-off programmes of their own and have since appeared on several albums, notably for Viper. You can now find them on Spotify. If I've done nothing else, I have at least made these tracks public.

I therefore spent much of my spare time in 1980 talking to Merseybeat personalities: There was Cilla Black (who offered me champagne), Gerry Marsden, Billy J Kramer, the Searchers and the Swinging Blue Jeans. I talked to Dave May who had shown Stuart Sutcliffe how to play a bass guitar and I recorded Allan Williams' comprehensive account of how he took the Beatles to Hamburg.

Bob Wooler wouldn't speak to me. I had written about that first Beatles' convention for *Lancashire Life* and he thought I had mocked Allan and himself for promoting Tommy Moore as a real live Beatle instead of as a casual drummer. I said, "That's okay. I've got enough people anyway." That caused him to change his mind. It was just Bob being Bob – he made a drama out of everything.

Freddie Starr had come up through the Merseybeat scene with Howie Casey and the Seniors and then with the Midnighters, Bob Wooler told me that Ray McFall loathed having Freddie Starr at the Cavern as his humour was cruel and dirty. When Jim Reeves died in a plane crash in 1964, Freddie Starr lay on the stage and said, "My impression of Jim Reeves". Ray McFall banned him for life.

When playing Liverpool in 1980, Freddie Starr visited Radio Merseyside for the afternoon show with Bob Azurdia. Janice Long was on the other side of the glass reading the news and as she did, Freddie unzipped and pretended to masturbate. Janice laughed and the station manager Ian Judson heard the laugh on the news. He rushed to the studio and shouted at Freddie Starr, "Put it away and get out!" Bob said, "But I've announced him as my guest. "All right," said Ian Judson, "You sit there and behave yourself!"

I was seeing Freddie at the Atlantic Tower Hotel at 6pm. He was drying his hair and he said, "Put your recorder on and we'll say we're recording this in a hurricane." Freddie grabbed my balls and said, "Let's have some fun." He told me he hated the Hollies "and when Graham Nash left his acoustic guitar in the dressing-room, I crapped in it." When we'd finished (the interview, that is), I left his room and noticed, looking back, that he was admiring himself in the mirror. I'd got off lightly.

That quote about Graham Nash didn't make the series, but Freddie Starr wasn't completely without charm. When I told him that he had still got Eddy Parry's mackintosh, he said, "Oh, I lent it to Columbo."

In truth, I interviewed far too many speakers for a radio series as if you have more than 20 voices in a one-hour programme, nobody knows what is going on. For a twelve-week series, the number of guests would normally be about 50 but I was well over 100. However, this bank of interviews was going to be mined continuously. It is the bedrock of my Liverpool work.

I found out many things. In 1963 Oriole Records had brought a mobile recording unit to the Rialto Ballroom in Toxteth and recorded two albums featuring one Mersey group after another. Each album sold 20,000 copies but I discovered no one had received any money. Years later, I told Kenny Johnson that I was going to interview Oriole's producer, John Schroeder, and he said, "Hit him from me!" John said he was surprised that nobody was paid but it was nothing to do with him.

On the other hand, the NEMS artists had all been treated fairly. Unlike Larry Parnes, Tito Burns, Don Arden or Oriole Records, Brian Epstein was a good guy, paying his artists what they were owed and not overworking them. That was rare in the 60s. Quite simply, the managers wanted young, naïve singers because they knew nothing about business.

By December I had over 200 fifteen-minute interview tapes and as it was taking an hour to transcribe each tape, it was time-consuming. I would cut-and-paste my transcripts and arrive at 12 themes with workable running orders.

Some musicians liked prevaricating, one of them being Mike McCartney of Scaffold. On my fourth attempt, he said I could see him at his home in the Wirral at 6pm on 9 December 1980. I was looking forward to that:

I knew I could get him to talk about Scaffold and I hoped that there would be occasional mentions of 'our kid'. Mike never referred to Paul by name, same as Noel Gallagher with Liam and Albert Wycherley with his brother, Billy Fury. I always wanted to get them together for the 'our kid' sessions. Although all my Mike McCartney interviews have been strange, they are also wonderfully entertaining. He is a master storyteller and Mike's eccentricity is a part of his charm.

Around the time I was working on this series, I went to bed as usual at 11pm on the night before and woke to the news that John Lennon had been shot in the foyer of the Dakota building where he lived. Only days earlier he had released *Double Fantasy*, his first album for five years and there had been rumours of a world tour. The shooting was such unexpected and heartbreaking news, but I took the train to work as usual. The carriage was eerily quiet as everybody was assimilating what they'd heard. Liverpool's most famous citizen had died.

It was the same at work. I was working in quotations for company pension schemes and I reported to Gerry Forrester, a sombre actuary and hard taskmaster who regarded praise as a sign of weakness. You were there to work: you did your job and that was the end of it. He was supremely capable himself and he expected everybody to work to the same standards, an actuarial Geoffrey Boycott if you like. I was in his office when two staff members walked past, the young lad putting his hand on the girl's bottom. Gerry was shocked: "Are those two married?" he asked. "Yes," I replied, "but not to each other."

This was a strange morning and maybe Gerry should have liked it as everybody was working, but he could sense that it was an office of automatons. He said to me, "Why does it feel so different today?" I said, "John Lennon's been shot." "He's just a pop singer," said Gerry, "They'll get over it. Tell them to behave properly." I said, "I feel the same as they do so you tell them, but it's not a good idea."

For once, Gerry backed away as even he appreciated that this was a moment that would change the world.

Back then, very few Beatle sites had been recognised in Liverpool and certainly not in the city centre. In the lunch hour, I went to Mathew Street. The Cavern had been filled in, the building above it demolished, and the site was a car park, but now the entrance was covered in flowers. I saw my Uncle Noel, who was a retired headmaster, and he told a BBC reporter, "I couldn't think of anywhere else to go." Everybody would be saying the same thing – John should never have moved to America: he'd have been safe here.

Bob Wooler: "I don't have much to say about the day of Lennon's death itself except that I had a fearful cold. I wasn't on the 'phone and didn't hear of his assassination until I caught the midday news on the radio. I went to the Grapes in Mathew Street and Bob Cook, the manager, said, 'Thank God you're here. Everyone's looking for you.' Allan had been at Radio Merseyside since dawn and done one interview after another. I then did all sorts of programmes and interviews for the newspapers, radio and TV."

That afternoon I rang Mike McCartney, sure that he would be calling off the interview. Quite the reverse: he said, "Come round, what else am I going to do?" It was a fine interview especially as Mike remembered a few incidents with John. Paul rang as we were speaking and they were discussing what had happened for half an hour.

Gerry Forrester's attitude towards John Lennon was odd because they were both born in 1940 and it seemed the attitude of someone much older, the attitude of the city council, in fact. The city refused to recognise its Beatle heritage during the 1970s and the plans for a Beatles statue were dismissed with little debate. I thought that things would start moving once the councillors were of the same generation as the Beatles. It is both cynical and true to say that the assassination of John Lennon in December 1980 kick-started the city's celebration of its most famous son.

Fed up with being mocked in the UK, John and Yoko had moved to New York in 1971. They felt their radical ideas would be more readily accepted there. Little did John know that he would never set foot in the UK again. Because of a drugs conviction, he was caught in a legal battle for a Green Card so that he could travel freely. He won his appeal in 1976 and visited several countries the following year. He didn't immediately come to the UK but then he didn't know that he would be gunned down in December 1980.

John kept a box marked "Liverpool" in the Dakota and shortly before he died, he told Brian Epstein's friend, Joe Flannery, that he wanted to return home. Music writer, Paul Du Noyer, also from Liverpool, comments: "You can take the boy out of Liverpool but you can't take Liverpool out of the boy. John was very proud of his roots, particularly in his last years when he was living in New York. He got very homesick, and he regarded New York as a Liverpool that had got its act together. He was set to return and he was going to do a world tour in 1981."

John was aware of the trends and would have known that the punk bands had initiated a Year Zero approach. On the B-side of their début single, '1977', the Clash sang, "No Beatles, Elvis or the Rolling Stones." Glen Matlock was allegedly sacked from the Sex Pistols for talking about the Beatles. It was all a pose, and in an interview, Paul Weller's mum went off-message to reveal how her son had collected the monthly *Beatles Book*.

This presumed aversion to the Beatles was accentuated in Liverpool. Most new bands were determined not to sound like the Beatles. After all, how could a new band become the best act in the UK when it was impossible to even be the best band from their home city?

Ian McNabb from the Icicle Works says, "When I started in a band in 1975, the Beatles were a curse as the shadow that they cast was so huge. If you tried to get a record deal, the companies would say, 'Oh, Beatles' which killed it. What goes around comes around and towards the end of the 70s when the New Wave was around, you had successful bands from Liverpool like Wah! Heat, Echo and the Bunnymen and The Teardrop Explodes and it became a baptism of fire. It killed off the Beatles comparison as the bands sounded like they came from Los Angeles or New York. The spell was broken. The musicians didn't speak much about the Beatles in the 80s, but they were always there. Then Oasis came along and that got a new generation into them."

After Lennon's death, the messages and poems in his memory stayed in the Cavern's car park for weeks. Sam Leach arranged a candlelight vigil on the Sunday after his death. Thousands gathered outside St George's Hall on Lime Street. Sam's would not be the obvious 'go to' name for an event of this magnitude but he brought it off perfectly.

Bob Wooler surmised, "It's extraordinary really but from the moment that John Lennon was shot by a crackpot, the whole attitude towards the Beatles changed. Everyone became

Beatleised, and Beatle Conventions have done very well since that date. When we stood on the steps leading up to St. George's Hall with the Bishop of Liverpool, there was a two-minute silence, although the traffic didn't stop. The weather was kind to us, and it was very touching. I felt then that there was a rebirth and there was going to be a fantastic renaissance for the Beatles."

The Liverpool playwright Alan Bleasdale was in a pub that night and some old-timer said, "They're making all this fuss over John Lennon. Just think what'll happen when Ken Dodd dies."

In 1981 the Everyman Theatre staged *Lennon,* written by Bob Eaton and starring Mark McGann: Mark McGann: "Bob Eaton already had the play and then John Lennon was shot dead. It was just fate that they had that script and now they knew how to end it. There have been many plays about John Lennon but this was the first and it has become the definitive one." It was an extraordinary play to see. A shot rang out followed by silence, and it was so dramatic that you could hear members of the audience crying.

CHAPTER 33

Disaster Arias

A concert by Victor Borge is a special event. The audience is laughing before the house lights are dimmed. Everyone is wondering what his opening remark will be. I first saw him in a theatre that was only half full. "There's a lot of gentlemen here tonight in red suits," he remarked, "Oh no, that's only the upholstery."

But tonight at Southport Theatre, it's a full house. When he steps on stage he dolefully announces, "We're going to be having an interval pretty soon." The audience erupts. "I've been looking forward to this concert ever since… seven o'clock." He scolds latecomers, "I got here on time, so why can't you?" He tells two honeymooners, "I'll make this show as short as I can."

Borge's rich, accentuated speech makes even the slightest quip devastatingly funny, even if we have heard it before. "Look at this piano they have given me. I think it's been in a fight…and lost."

As someone is laughing longer and louder than anybody else, Borge addresses him directly, "Sir, would you be kind enough to laugh with the rest of the audience? If everybody decides to laugh individually, we are never going to get out of here."

Victor Borge is a concert pianist with a difference as he deflates the pomp and solemnity of classical music. "This is by

Mozart in the key of C." He looks baffled. "Now, where is C? I can't find it. Long time no C."

Borge keeps up these witticisms for two hours and then comes to his most famous routine, "I hope you recognise this. Otherwise, it is not as popular as I thought." It is *Phonetic Punctuation* which advocates the use of punctuation marks when we speak. He receives a standing ovation and ends, "Drive carefully when you leave because I shall be walking to the hotel."

I got to interview him later at the Royal Clifton Hotel, where he was staying in Southport. "Did you take the lift?" he asks. "It is so small that it only takes one leg at a time. This room isn't much bigger. I put my key in the door and the window broke."

Victor Borge was born in Copenhagen in 1909, the son of the first violinist with the Royal Danish Symphony Orchestra. He made his concert début as a pianist when only eight and the comedy came by accident when he was 14. "I was the soloist for a performance of Rachmaninov's Second Piano Concerto. The conductor didn't know the score well and the orchestra went to pieces. I stopped playing, went up to the podium and pointed to the score. I said, 'I am here. Shall we do it together now?'"

Does he mind that his classical career has been upstaged by the comedy? "Not at all. I enjoy what I do. A happy smile is my reward. The rest goes to the Government."

I mention the man with the mad laugh. "Oh, a lot of the audience will go home convinced I had him there deliberately, but I would have preferred him to have gone to the cinema tonight. I am lucky because every situation is so familiar to me. It is just me and a piano and I can turn to the audience and know that something will happen."

CHAPTER 34

Let's Go Down The Cavern

The 12-part radio series, *Let's Go Down The Cavern,* was broadcast on BBC Radio Merseyside. The title came from a Mike Hart song, and it sounded like a Famous Five adventure, which was my intention. After all, the fans and the musicians were going to this wonderful underground venue to hear something special.

The highly competent Jenny Collins was assigned to produce it and she was always very pleasant, although it must have been a nightmare. In each 55 minute programme there would be extracts from a dozen records and perhaps 30 clips of speech. Each time I wanted a clip the tape was lined up and the appropriate section dubbed. We might end up with 40 minutes of speech for each episode which was edited with razor blades (yes!) to cut out er's, um's and waffle where it didn't interrupt the flow. We had 30 minutes of tightly-edited speech, 20 minutes of music, 5 minutes of links and *et voilà,* a radio programme.

I didn't possess all the records I wanted but, unlike Radio City, we had access to the BBC Gramophone Library, a wonderful institution which would loan us what we lacked.

It was a long process and it must have seemed unending to poor Jenny but we made 12 programmes which started on 30 May 1981 (replacing football) and were very well received. The series was repeated twice in quick succession and even though it was based around Merseyside, another 14 local radio stations took it – despite the Liverpool accents. The programmes are now on-line with the British Library and Liverpool Central Library. They are history because so many of the contributors have died.

Merseybeat musicians had been interviewed before, notably by Billy Butler, but this was the first time that we got, say, three people's versions of the same event.

Some people have said to me, "Why didn't you give your tapes to Radio 2 and let them make the programmes?", but I didn't think they would do it right. About 10 years later, Radio 2 asked me for some material for a two-part Gerry Marsden series about Merseybeat, but it was all wrong as Gerry, rather than reading the script, chose to comment on what the others were saying. Entertaining, sure, but it was a skewed portrait of Merseybeat.

In a way, *Let's Go Down the Cavern* threw up more questions than answers. As I was editing it, I was thinking, "I'd like to know more about this" or "I'd like to know more about that". And that's what I've done over the years. Merseybeat has been the gift that keeps on giving. It would be possible to take all my interviews and write a 3,000 page history of Merseybeat but who but me would read it? Indeed, just to the left of me as I write, there is shelving containing printed copies of my interviews and they cover 20,000 pages. That's a lot of speech.

The death of John Lennon had prompted the architect David Backhouse to think that something should be done with the Cavern site in Mathew Street. The Cavern was closed because British Railways needed the space for ventilation shafts for the underground and it was subject to a Compulsory Purchase Order, BR was as hopeless as Network Rail today: no sooner had they acquired the line than they decided they didn't need it anyway. The Cavern should never have closed at all.

CHAPTER 35

Just Like Starting Over

Most musicians don't give up. Even if they stop playing professionally, they still entertain their families or their friends down the pub.

In Liverpool, the Merseycats charity has been successful in finding musicians of the 1960s and coaxing them back on stage to strut their stuff through 'Roll Over Beethoven', 'What'd I Say' and 'Some Other Guy'. The musicians include members of the Undertakers, the Fourmost, Ian and the Zodiacs, the Remo Four and Denny Seyton and the Sabres: the list is endless. Almost.

Few musicians have resisted the call to appear at a Merseycats reunion, but John Lennon has always said no.

John Lennon, you may remember, was a leading figure in the Beatles - maybe even the leader - until that fateful date on August 16, 1962 when he was sacked by Brian Epstein.

The Beatles were on the verge of a national breakthrough - and Paul, George and Pete with a new vocalist, the effervescent Gerry Marsden, achieved worldwide success with 'How Do You Do It' and then 'I Like It'. Paul's melodic flair was brought out in the million-selling 'Yesterdays', although if John were around, Paul would never have rhymed 'yesterdays' with 'sequesterdays' in what was thought to be the most inspired couplet of the 60s.

John and Eppy never got on. John hated him saying that the

Beatles would be bigger than Elvis. "Come on, Eppy," he would shout, "even Cliff could make a better film than *G.I. Blues*."

He rebelled when Epstein wanted to replace the raucous, American rhythm and blues from their act ('Twist And Shout', 'Money') with cheerful, Tin Pan Alley, three-chord pop. John was adamant; "If you want The Beatles to sing 'How Do You Do It', Eppy," he said, throwing him his Rickenbacker, "you can take my place - but have some singing lessons first."

Then there was Cynthia. Brian had wanted to market four desirable, unattached young men…and here was John with a pregnant girlfriend. He told John that a married Beatle would be disastrous for their following but John, even though a nonconformist, did not want his child born out of wedlock.

Many recall the outburst at the Cavern on 15 August 1962. Eppy was red-faced about John sabotaging his plans, and John chided him, "You're the mistake, Eppy. We should have stayed with Allan Williams."

Albert Goldman's infamous hatchet job on Paul McCartney states that Paul, forever ambitious for the Beatles, shared Epstein's thoughts that night and agreed that John should go. Epstein asked John to call into his Whitechapel office the following morning. No one has ever repeated that conversation, but John went into the Grapes and announced, "I'm not a Beatle anymore."

At first, John with typical Merseyside arrogance said, "I'm going to do it on my own." He'd heard the new American folksinger, Bob Dylan, and he decided on something similar. Too similar unfortunately as the melody of his first and only single, 'Working Class Hero', lent heavily on Dylan's own 'Masters of War' and he was sued for plagiarism. "Of course, I pinched the bloody tune," said Lennon in court, "Folk songs are for the people: there shouldn't be such a thing as copyright." That didn't go down well. His record company lost and after Lennon had had 'a visit from the boys', he decided that he wanted nothing further to do with 'capitalist record companies'.

There was nothing to report: John never played his guitar, never wrote songs, never jammed with another band. He never did anything: long before the term was fashionable, he was a househusband, looking after his son while his wife worked as a designer.

Although the only tracks on record by John Lennon are 'Working Class Hero', its Utopian B-side 'Imagine', and some rock'n'roll that the Beatles cut with Tony Sheridan in Hamburg, a cult surrounds him. Beatlefans long to meet the group's original lead singer and rhythm guitarist. "I love looking at photos of George, Paul, Gerry and Pete," says Lee Mavers from the Beatles Fan Club, "but look at this photo of the Beatles from 1962 and it is John's face that you are drawn to first. I can't understand why he gave it all up."

Eventually, after calls to the *Liverpool Echo*, John Lennon was found, living off his Giro in Birkenhead: his marriage had ended, following his affair with a Japanese artist. "That was just an excuse," says John, "The truth is, there is no call for househusbands once your kid has left home."

After all this time, John Lennon has been persuaded to perform again. Tonight, after 40 years, John is going to be playing the Cavern in a band which includes Ringo Starr from the Hurricanes on drums, his son Julian and a few former Quarry Men. "I have nothing to prove," he insists, "It's just a way of spending some time. I know I was the best. The Beatles are the nowhere men, not me. They're the ones on the fucking Flying Music tours."

No one knows how good John Lennon will be. The Grapes is across the road. He might drink too much. He might curse the

80@80

audience. No one will mind. Everyone is waiting for the moment when Paul's former partner steps on to the stage. Paul has sent a goodwill message to the Cavern. "Well, he would, wouldn't he?" is John Lennon's savage rejoinder.

CHAPTER 36

Days In The Life: 1981-1983

After the success of *Let's Go Down the Cavern,* I had ideas for other series and I wanted to make one about Liverpool's folk music heritage. After all, the Spinners came up at the same time as the Beatles and achieved national fame. There is a promotional film made by the town council in 1963 which disregards the Beatles but praises the Spinners. Those in authority had reservations about beat music and they wanted to show the 'real' Liverpool. "I was surprised," says Hughie Jones of the Spinners, "as we also had long hair."

I was delighted to meet Stan Hugill from Hoylake who now lived in Wales. He was a retired sailor who collected shanties and had published the almost definitive *Shanties from the Seven Seas*, published by Routledge in 1961. I say 'almost' because Routledge did not print the bawdy lyrics sung by the sailors as they worked. Stan never updated his work, and if possible, there should be a new, unexpurgated edition. Still, Stan's book was a colossal achievement, and among the shanties emanating from Liverpool are 'Maggie May', 'The Leaving of Liverpool' and 'Liverpool Judies'.

It was great to meet Stan and his family at their home in Aberdovey and to record his wonderful stories. He was an artist, painting tall ships and we bought one that is now in our hall.

Anne asked him if he ever painted storms at sea and he rang a month later to say that he had painted one and would we like that too. It is at the top of our stairs, so we think of Stan every day.

I saw him perform in folk clubs and once, on board a ship, he couldn't resist the temptation to climb the rigging even though he was over 80. He was a marvellous man.

Around the same time as we went to Aberdovey, I had an opportunity to interview Billy Fury who lived on his bird sanctuary in Wales. He was returning to the business with new recordings produced by Stuart Colman. I can remember thinking, "Where shall we go this weekend?" – it could be Billy Fury or Stan Hugill. We chose Stan Hugill as he was 30 years older than Billy but Billy died shortly afterwards and we should have gone there. Billy died because his heart had been damaged by rheumatic fever as a child: he had spotted an injured seagull and had taken the wet bird home under his coat, hence his illness. I never met Billy and I could, instead, have spoken to Stan a few months later, but we aren't to know these things.

I had gone to Radio Merseyside in a lunch hour to pick up some mail and someone said, "Spencer, go to the studio quickly." The news had come through that Billy Fury had died, and Steve Kaye had lined up a record, 'Halfway to Paradise', not perhaps the most sensitive choice. Steve Kaye was a good presenter who hosted programmes under different names around the country. I wondered if he changed his voice for these identities.

Like Steve Kaye, I never knew what was coming next. Reader's Digest asked me if I would write the sleeve notes for a 4-LP box-set by Harry Secombe, mostly of operatic arias. I regarded this as a challenge but they gave me Harry's phone number and so my shortcomings were hidden by Harry's comments. He was a joy to interview and I'm very glad to have done it.

Reader's Digest packaging was exemplary, and I did many sets for them, all of which were sold by mail order. Titles like *Easy Listening Country, Country Harmony, Golden Memories of the 60s* and *Songs Of Joy* are crass but the sound quality and the presentation were superb. They knew their market and they made sure that they had obtained the correct versions of the oldies.

There was great delight when, after many years, the Beatles and Queen allowed themselves to be licensed for compilations from Reader's Digest and subsequently, other labels. The ruling was that if you had a track by the Beatles or Queen, it had to be Track 1 on the first album, but I don't know what happened if you wanted both Beatles and Queen on your compilation.

Reader's Digest paid well too and always send me a Reader's Digest publication for Christmas like *Facts at Your Fingertips*.

I was asked to write extensive notes for a series of Edsel albums in 1982, a label that was partly owned by Elvis Costello. I did the notes for the Big Three, the Escorts, the Merseybeats and the Mojos and a various artists compilation of Oriole tracks. Costello was so impressed with the Escorts' 'Nighttime' that he recorded it himself.

I was doing some country music sleeves for Lee Simmonds at RCA and, even today in 2024, he may ask for a CD note for his Morello label. I'm impressed that he knows how to reach people who still buy CDs.

Colin Miles had an excellent reissue label See For Miles and I wrote several liner notes including the Zombies in 1984. That year I went to Amsterdam for an insurance conference and I found the album for sale in CD format in one of the shops. I'd not got a player but I brought the disc nevertheless, my first CD. Colin then issued a CD version of a Freddie and the Dreamers LP but the CD booklet was unreadable as the print was way too small. Great label though and I was so sorry when it went under.

In 1982 there was excitement around New Hall Place, We looked out onto the Mersey and we could see Barbra Streisand filming *Yentl* at the Pier Head. The Isle of Man steamer was repainted for filming. It seemed that half of Liverpool had been recruited as extras. As the star, writer, director and producer, Streisand kept to herself and probably didn't have any spare moments. She had a Rolls to take her from Atlantic Tower to the Pier Head every day, some 200 yards.

Just as well as she might have encountered a lad working at the Royal who must be the only person to knock a motorcyclist over on his driving test and pass. The examiner said it wasn't his fault. He lived in Crosby in a road with a grass verge on either side. He told his mother that he had passed and so they went for a drive. As soon as he was through the gates, he hit a tree. He reversed and hit the gatepost. The next day he took his father to the pub and reversed into a wall.

Royal Life got into TV advertising as there was a new Government scheme to provide mortgage interest relief at source (known as MIRAS) and we were having TV advertising for this, targeted at TV-am, although a telephone number at 8am was not the best of ideas. Nevertheless, the ads were successful, but there was a PR problem when it was revealed that the narrator had been convicted for theft.

The ad was written by the man who wrote the ad, "Domestos kills all known germs." Actually, his original slogan was "Domestos kills all germs dead" but the broadcasting authorities didn't like the word 'dead' in an advert ('kill' was all right) and they wondered about germs that weren't known, hence the amendments.

The insurance executive David Parry had to do everything first – he probably celebrated Christmas at the beginning of

December. However, he couldn't make a Christmas get-together with the Abbey National Building Society in Baker Street. He said, "Spencer can you go in my place? It's easy. All you have to do is drink their brandy, smoke their cigars, and say we expect £20m of business from them next year." I said, "I can deliver the message, but I don't drink and I don't smoke, so it had better be somebody else." I didn't suggest Peter Lawrence as he had fallen asleep at a meeting the day before and Parry just glared at him before waking him up.

When promotional shots were wanted of Head Office, the photographers had decided upon Peter Lawrence's desk but he went AWOL that day and I was asked to sit there instead. Hence, there was a publicity photograph of our lovely new office with me surrounded by pipes and tobacco tins.

For the summer in 1982, I did a 12-week series, *Almost Saturday Night*, for BBC Radio Merseyside, one-off interview programmes with music. The title song was written and first recorded by John Fogerty and each week I could pick the most appropriate version from Fogerty, the Searchers, Rick Nelson and the Burrito Brothers. The series featured Joe Brown, Alvin Stardust, the Searchers, Scaffold, Richard Thompson and Fairport Convention, all of whom I interviewed several times over the years. We saw Dave Edmunds at Liverpool University and we had never heard anything so loud. There was the unfairly neglected Paul Kennerly from the Wirral: he loved country music and wrote the concept albums, *White Mansions* and *The Legend of Jesse James*, recorded with top US names like Emmylou Harris and Waylon Jennings.

Among one-off appearances, I appeared on the Radio Merseyside show, *It's Saturday*. The presenter had a skill for asking local businesses for good prizes, but unfortunately, he made up the winners' names. The station manager visited his house and found it like a warehouse stuffed with the station's goodies.

My folk music series, *In My Liverpool Home*, was very different from *Let's Go Down the Cavern* as I had so many born raconteurs such as Mike Harding, Bob Williamson and Bernard Wrigley, the Bolton Bullfrog. I included American folk singers - Tom Paxton, Ramblin' Jack Elliott and Judy Collins - and the series continued my love with Fairport Convention and Steeleye Span, not to mention the Spinners and Jacqui and Bridie. Folk songs by definition told stories and these folk knew how to tell them.

It was good to befriend Pete McGovern, a railway worker at Lime Street Station, who wrote 'In My Liverpool Home'. Well, he put new lyrics to 'The Strawberry Roan', an American cowboy song he had heard by Marty Robbins. 'In My Liverpool Home' was made famous by the Spinners, and Pete kept on writing it. When I started the weekly *On The Beat* in 1985, I asked Pete to come in from time to time with new verses. He enjoyed the challenge and I doubt if any song has a longer lyric than 'In My Liverpool Home'.

CHAPTER 37

Cat O'Nine Tales

A book based on my radio series, *Let's Go Down the Cavern*, was published by Hutchinson in 1984. The concept was to print the book with *Merseybeat Family Trees* drawn by Pete Frame but he found them complicated as no one seemed to last in a group more than five minutes. They couldn't be completed before the deadline and so he gave us Merseybeat timelines instead, which were still terrific but were really handwritten prose. The *Rock Family Trees* were eventually published by Omnibus in 1992 in *The Beatles and Some Other Guys* and were well worth the wait, a brilliant way of showing Merseybeat history.

Despite thorough research, Pete included little jokes and mistakes in his trees so that he would know when people were copying his research. In *Cavern Kids 3*, for example, Pete added a new member to the little-known Delameres, Ambrose Mogg, who left to go to the States. Untrue. Ambrose Mogg was our cat and his story was told in an April Fool's Day *On The Beat* in 1989 where I asked musicians like Freddie Garrity and Dave Berry to make up stories about him. This led to an entry in the *The Guinness Encyclopedia of Popular Music* and it is still there for all to see online and with additions on the *All Music* website.

"Ambrose Mogg b. Andrew Morgan, 1 April 1941, Liverpool, England. Mogg, a catalyst amongst Merseybeat musicians, formed the Caterwaulers in the early 60s and enjoyed local success with 'The Cat Came Back' and other feline songs. He refused to sign with HMV Records because of the picture of the dog on the label. However, his short time with Decca Records in 1963 was fraught with problems. Forced to use pugnacious session musicians, Jackie Russell, Gordie Setter and 'Bulldog' Drummer, Mogg's desire to escape from the studio turned 'Mean Dog Blues' into a frantic rockabilly classic. Unfortunately for Mogg, the pressing plant was closing for its annual holiday and careless workers approved the record without a hole in its centre. Mogg raged at Decca, who cancelled his contract on grounds of insubordination, saying he should take lessons in manners from the Rolling Stones. A few weeks later, Mogg lost a leg at the Cavern when passionate fans pulled him first one way and then the other. He disappeared into the Catskill Mountains, while 'Mean Dog Blues' became a cult single although the drilling of the holes by collectors is rarely accurate. George Harrison referred to Mogg as an early influence in the biography *The Quiet One* written by Alan Clayson. Mogg returned to Liverpool in 1989 with nothing in the kitty, but he is clawing his way back into the limelight with sterling work for the Merseycats charity. Music writer Pete Frame and *Record Collector* editor Peter Doggett have both lectured and written about Mogg's standing in the music world. Mogg's reappraisal has been largely due to the writer and broadcaster Spencer Leigh, who has been a major crusader of his work over the past two decades."

For a time there were Ambrose Mogg T-shirts with the Merseycats charity and at one concert at the Philharmonic Hall Davy Edge played Ambrose Mogg with Freddie Marsden on drums. I am amazed that Ambrose Mogg lives on but of course 'Mean Dog Blues' is a classic.

CHAPTER 38

Days In The Life: 1984

We've now reached the famous Orwellian year of 1984, which had the potential for being just as grim in reality for Liverpool and its city region. Derek Hatton and Militant were causing havoc in their pursuit of a national goal to topple Margaret Thatcher.

Liverpool City Council was a pawn in the game and John Hamilton, the leader of Liverpool City Council, was a decent but broken man unable to control the rebels. Looking at the events now, I'm surprised that John Hamilton was only 61 as he seemed so much older. All the tension and arguments could have aged him.

Neil Kinnock's main task as the leader of the opposition was to oust Thatcher and he had to rein in Militant or he would never gain power. It culminated in his fiery speech at the 1985 Labour Conference when Hatton and his associates were expelled.

Nowhere was the tussle between Militant and the Labour Party more keenly felt than in Liverpool. The city had problems and yet there were positive signs about its future.

Margaret Thatcher saw Michael Heseltine as the threat to her leadership and probably to keep him out of London she appointed him Minister for Merseyside, someone who could restore its fortunes and reputation. He was a remarkably good choice as he loved the region and he knew how to get things done. After much planning, he initiated the Garden Festival, a wonderful example of restoring barren land (albeit, nobody knew what to do with it once it was over) and he negotiated for the Tall Ships to come to Liverpool, another major tourist attraction, and both in 1984.

And then there was Cavern Walks.

Straight after John Lennon died, the architect and former Cavernite, David Backhouse, saw how the Cavern itself could be restored as a tribute to John Lennon. Even though it was a narrow street, he envisaged a large, high building on the site with a new club in its basement. It was effectively in the same place as the old one but because of fire regulations, the main entrance could not be in the same position.

Backhouse proposed Cavern Walks with a frontage that was influenced by the Dakota building in which John and Yoko lived. The brickwork was bright and the ceramics around the archways were designed by John's first wife, Cynthia. They are not credited, and many tourists miss them completely.

At ground level, there were quality shops, a statue of the Beatles by John Doubleday, and the Abbey Road pub. There were nine floors of offices but there were problems in occupation as there was so much office space already available in the city: indeed, that never really worked and the current plan to turn Cavern Walks into a luxury hotel is the best to date.

In the basement was the new Cavern. Although it was intended to use the old bricks in the recreation of the club, they were not in sufficiently good condition. Instead, they were sold individually for charity with a plaque signed by Ray McFall as the founding owner (he wasn't) and the Royal actuary, Hugo Johnson. I bought one for £5 but Anne was wary about having it on display as it might have come from the toilets – and she could have been right. I eventually sold my brick for £120 in the annual Beatles auction so it is unquestionably the best investment I have ever made – I wish I had bought a wall although that might have given my postman a hernia.

The new Cavern was much deeper than the original but it looked the same. It had three arches and the groups would perform on the stage at the back of the middle arch. The architect David Backhouse told me that its length was 'half an inch shorter' than the original Cavern.

Some books say that a thousand people would see the Beatles at the Cavern – rubbish, Even if you piled everybody in there, it would be difficult to top 700 and anyway, only half of them would see the Beatles as the arches cut off views of the stage. If you did see the Beatles at the Cavern, you were certainly privileged.

Shortly before the new Cavern opened, it was decided to duplicate the wall at the back of the original club by having it signed by the 60s groups. I invited the ones I knew to the Cavern one Sunday afternoon in March 1984 to sign the wall and asked them to bring other musicians along. It was a joyous occasion.

Norman Kuhlke of the Swinging Blue Jeans was stopped outside the club by someone who said, "You'll get free booze if you go through that entrance and say you played in a group." Fortunately, all the signatures on the wall are authentic.

Whenever someone aged between 35 and 45 entered, there was widespread speculation: "What group was he in?" A cheer marked Bob Wooler's arrival. I had assumed that the musicians would still recognise each other but this was not so. They'd not seen each other in years and indeed, some were meeting for the first time because there had been so many groups and venues on Merseyside.

It was like watching umpteen editions of *This Is Your Life*.

Musicians who hadn't met in twenty years hugged each other, but every conversation was interrupted by another old friend. There was catching-up to be done, especially as several musicians brought along their wives, children and even grandchildren. A lot of musicians had married their fans.

After all this time, some had difficulty recognising old friends. Clive Hornby was a familiar face as Jack Sugden in *Emmerdale Farm*. Everyone was saying, "Hello, Clive", and he was frantically trying to work out who they were. Another Dennison, Steve McLaren, looked scarcely 25, while age had taken its toll on others. Gus Travis with his sleek black hair had worked on his appearance and singer Lee Curtis in white tux and medallion looked a star entertainer.

A young boy blocked the photographer's view as Lee Curtis was about to sign the wall. He was asked to move and replied, "It's alright. It's only Grandad."

Whenever possible, groups assembled in their original line-up to sign the coloured squares. The Swinging Blue Jeans went up to the stage, followed by the Dennisons, the Undertakers, the Merseybeats and the Fourmost. Hank Walters was with his Dusty Road Ramblers and said, "I've signed for a couple of the lads who've died. They'd have wanted to be included."

Roy Brooks of the Dions watched quietly as better-known musicians signed the wall. When his turn came, he chose one of the larger boxes and in bold lettering wrote 'ROY BROOKS AND THE DIONS', close to, and bigger than, the Beatles' name. That sheer cheek is the very essence of Merseybeat.

My cousin, Jenny Johns, had married John Cochrane, the former drummer from Wump and his Werbles. They had been the first rock'n'roll band to play the Cavern (6 July 1960) and the hardcore jazz fans threatened to beat them up. They wisely stayed behind until they had left, but feelings ran high. John, a librarian, kept a list of what other bands, including the Beatles, were playing in 1961. It is now an important historical document. In the 1980s John played for the Irish tenor, Josef Locke, who would sing on the mainland as Mr X to avoid paying taxes. "He never said who he was," said John, "but if you were behind him and said, 'Hey, Joe', he would turn around."

The goodwill around this event signing led to the formation of the good-natured Merseycats charity, founded by Don Andrew from the Remo Four. They even had benefit concerts at the Philharmonic Hall, a place that they certainly wouldn't have been playing in the early 1960s.

The Mersey Cats also supplied bands to the Garden Festival. The performance space had a stone floor but that didn't deter Faron who fell to his knees as per usual. How his knees have survived such mistreatment I don't know.

The hard man of Liverpool FC, Tommy Smith, however, had knees that had certainly given way although he was still the tough guy. He was the manager of both the Abbey Road pub and the Cavern and when I was talking to Tommy once, there was trouble nearby. Tommy got hold of this feller and told him to behave himself. There was no need for a bouncer with Tommy around, but he could be very pleasant. He told me once that he had sung on Liverpool FC's hit single – no electronic trickery there.

Although the Abbey Road pub was very successful, he was the wrong person for the Cavern – or at least he should have recruited someone who knew how to respect the old music and how to promote the new: a difficult balance and one that has only been managed in recent years by the current management.

Although I am writing mostly about my extra curricular activities, I was still working at Royal Life, but because they owned Cavern Walks, they let me have time off to help promote their new investment.

In 1983 I had been on a Budget special on BBC Radio Merseyside to talk about the proposed withdrawal of Life Assurance Premium Relief (LAPR). Up until then, the Government encouraged its citizens to effect life assurance policies by reducing their premiums. This was to come to an end in 1984, a black day for life assurance companies as it would be harder to persuade people to protect themselves and their families. During the final week, we were working until 10pm to process the new business.

On the final night I was on Alan Jackson's early evening programme and David Parry told me to stress that Royal Life was going to be open until midnight to accept new business. I grabbed a stack of proposals and put up a notice that this was the last chance to take out a new policy with tax relief. Even if you hadn't got a mortgage, it was worth getting on the ladder or taking a policy out as an investment. By 9.30pm, I'd received a handful of completed proposals from the station's staff and I took them to New Hall Place for acceptance. I didn't accept them myself as that would have been a conflict of interest. However, I did everybody a favour that night, a genuine win-win situation.

While all this was happening in my day job, the series that I was working on at BBC Radio Merseyside was *Try to See It My Way*, an analytical look at the Beatles' recordings. In a joint sponsorship, Royal Life had printed forms for a Beatles quiz and they had been available from Radio Merseyside and elsewhere. The answers were given in the final part of *Try to See It My Way* and the winners announced. Participants had also been asked for a name for the block of shops, offices and Cavern club in Mathew Street, and 'Cavern Walks' was the winner. There were clever ones but a straightforward, unambiguous one was thought best.

I would go to work in a suit and tie and might stay in town for an interview before I went home. I went to the Neptune Theatre to talk to Allen Ginsberg, who was giving a poetry reading. Ginsberg had come from Manchester with John Cooper Clarke and the singer Nico, JCC's girlfriend at the time or at least they had a love of the same substances. I introduced myself but before I got started, Adrian Henri dropped in to see Allen and they kissed each other on the lips, a very unusual sight in 1984. I thought the interview went okay but some years later somebody wrote a book about Nico which talked about her time in the north-west and laughed about this very unhip guy they had met at the Neptune. There was no doubt that it was me, and it was myself as others saw me.

Anne and I also had the strange honour of being acknowledged in an Alan Bleasdale play, *Robbin' the Leighs*, on Channel 4. In the play Anne and I kept the footballs that were coming over into our garden, and the lads wanted to get them back. There was a memorable scene where the lads opened a cupboard and hundreds of balls came tumbling out. None of this was true.

During the year, I was at Southport Theatre for an interview and the manager of Southport Theatre, Phil King, said to me, "Come in the Floral Hall and meet Giant Haystacks." Mr Haystacks was wrestling that night. I had never met a man who was 43 stone before. Indeed, I did wonder if my hand would survive his handshake. He was very pleasant and told me that he had a role in Paul McCartney's new film, *Give My Regards to Broad Street*.

At the end of the year, Paul McCartney came to Liverpool and was given the Freedom of the City in a short ceremony in the Central Library. He was in good humour, joking with friends he saw in the audience like Freddie Marsden and if there had been guitars and drums, I'm sure they would have jammed. It was less successful in the evening when he and Linda attended the première of *Give My Regards to Broad Street* at the Odeon. The music was fine but the acting was dreadful as though nobody believed in what they were doing, not even Giant Haystacks.

NEPTUNE THEATRE
LIVERPOOL

An Evening of Poetry
WITH
Allen Ginsberg
PLUS
JOHN COOPER-CLARKE
PLUS
JIMMY KELLY
on THURSDAY, 19th APRIL
at 7.30pm

Tickets £3.50

AVAILABLE FROM:
NEPTUNE BOX OFFICE, ROYAL COURT BOX OFFICE
PROBE and PENNY LANE.

CHAPTER 39

Cavern Of Dreams

Looking back, I can see that 1984 was the busiest year of my life, but I didn't feel under pressure as it was all so positive and such fun. I wondered what Royal Life's management thought of my extra-curricular activities but because they had acquired the Cavern site and built a new Cavern, it was useful to have a Merseybeat enthusiast on the spot and it was beneficial to all.

To promote the new Cavern, I wrote the text for a heritage brochure that described what had happened on the site and what was happening now. Much as I joke about David Parry's behaviour in this book, he approved of Royal Life publishing the brochure when the chief actuary Tony Baker was uncertain whether it would lead to more business. It was available for free from BBC Radio Merseyside and 3,500 copies were given away in the first week, so that was a win-win situation.

Several thousand copies were distributed around Merseyside and they now sell at Beatle Conventions for £30. I should have picked up a box and preserved them in the loft. It was far more successful than Royal Insurance's official history.

Adam Faith was starring in a stage production of *Alfie* at the Liverpool Playhouse and I interviewed him after a rehearsal. I presumed that he would be in town overnight and might like the brochure. However, he was leading a secret life and was dashing off to his new girlfriend, tennis player Chris Evert. Adam Faith was a great success in *Alfie,* but the play called for asides to the audience and Adam might improvise. It made it difficult for the cast to know where to pick up.

Adam left the brochure behind. One of the resident directors at the Playhouse, Bill Morrison, read it. He had been born in 1940 and he enjoyed the quotes from Merseybeat musicians. He called me and said, "This will be perfect for our summer production. Can you come and see me immediately?"

I gave Bill the full text of my book, *Let's Go Down the Cavern,* which was being published by Hutchinson in October. He got a green light from them, and a play based on the book would run at Liverpool Playhouse from August 3 to September 22. I was given £500 and was allowed to have as many free tickets as I wanted (within reason!).

The poet and philosophy graduate Carol Ann Duffy was living in Mount Street with Adrian Henri and was a resident playwright at the Playhouse. She wrote the script which was about defying convention and what it meant to be in Liverpool in the early 1960s. I had compiled a Merseybeat timeline and a fictitious group Billy and the Dingles was inserted into it. Several of the funny stories in *Let's Go Down the Cavern* would now happen to Billy and the Dingles.

For example, in January 1960 Rory Storm and the Hurricanes were booked as a skiffle group for the Liverpool Jazz Festival at the Cavern. Skiffle was tolerated by the hardline jazzers because of its connection to American blues, but Rory couldn't resist going into 'Whole Lotta Shakin' Goin' On'. The hardliners were furious and threw those big old pennies at them. This now happened to Billy and the Dingles.

Carol wrote a great script and Billy and the Dingles were Ian

Hart (Billy), Andrew Schofield (lead guitarist), John Wild (bass), Mickey Starke (rhythm guitar) and Paul Codman (drums). They were excellent in rehearsal and we had fun choosing the songs. In the script, Billy and the Dingles had a one-off hit in 1963 and I came up with the unreleased 'Back Again to Me', written by Earl Preston and recorded with his group, the TT's. It was so obviously Merseybeat and was also a good song. We gave away Billy and the Dingles' version as a flexidisc with the programme.

The second song on the flexidisc was by Sadie White (Jeanette Dobson) with 'Please Stay', a Burt Bacharach song which had been recorded by a Liverpool group, the Cryin' Shames. Praise too for the musical director, Rick Juckes, who coped with 40 different songs or snatches of them in the production.

The cast included Roy Brandon (an excellent comic who was full of fun), Richard Tate (who in 1962 had been sent a letter from Brian Epstein's solicitor telling him not to call Epstein a homosexual), John McArdle (excellent but underused as Bob Wooler) and Majella Reynolds (from the hit-making Reynolds Girls).

The opening night was a triumph and musicians like Earl Preston, Fred Marsden (Pacemakers) and Ralph Ellis (Swinging Blue Jeans) said how authentic it was. However, Ralph did add, "We never swore like that. The language was appalling." I'd agree as it was unnecessary.

The theatre critic at BBC Radio Merseyside Colin Voake (whom I didn't know) hated the production – it was too loud and wasn't real theatre. This was a little worrying, but the reviews otherwise were generally very good. However, *The Guardian* said it was "Working class people paraded to middle class people for laughs." I don't think any of us had thought that way.

The Daily Telegraph thought that the music was mimed, which was ridiculous. If it was, how come Billy and the Dingles were good enough to appear alongside real Merseybeat practitioners on a Sunday night charity show at Liverpool Empire?

Balcony seats were only £1, a great idea as it meant that teenagers could go again and again and this created a following for Billy and the Dingles, who got audience screams. The production did very well, and Bill Morrison hoped for a tour but bookers were wary of a show without star names and about Liverpool, which had a bad reputation at that time.

Bill Kenwright wanted to film it but with a script from Alan Bleasdale. Carol Ann, quite legitimately, would not agree and after all, she did become Poet Laureate. Hutchinson also wanted a bigger cut for the film rights, this from a book they had yet to publish. Indeed, I had wanted to bring the publication of *Let's Go Down the Cavern* forward for sales at the theatre but they weren't as flexible as the Playhouse.

Cavern of Dreams was a very enjoyable experience and I wish that it had gone to the West End as the production was so good and the acting so strong. What's more, it could have set the template for musical biopics. As it is, it started a couple of years later with *Buddy*.

CHAPTER 40

Sexuality

I had first worked in Life Underwriting in the mid-1970s because Cliff Jaggers, an actuary and the Chief Underwriter, was heading for retirement and nobody was sure of the actuarial content of his work. I had to find out what he did, and he passed over good advice with his files. He was replaced as Chief Underwriter by a non-actuary, Ken Macphail. Ken was a delightful man and tried to be 'with it' but did think that the pop star was called Lloyd George – we never wanted to correct him.

Effectively, I had gone back to an actuarial department with Cliff's work while Ken supervised the day-to-day business and he would see me for actuarial input. The company's idea was that actuaries should move around for experience but somehow, I retained the brief of dealing with Cliff's work as I was shuffled around.

One of my regular jobs was to determine how many of our policyholders were expected to die in the previous year and how this contrasted with our actual experience. We could break the experience down by age and sex and whether they had been charged extra premiums for ill-health. We charged extra premiums when there was a known health risk, say, being overweight or an insulin-dependent diabetic. We could determine whether the extra premiums were in line with the additional claims we were paying. Thus, we could determine if our premium rates were fair and whether we should make any changes for new business.

Then, in the early 1980s, a new deadly disease AIDS came along and the medical profession soon determined that the main risk was with those who practised anal sex. We were used to asking intimate medical questions on proposal forms, but it was highly contentious as to whether we should ask proposers about their sexual habits.

The industry's trade association, the Association of British Insurers, normally determined guidelines, but in this instance, it said that individual offices should determine their own strategy. I argued that if we do put questions about sexuality on proposal forms, we might offend some people, but if we didn't, we ran the risk of accepting proposers whose behaviour might lead to early death. This would mean additional death claims. We had no idea how big the epidemic would be and the cost could run into millions of pounds before a cure was found.

As the ABI was prevaricating, I was told to invite the chief underwriters from our main competitors to Liverpool for an all-day conference to seek common ground and hopefully, reach an agreement. If the 12 offices who controlled the bulk of the market reached a decision, then other offices would follow as they wouldn't want to be left behind. We had to be careful that we weren't breaching trade regulations but something had to be done and fast. We all agreed that we had the same problem.

Someone said that we could solve the whole issue with just one additional question on the proposal form, "Are you prepared to have an HIV test?" That was a gloriously *Catch-22* question, namely, anyone who answered 'No' would be asked to go for one. HIV tests cost £13 so we wanted to use them sparingly.

We drafted a candid questionnaire about sexuality and

automatically tested single males if the proposal was over £150,000 cover. We had a £250,000 limit for females and married men. This wasn't perfect, but it worked. We were criticised in the press especially by one insurance broker, Ivan Massow, who specialised in gay clients. I was described as "a vindictive life assurance underwriter who was passing judgement on homosexuals". Not at all. I was protecting our funds from financial problems that would impinge on our profitability and hence, the bonuses for other policyholders.

Financially, we made the right move, but I wonder what would happen if there were a similar situation today. In this woke age, the offices would face immense criticism in the press and be accused of victimisation.

CHAPTER 41

Daydream Believer

I was pleasantly surprised when BBC Radio Merseyside's chief engineer Bill Holt told me that American singer songwriter John Stewart had been booked for the Floral Pavilion, New Brighton on Sunday 5 August 1984 and that the concert would be recorded for broadcast.

To promote the concert, John Stewart's albums had been obtained from the BBC's Gramophone Library and were being handed from presenter to presenter to give him airplay in the days leading up to the concert. John could be heard almost as regularly as the news, and I presented a half-hour appreciation, *Fire in the Wind*.

John Stewart had been part of the Kingston Trio and sung on 'Where Have All the Flowers Gone?' but he was little-known, although there was a cult around his albums, *California Bloodlines* and *Phoenix Concerts* and he had written the Monkees' No.1 'Daydream Believer'. His live album showed his speech was as mesmerising as his singing.

John Stewart, his wife Buffy Ford, and their son Luke were duly booked into the Holiday Inn. I met him at midday on the Sunday and took him across the road for an interview. I planned a half-hour conversation to which I would add music and broadcast it in my series, *Almost Saturday Night*.

I was with my friend, photographer and John Stewart devotee, Andrew Doble. We got underway with a coffee and John signed some albums, usually with a pertinent quip. On *California Bloodlines*, he wrote, "Why is this man laughing?" On *Phoenix Concerts*, "Would you invite these men to dinner?"

The interview was long enough for two programmes and Andrew and I gave John a quick tour of the city centre. He called the Cavern 'holy ground' and Andy took a photograph of him offering a cigarette to Tommy Steele's statue of Eleanor Rigby.

Back at the Holiday Inn, we ate with John, Buffy and Luke. There was more good conversation as John described Bruce Springsteen as "a mixture of Bob Dylan and Dion". He thought he'd like Elvis Costello's songs "but I never listen hard enough. I can't stand his voice." The first time he heard the Police's 'Every Breath I Take', he thought, "When I did do that?" The New Brighton concert was excellent and John was amused by the support act, Hank Walters and his Dusty Road Ramblers.

Over 600 people came to the concert, a testimony to the power of local radio (at least, back in those times). Hank brought in some country fans but John wasn't really singing country music. The following day a taxi driver called out and showed me the John Stewart albums he'd just bought.

Here are some snatches from the John Stewart interview:

"I saw Elvis Presley at the Pan-Pacific Auditorium in LA right when 'Hound Dog' was out. He still had the stand-up bass and it was unbelievable. I was shaken by the concert. I had never seen anything like that in my life. There was so much energy coming from the stage; his voice was so strong and he was having so much fun."

"When Eddie Cochran's 'Summertime Blues' came out, I thought, 'Oh my God, who is this guy? He's great.' Same with the Everly Brothers – one hit after another and each one different from the one before. That's what I miss now, Spencer - a record used to come and totally blow me away. I mean, I would be shaken by it. The world would always look different to me because of that record, and that doesn't happen anymore."

"'Where Have All the Flowers Gone?' will always be relevant. It would have been relevant 10,000 years ago and it is relevant today."

"'Blowin' in the Wind' was the first Dylan song that really caught me and then I heard 'The Times They Are A-Changin'', which is one of the most powerful records ever made by anyone, and it is just one guitar with one voice.

"'Daydream Believer' was written as a folk song and I can remember thinking, 'I didn't get much done today – all I did was write 'Daydream Believer'. A friend of mine, Chip Douglas, produced the Monkees and he thought it would be right for them. They did it in rock'n'roll mode with a 'Help Me Rhonda' horn line. If you play 'Daydream Believer' with one guitar, it's a folk song. If you play it with a band, it's a rock'n'roll song, so can you tell me what rock'n'roll is? It all depends on what you put behind it."

"A lot of people got the wrong idea about 'Armstrong'. It wasn't a putdown of the Moonshot. The message of the song was that even though there are ghettos in Chicago and people are starving in China and we've ravaged the planet, we could for just one moment sit there and watch one of our kind walk upon the moon."

The concert was broadcast on BBC Radio Merseyside. My interview was broadcast in *Almost Saturday Night* and the full text appeared in the Autumn 1984 edition of the singer/songwriter magazine, *Omaha Rainbow*, edited by the dedicated Peter O'Brien.

CHAPTER 42

Days In The Life: 1985-1986

By 1985 I was going to insurance meetings in Cheltenham (an inter-office society called Select 74, hosted by our main reassurers, Mercantile & General) and in London (Assurance Medical Society, Life Underwriters Club). Even though I led the rebellion against the Association of British Insurers' stance (or rather non-stance) on AIDS, they invited me to join one of their committees, probably thinking it was better to have me inside than out. I was also on the mortality committee of the Institute of Actuaries and was deputy editor of their Journal, so you can see how easily I could brighten up a room.

Following Ken Macphail's retirement, I was the Chief Underwriter for Royal Life. Because I had had an actuarial qualification, I could get some exemptions from the general insurance qualification with the Chartered Insurance Institute and just by taking three papers, I became a fellow of their institute, and I made it a hattrick by becoming a Fellow of the Royal Statistical Society purely on recommendations. I could now write FIA, FCII and FSS after my name and I used to wonder in what order they should be.

A couple of years into being Chief Underwriter, I was made a fellow of the Assurance Medical Society and then they gave me a diploma in medical underwriting as well. That made my total haul FIA, FSS, FCII, FAMS, DMU (AMS). That was longer than my full name of Thomas Spencer Leigh, which amused me. I used the full quota if I was presenting an insurance paper but otherwise, it didn't mean much.

The meeting in Liverpool I had called with the chief underwriters of the main offices bore unexpected fruit. We decided to continue with our meetings on a six-monthly basis to discuss not only AIDS but also issues which affected us all. This proved productive in terms of the common good without stifling competition.

When I went to Friends Provident's head office in Salisbury. I got in early and walked around the city. Next to the cathedral was a tranquil, tree-lined road but why was there a policeman outside one of the houses? When I bought some postcards in the gift shop, I learnt that it was Edward Heath's house. As a former Prime Minister, he had 24-hour police protection.

One advantage of going to meetings in London (or indeed elsewhere) was that I could usually sneak in an interview or two before returning home. It is nearly always better to interview people face to face.

One day I went to Highgate Cemetery but not to see Karl Marx or Billy Fury's grave. I was stopping off nearby to interview Viv Stanshall, noted eccentric and former lead singer of the Bonzo Dog Band. I had arranged to go there at 4pm and I rang the bell. No reply. I knocked. No reply. I rang the bell again. Eventually he answered the door. "No, I don't want any insurance today, thank you!" "But we arranged an interview," I said. "You look like an insurance man to me." "Well," I admitted, "I came to London for an insurance meeting and that is why I'm in a suit and tie, but I also have a radio programme and you've agreed to be on it." He welcomed me inside. "Don't give me any more shocks like that," he said, clearly having a downer on insurance men. "I've just been sorting these out. What shall I do with them?"

Viv handed me a bag containing his father's personal effects. I could see a set of false teeth. "You could give them to Roger Ruskin Spear," I suggested – he created the special effects for the Bonzos, which included chattering teeth. "No," he said, "I think I will paint them."

Viv took me into his cluttered studio. He was halfway through a painting that resembled Edvard Munch's *The Scream*. "It's very good," I said. "The eyes aren't right," Viv replied in that wonderfully plummy voice, "Hang on, look at me, yes, yes, you've got the very eyes I want. Sit there and let me paint them." I said, "Okay, but I'm getting a train to Liverpool at 7pm. Can I put on the recorder, and we can talk while you're doing it?" It was one of my strangest interviews but entirely in keeping with the man himself. He said, "If I make another album, it will be an untribute to Elvis and I'll call it *Unfun in Acapulco*."

I was with Viv for 90 minutes so it worked out well. I contrast it with saxophonist and writer Mike Evans who was living in Liverpool and was offered an interview in London with Chuck Berry who was promoting his autobiography. When Mike got there, he was told that Chuck Berry could only give him three minutes of his time. When he went into the room, Chuck Berry turned on a stopwatch, so Mike cut the pleasantries and went into his first question. "I beg your pardon," said Mr Berry, "Can you say that again?" Three minutes and I don't think Mike got past the first question.

I had a second interview with Adam Faith at Fortnum and Mason's on Piccadilly. He didn't have a London office and he held business meetings in the tea room. I brought an LP, *Not Just a Memory*, a hits collection on See For Miles. I'd written the sleeve notes and I thought he might not have seen it. Adam thanked me and looked down the contents, making the most savage indictment I've heard anyone make of his own hit records, "Who buys this crap?" It was sad that he had no satisfaction about what he had done – although, admittedly, many people would say he was right.

Adam had a financial column in the *Daily Mail*. One week he asked, "Do you want to be a millionaire?" If you invested £6,000 in Roger Levitt's company, you could be a millionaire in 10 years. Nobody looked up and saw the pigs flying by.

After a few years the company went into liquidation collapsing with debts of £30 million. Faith was lucky to avoid jail but he had been duped alongside the others. Levitt latched onto Faith because he had contacts including Michael Winner, who lost millions. Faith lost his own money but it was through his naivety.

Later, I did an interview with Anthony Newley who had returned to England for a tour in *Scrooge*. He told me, "It's amazing. I come back to England and I find that Adam Faith is regarded as a financial wizard." I said, quite alarmed, "Don't give him any money. He's been discredited. Remember you're playing Scrooge!"

A disillusioned performer, Phil Ochs, had killed himself in 1976, ironically being the composer of 'There but for Fortune'. Michael, his brother and manager, ran the Michael Ochs Archives. He had acquired the right to hundreds of rock photographs, often from the mid-1950s, which led to an excellent book, *Rock Archives*. He came to the UK to promote it and he signed my copy, "Enjoy the first rock book that fully explains why the girl couldn't help it." Unlike his brother, he had faith in what he was doing.

Michael was in Liverpool to talk about the book, first with

Billy Butler and then with me, both at BBC Radio Merseyside, and we all went for coffee to the Holiday Inn. While we were there, Chris Curtis, the former drummer of the Searchers, came in. He'd heard Billy Butler's show and determined that Michael Ochs should be the repository for his Searchers memorabilia. He handed him two bags stuffed with wonderful material. Billy and I watched aghast but there was nothing we could do. Michael quickly made his excuses and left, carrying the bags of course and probably wanting to exit before Chris changed his mind.

CHAPTER 43

The Man Who Wasn't There

Telephone rings. "Hello, this is Trevor Stanford, Russ Conway's management, how can I help?"

"Hello, Trevor. It's Spencer Leigh here, BBC Radio Merseyside."

"Oh Spencer, good to hear from you. Everything OK in Liverpool? Russ is coming to New Brighton next Friday."

"I know. I was hoping I could interview him for 20 minutes before the show."

"That should be okay but he's here with me now. I'll go and ask him." (Footsteps, muttering in background, footsteps return.)

"Hello, Spencer, it's Russ here. Trevor says you'd like to talk to me." (There was no change in the voice: you'd almost swear it was the same person.)

"Yes please, next Friday in New Brighton if possible."

"Shall we say six o'clock?"

"I'll be there."

"Okay, I'll see you then, and Trevor sends his best wishes."

"Yes, I hope to meet him someday."

"That'd be nice, but he hardly has time to get out of the office, poor dear."

"Bye, Russ."

"Goodbye from me and goodbye from Trevor too."

SPENCER LEIGH

CHAPTER 44

Days In The Life: 1986-1988

Things were going okay. I'd had a second series of *Almost Saturday Night* and often broadcast book reviews for *A New Leaf* as well doing a few interviews for *Folkscene*. In addition, I was carrying out interviews for a new summer series for 1986, *Shakin' All Over,* the story of British popular music before the Beatles. The series had a Merseyside content with Lita Roza, Russ Hamilton, Michael Holliday, Billy Fury and Michael Cox under scrutiny.

Chis Barber who had been playing trombone since 1948 and leading his jazz and blues band since 1950. He had been an actuarial student with Clerical, Medical and General, so as well as interviewing him for radio, I wrote something for the Institute of Actuaries' monthly house organ, *Fiasco*. He was surprised to be asked specifically about his actuarial career and he said when he studied determinants, he had no real interest in them or even of their application. Far better to stick to the trombone, so he became a professional musician.

Then the BBC Radio Merseyside station manager, Ian Judson, asked me if I'd like a weekly series. It would be a record show for £30 a week as there was no budget for interviews and I'd have to do everything myself.

I said okay but I'd rather broadcast interviews and as long as the interviews remained my property, I wouldn't claim any expenses and do the editing myself. Ian was fine with that and it worked out well for both sides.

There was a trial run of five shows going up to Christmas and if okay, I would have a continuous series from March 1986. For no other reason than impressing management, I had 12 guests in those shows, all recorded in advance so nothing could go wrong: I didn't want live guests until I was established. There was Jess Conrad (why on earth did I start with him?), Brian Poole (with unreleased tracks), Billy Bragg, Alexei Sayle, Hal Carter (on managing Billy Fury), Ken Pitt (on managing David Bowie), Michael Ochs (on his rock archives), Pete Best (on being a Beatle) and rock authors Mark Lewisohn and Ray Coleman (both on the Beatles) and Stanley Booth (on the Rolling Stones). Alan Bleasdale talked about his new film, *No Surrender*.

When *On The Beat* began its continuous run in March 1986, I generally had one guest per programme, and I couldn't go wrong with Alan Freeman talking about presenting radio shows in the first episode. He described coming from Australia to work in the UK: "I'd been broadcasting in Australia between 1953 and 1957 and, like American radio, it was fast and breezy and exciting. I came over here and they were saying, 'That was a terribly nice record and here's another terribly nice record.' It sounded professional but it was scripted and quiet. I thought, 'We can't have any of that.'"

I talked to one of America's greatest songwriters, Doc Pomus, and he chose 'A World without Love' as his favourite Lennon and McCartney song. In retrospect, I can see why. Lennon and McCartney said they would like to be like Brill Building songwriters and that song is similar with its comparisons to nature, "Birds sing out of tune and rain clouds hide the moon".

The Beatles' press officer Tony Barrow, originally from

Crosby, had returned north to Morecambe and we had a phone-in (my first!) and he was amazed to find old friends, including a girlfriend, calling him up.

Petula Clark was marvellous and generous with her time, being possessed of a very good memory and not exaggerating her achievements. It's always fun interviewing stars at home as they are relaxed and they may show you memorabilia. There is an American author I won't name who told me that he liked interviewing stars at home but because he could take, or actually steal, a souvenir or two: George Harrison and Pete Townshend were victims.

Mind you, the stars themselves could be as grasping. When I saw Brook Benton, I asked him to sign a UK LP that he'd never seen before. He wanted it for his collection and that became a condition for the interview. Fair enough, he gave me a good interview, but he could have been diplomatic, and I would have given it to him anyway.

When I was talking to Mike Batt, he received a fax from Sir John Gielgud, who agreed to appear on a musical album based on Lewis Carroll's *The Hunting of the Snark*. Mike couldn't believe his good luck and I couldn't have interviewed him at a better moment.

Dave Clark rarely talked about his hits but he agreed to a two part interview – one about the West End musical he was producing, *Time,* with Cliff Richard and another about the Dave Clark 5. He insisted that he played drums on all the Dave Clark 5 records, but I wouldn't put money on it.

Millie of 'My Boy Lollipop' fame was breastfeeding while I spoke to her and if you listened hard, you could hear the baby gurgling.

Eric Bogle would be featured on folk programmes and so I

was happy to give him a more general outing and listeners were stunned by his anti-war song 'And the Band Played Waltzing Matilda'. I was doing a public service by playing that record. Similarly, Pete Seeger brilliantly explained how he came to be associated with 'Where Have All the Flowers Gone?', 'Turn! Turn! Turn!', 'Little Boxes' and 'Guantanamera'. I was never happier than when I was talking to songwriters.

Anne didn't normally travel with me but she did come to Nottingham to meet Pat Boone. I'm glad we did as we saw the kitchen we wanted and it is still looking good 40 years on. Although I have my reservations about his rock'n'roll records, Pat Boone was a wonderful interviewee and a warm and friendly man. Like Johnny Mathis, he arranged his touring dates around golf courses, so he could play in the day and sing in the evening. He was very sporty, even trying cricket, and in 1963 he caught the England captain Ted Dexter in a charity match: how impressive is that?

I met another rock'n'roller Ronnie Hawkins in a London hotel where a girl was playing the harp in the lounge. Very adept at coming out with a good chat-up line, Ronnie went up to her and said, "Hey, you sweet young thing, how would you like a gig tomorrow night?"

Another American rock'n'roll performer, Ben Hewitt, came to St Helens as the guest of Geoff Taggart who had written for the Shadows ('Break Thru') and played in a local band, the Zephyrs. He wrote songs with Jim Newcombe, a St Helens lad who had emigrated to Canada, and they were recorded by Rayburn Anthony, Ben Hewitt and Shakin' Stevens. Jim may have emigrated to Canada but I'd hear him if he shouted loud enough: you had to have the controls right if he was on the show.

So, that is how *On the Beat* started. Soon I developed *Juke Box*

Jury programmes where I invited local guests discussing new releases and I identified those who were very good with instant opinions – Tim Adams, Chris Beazer, Bryan Biggs, Jean Catharell, Pete Cowley, Geoffrey Davis, Steve Dinwoodie, Frank Donovan, Ron Ellis, Peter Grant, Billy Hatton (Fourmost), Colin Hall, Sylvia Hall, Brian O'Connell, Mick O'Toole, Mick Ord (station manager), Norman Killon, Colin McCourt, Clive Pownceby, Melissa Storey and Geoff Taggart.

Ron Ellis wrote crime novels around the 1960s featuring his detective Johnny Ace. I interviewed Ron on air about his new novel, *Grave Mistake*. "It's the wrong title," I said. "What's wrong with it?" Ron asked. "Well, right from page one, I knew the wrong person was going to be in the grave."

I had a regular team of performers too including Davy Edge, Dean Johnson (everybody's favourite opening act), Gavin Stanley (who when he started was a like a teenage Billy Fury with the best hair in Liverpool).

My most controversial guest was Albert Goldman. Albert was a New York academic who had written a scurrilous biography of Elvis Presley, which really was a northerner saying how he hated the south. The author Barry Miles said Albert was a frustrated comedian and you can see the book as a long Jackie Mason routine.

Albert asked if I would help with the Liverpool interviews for a biography of John Lennon. I wasn't keen as I associated with these people, and what they said might be distorted. However, I did recommend that he should put the Beatles into the context of the Merseybeat era. Albert sent me $100 and asked me to send him Merseybeat records, which I did.

When Albert had come to Liverpool, he seemed reluctant to leave the Holiday Inn and said he had been threatened over his

Elvis book. He had a stentorian voice and laughed heartily as he told unrepeatable tales of sexual escapades among the famous. Who knows what the people at nearby tables thought? It was odd behaviour from someone who had travelled incognito since the Elvis book.

Ron Ellis agreed to conduct interviews on his behalf. He got some very good material. Albert edited and rewrote the interviews as part of another scurrilous book, *The Lives of John Lennon*, in 1988. If anything, Albert hated John Lennon even more than Elvis Presley.

At the Beatles Convention in August 1988, *The Lives of John Lennon* was publicly burned in front of a cheering crowd at the Adelphi. Inside, on the interview stage, I commented on this and said, "This year Albert Goldman's book: next year Albert Goldman." It was just me being silly but it was taken seriously and there was a huge cheer throughout the hall. "My god," I thought, "This is how revolutions start."

CHAPTER 45

Be Bop A Lula

The play, *Cavern of Dreams*, with its young, vibrant cast had been successful for the Liverpool Playhouse in 1984 and even though it was about the 1960s, it brought teenagers into the theatre. Anne and I admired the large poster on the outside of the theatre with Andrew Schofield's face, and Anne thought he would make a wonderful Gene Vincent: she was proved right.

The thought of Andrew, or "Drew" as we called him, playing Gene Vincent was attractive but what was the angle? Why would the Playhouse want to do something about a 1950s American rocker, famous really for just one song, 'Be Bop A Lula'.

By 1987 I had a plan and I asked Bill Morrison if I could call round. As I rang his bell, I held up a photograph of Gene Vincent. "Who's that?" I asked. "Blimey, it's Drew," Bill replied.

I told Bill the story of Gene Vincent and Eddie Cochran's ill-fated UK tour from January to April 1960. The tour had come about because Vincent had problems in the US: his group, the Blue Caps, had deserted him and as he had been sanctioned by the union, he could only accept scratch gigs with non-union bands. The possibility of UK dates, both on stage (promoted by Larry Parnes) and TV (Jack Good's *Boy Meets Girls*). was a lifeline.

Norm Riley who was handling Gene Vincent's business also recommended Eddie Cochran, so Parnes devised a UK tour in which they would be supported by British acts whom he managed: Billy Fury, Joe Brown and Georgie Fame. His road manager was a Liverpool lad, Hal Carter.

Eddie Cochran had had hits with 'Summertime Blues' and 'C'mon Everybody' and had so much potential. Gene Vincent was a spent force with an injured leg but Jack Good, inspired by a university production of *Richard III*, dressed him in black leather and gave him that biker image.

Eddie knew Gene from a tour with Little Richard in Australia and had seen him in Los Angeles but they didn't know each other well. Eddie didn't know how wrecked he had become, how much he drank and how wild his behaviour could be. Vincent could erupt and threaten people with guns and knives.

Instead of touring with a great mate, Eddie was having to keep Gene in check – and Eddie was homesick. He came from LA and he couldn't adjust to British weather. His girlfriend, the songwriter Sharon Sheeley joined the tour: she wanted to marry Eddie but he wasn't so sure.

Eddie and Gene were strangers in a strange land, but they were two great practitioners of rock'n'roll and the supporting musicians wanted to learn from them. Billy Fury learned about stage presence from Eddie Cochran, while Joe Brown admired his guitar playing - and that Gretsch Sunburst G6120 looked great.

On the last night of the tour, Eddie and Gene wanted to return to London. The taxi-driver drove fast and lost control at Chippenham and crashed. Eddie died and Gene had more injuries.

"That's your surprise ending," said Bill, "Throughout the play, they'll be thinking that something might happen to Gene but it's Eddie who dies." I thought we'd be appealing to people who knew the story anyway, but Bill saw the market for a younger audience too.

Bill got the go ahead from Ian Kellgren, the producer at the Playhouse. I assembled background material, mostly by talking to the participants. Bill wanted to know what they had for breakfast, how much they drank, who was friendly with whom, what they read, anything really, so that if he had two characters on stage together, he knew what they thought about each other. For example, Georgie Fame told me that he was only 16 when the tour began: he knew how to play rock'n'roll but his hands weren't big enough to stretch over the keys. Everyday he was hoping they had grown a little more. Georgie Fame wouldn't have a big role in *Be Bop A Lula* but this insight gave Chris Garner something to work with.

By April, Bill Morrison had a working script and auditions could start. Drew was perfect for Gene Vincent and he soon mastered the singer's voice.

I said to Bill, "I'd love to see you do that Hollywood thing and say, 'You're hired!'" He said, "Come at lunchtime tomorrow and you'll see just that." I had seen Tim Whitnall in Jack Good's show about Elvis in 1977. He had been very good as the young Elvis – and sometimes when P J Proby didn't appear as the old Elvis too! Tim did a marvellous Eddie Cochran on the Playhouse stage and was perfectly cast. He bought a Gretsch guitar just like Eddie's so there was great attention to detail.

Steven McGann was originally going to be Billy Fury but terms couldn't be reached. The role went to Gary Mavers, a Liverpool actor with a good singing voice who would later star in *Peak Practice*. His brother Lee was in a Liverpool band with a lot of potential, the La's.

Jack Good had created a stage setting for 'Wondrous Place' with a single spot on Billy's face and a slow, eerie accompaniment, and we copied it. Billy would hold a cigarette and when he got to the title line, he'd sing "Ooh, ahh, a wondrous place" and tip ash on the floor. Gary was getting screams like Billy Fury and teenage girls came to the show over and over. I was in Gary's dressing-room one night and he said, "Look at these letters." They were from girls who were desperate for a one-on-one. I said, "You're only playing Billy Fury. Imagine what the real thing got." Indeed, Billy's brother Albie told me that Billy had 18 girlfriends in 18 months. This man was sex on legs.

We asked vintage musicians to see the rehearsals to see how authentic the music sounded. We had Johnny Gentle, Duffy Power and the American Ben Hewitt, who recorded demos for Elvis. When Billy's brother, Albie Wycherley came to a rehearsal, he said that Billy was going to throw his shirt out of the window to the fans. "I said, 'That's a great shirt, Bill, give it to me and throw mine out instead.'" That found its way into the script.

The title I suggested for the play was Eddie's *Three Steps to Heaven*, but Bill thought it far better to call it *Be Bop A Lula*. The audience would come in and the curtains were closed. The lights would go down and a black gloved hand would reach through the curtains for the microphone. The curtains would open and Drew would go, "Wel-l-l-l-l, Be Bop A Lula, she's my baby."

Rob Jarvis was cast as Joe Brown – admittedly six inches too short but nothing we could do about that. Joe was coming to Liverpool and staying with his wife's family. I asked Rob if he wanted to meet him. He certainly did. Joe told him about the tour and when he left the house, Rob was saying, "How about this?" and "Is this right?" as he had been noticing his facial expressions. They went straight into his performance and the audience forgot his size and thought, "This *is* Joe Brown".

Similarly, I took Paul Codman to meet the drummer Brian Bennett who explained his drumming technique. Brian had a colour photograph of the jumper that he had worn off-stage while touring and someone in the costume department recreated it, which was wonderful as I loved that detail. Brian thought it was hilarious when he saw it on opening night.

There was also excellent staging from Candida Boyes, costumes from Anne-Marie Allison, and music direction from Rick Juckes. I was there the day they gave Drew the leg iron, a reproduction of the one Gene Vincent needed because of his disability. He said, "Spen, let's go for a walk" and he walked up and down the main street in Liverpool.

Eddie's girlfriend Sharon Sheeley was played by Catherine Roman. Sharon had been against the play as she had been angling for a Hollywood biopic. I don't think she could have stopped our production, but she might have been able to have her character removed from the script. I persuaded her that this was a loving portrait of Eddie Cochran and their relationship, and it wouldn't harm her plans at all.

The road manager Hal Carter was played by Mickey Starke, who had been in *Cavern of Dreams* and was making a name for himself. He landed the role of Sinbad in *Brookside* while *Be Bop A Lula* was playing. Hal Carter was a larger-than-life Scouser (just like Mickey) and had had several run-ins while trying to discipline Gene Vincent. On one coach journey, Vincent cut his suit into pieces… while he was wearing it.

Mickey and Drew were best mates and they referred to Tim Whitnall as Mr Professional. They would go home and relax before the next show but not Tim. He might shoot off to London to record a commercial or narrate a children's programme. He narrated *The Teletubbies*. You might have thought he would have been whacked out, but he had a really high energy level.

In the run-up to opening night, I got a telephone call from

Larry Parnes' partner. He said, "Larry wants to come to Liverpool but is there anything that will embarrass him?" I presume he was worried about being outed. I said, "No, but the musicians on the road do talk about being underpaid." A few minutes later, Larry himself rang me. "I don't mind that," he said, "That is only schoolchildren talking about their headmaster." That reveals how he saw himself and his performers.

Larry was extremely pleasant at the opening, lavishing praise upon Davy Edge who played him and sending him a signed photograph. Marty Wilde was astounded when he learnt Larry bought the whole cast a drink, so he must have loved the production. Larry had one criticism. He said, "If I refer to someone who has died, I always say 'God rest his soul' as a little prayer." The next night Davy Edge had added, "God rest his soul."

When Larry talked to Jean Wycherley, Billy's mum, they were friendly, although Jean thought that he had worked Billy far too hard with his damaged heart. "It wasn't me," said Larry, "Billy wanted to do it."

Joe Brown couldn't come to the opening but came a few days' later. The play started and there was a huge laugh from Joe as Davy Edge came on stage. I asked Joe what that was about. He said, "I couldn't help it. That bloke playing Larry Parnes looked just like him – I thought Larry had come back to haunt me."

For the second year, Martin Glyn Murray of the Manchester band, the Mock Turtles, played Eddie Cochran and Paul Kissaun played Joe Brown. They played them well, but the original production had the spark. The *Be Bop A Lula* band did charity performances at the Liverpool Empire and the Philharmonic Hall and to this day, there is an annual performance at the Cavern. Martin was to make a name for himself in the daytime soap, *Families,* which took place in both Australia and the UK.

Bill Morrison and I got on very well except over the billing. He didn't want 'by Bill Morrison and Spencer Leigh' as he was the playwright, and it became 'Bill Morrison with Spencer Leigh' with my name in a lower typeface. Bill said that when he wrote a play about the missing racehorse, Shergar for BBC-TV, the researcher got a flat £500 and no credit on the script, and I was getting a much better deal.

I was offered 25% of the royalties and his agent, who said he would act for me, said Bill was being generous. I wasn't bothered. I wanted the play to be staged and with the 1988 and 1989 productions at the Playhouse and touring weeks in Brighton, Bristol, Hanley and Manchester, I did get £2,000 so I can't complain.

I might have felt differently if it had gone bigtime. There was talk of a West End production, but Bill Kenwright didn't like the final scene of Gene Vincent at the airport with Eddie Cochran's coffin. In his view, West End musicals needed to end with the cast on their feet.

Also, Bill Morrison had a girl with a saxophone, Sheri Gaubert, portraying Gene's blue moods. It worked well and she played great, but Bill Kenwright felt it was too negative and that audiences wouldn't get it. For the sake of the production, Bill Morrison could have met him halfway but they were both intransigent.

Bill Morrison wrote a film script based on the play but nothing came of it. In the opening scene, Gene Vincent is in an airport toilet, taping a revolver to his leg as Customs officials will think that the X-ray is picking up the leg-iron. To this day, there has not been a film about Gene and Eddie.

But there is a legacy to *Be Bop A Lula*. It led to *Buddy* in the West End as the director had seen *Be Bop A Lula* and knew where to take his show. It opened at Victoria Palace in London in 1989. I liked it very much, but it skirted over the more contentious aspects of Buddy's career (his falling out with the Crickets, the duplicity of Noman Petty). Now, pretty well any rock star is up for grabs and we have big lavish productions like *We Will Rock You*.

As for me, I wrote a book about the Gene and Eddie tour, *Things Do Go Wrong;* which was published by Finbarr International in 2008. It is good to have my research out there instead of being stored in files in the garage. I thought that everybody would get the book's title – it comes from 'Three Steps to Heaven' but they didn't.

CHAPTER 46

Days In The Life: 1988-91

I can't write about this section of my life without a mention of the tragic disasters that Liverpool football fans suffered during the second half of the 80s.

In 1985 there was the Heysel Stadium disaster when a riot broke out after some disorder in the stands which led to 39 deaths and over 600 injuries. Liverpool fans were banned from European games for some time and the stadium was rebuilt before it reopened in 1995. As if that was not enough, an even greater tragedy befell Liverpool FC and its fans only four years later.

In 1989 Liverpool and the whole Merseyside region had been shocked by the deaths of the Liverpool fans at the Hillsborough stadium in Sheffield. I haven't written about it because I don't have anything new to contribute. It is so hard to know what to say and I would point readers to the brilliant poem by David Charters on the Hillsborough memorial, which is opposite the World Museum in William Brown Street.

Tom Murphy's sculpture lists the victims and gives their ages. You, like me, will be taken by how young so many of them were. Normally when someone dies, you remember the past but here, faced with such youth, it is their future which has been lost. That is the substance of David's poem and how true that is.

On the day of the tragedy, I had presented my *On the Beat* programme at Saturday lunchtime with Tony Barrow, the NEMS' press officer, and the singer-songwriter Davy Edge. We had discussed Tony's sleeve notes on the Beatles' albums. The programme had finished at 2pm. I stayed behind to log my records for copyright payments and caught the train home. It was a perfectly normal day and then something happened that was so devastating that you wondered if the city would ever be normal again.

Hillsborough affected everybody in the city. Two of the victims worked at Royal Life on the unit-linked maintenance department: they were Peter Burkett (24) and Jon Owens (18). RIP.

Hugo Johnson was a Director at Royal Life. He was urbane and cultured and he hated it when Royal Life formed a partnership with Owen Oyston, the arrogant, uncouth estate agent who also owned Blackpool FC. Oyston's organisation would sell its clients the houses and the Royal would cover the loans with life assurance, for which Oyston would get commission, loads of it.

Whenever Oyston was coming to the office, Hugo would find something else to do. I don't think he wanted to be associated with a man who wore such gaudy clothes and was, ironically, very proud of the bulletproof windows on his Rolls-Royce. He thought that was a sign of success and if so, he was welcome to it. I can remember walking by Owen Oyston when he was in the office and he clicked his fingers and said to me, "Coffee". He'd got the measure of me immediately.

My dad enjoyed these stories of these larger-than-life characters, and I was glad that I could entertain him. He died in 1988 and he had been ill for some time, putting a strain on my mother. She was then on her own and was okay for a year or so.

Then I got a call from the cleaner that she wasn't answering the door. I got round as quickly as I could but she had collapsed on the landing. After hospital treatment, she went into a home in Southport, Ascot Lodge, and they looked after her well.

One day I arrived after work, just in time for the local news. The old dears were all in the lounge and who should appear on TV but my boss, David Parry. It was a truly surreal moment. Mum lasted until 1994, but she didn't know where she was at the end.

At the time, I was leading quite a busy life and it was a privilege to write so-called learned papers for the Institute of Actuaries. When I look at those papers now, I see that I was the first actuary to quote Leonard Cohen, Bob Dylan, Paul Simon and Loudon Wainwright in august publications. For one feature on AIDS, I began by quoting Leonard Cohen, "Everybody knows that the plague is coming, Everybody know that it's moving fast." I'm sure it helps to engage the reader.

We delivered our message as best we could, but some people did not want to listen. We were a major insurance company with our head offices in Liverpool and in 1990, Liverpool City Council passed a resolution attacking Royal Insurance for "discriminating against people suffering from major diseases such as AIDS".

I could imagine a maverick councillor or two voting against anything to do with a large corporation but to have the Council pass such a resolution meant that over half the councillors agreed with the stance. It was a misunderstanding of the principles of insurance. If it was their own money on the line, would they behave in the same way? Of course not.

Their resolution implied that we could continue to ask people about other medical conditions such as asthma or blood pressure and determine the premiums accordingly. However, the Council did not want us to ask anything about AIDS, so that those who had it would be paying less for life insurance than someone with a slightly raised blood pressure.

Insurance premiums have to be equitable, which means that we had to determine the risks involved in each case, taking into account age, sex (as women overall lived longer than men), health, hazardous occupations (scaffolders, racing drivers), hazardous pursuits (hang gliding, deep-sea diving) and now sexual practices.

I was asked to diffuse this situation with the Council and I took along our Chief Medical Officer, Bryan Walker as they could hardly disagree with a consultant physician. They were still unhappy, but I told them of reassurance companies who took on specialist risks. If the Council felt so strongly about it, they could set up their own reassurance arm whereby the risks that we found unacceptable would be reassured with them and they would meet the death claims. We never heard any more from them after that.

There was another issue fast coming down the track – genetics, whereby healthy people might learn that they are prone to a disease because it ran in the family. We had to head this one off at the pass, but we had no idea how it was going to develop.

In this regard, I found a great quote from Alexei Sayle: "They tell you that you're most likely to die of the same things that your grandparents did. So provided I steer clear of marauding Cossacks, I'll be fine."

And then there's Loudon Wainwright III's '1994': "There's been a brand new breakthrough, Though they're not sure what it means. We used to blame our parents, Now we can pin it on our genes."

Loudon was one of my guests in *On the Beat* and he illustrated my theory that songwriters often make the best guests as they know how to express themselves well and concisely. Sammy Cahn and Jimmy Webb wrote in very different styles and their interviews back this up. Cahn was in London and before I arrived, he was amusing himself by listening to contemporary songs on the radio and tightening up the lyrics: it was more fun than a crossword. He didn't like the line "Goin' where the weather suits my clothes" in 'Everybody's Talkin'' and preferred his alliterative "Goin' where the climate suits my clothes". He had heard 'Señor' by Bob Dylan with its rhymes of 'headin'' and 'Armageddon' and been unimpressed. He said, "I could never give that rhyme to Frank Sinatra."

I suggested it was good songwriting because it was such a surprise, Cahn said, "Surprising, yes, but lazy songwriting. You should work hard to get the rhymes right."

Another guest was Barry Mason, the lyricist from Wigan, who wrote for Tom Jones ('Delilah') and Engelbert Humperdinck ('The Last Waltz'). He said that a good songwriter should write as concisely as possible and he quoted from his own work with "I felt the knife in my hand and she laughed no more."

Justin Hayward of the Moody Blues came into Radio Merseyside with his guitar and asked if I wanted some songs. While he was singing a very cool version of Buddy Holly's 'Learning the Game', I was thinking, "What if he sends in a bill?" He didn't of course and as luck would have it, Rick Wakeman came in a couple of weeks later and said we could do the interview at the station's Steinway. Again, it worked out well and he played his part on David Bowie's 'Space Oddity' as an instrumental.

Although it's nothing to boast about now, Rolf Harris said he would draw my portrait as I talked to him. He gave me the picture and I had it framed and put it in the hall. It's a good piece of work but obviously, we thought of taking it down. However,

Gustav Klimt is still on display in galleries, so maybe the art can be distanced from the artist.

We booked a radio concert with Townes Van Zant who arrived at BBC Radio Merseyside in a dreadful state, totally wiped out. Kenny Johnson, who had seen much more of life than I had, said, "Take him into a studio and interview him. Don't let anybody see him." Especially the boss, Mick Ord. Townes was in no shape to face an audience, but Kenny returned with a bottle of whiskey and within an hour, Townes Van Zandt was okay and we got a fine concert. It was broadcast half in *Sounds Country*, half in *On the Beat*.

When we recorded a fifth anniversary concert for *On the Beat*, we had Bill Dees, Roy Orbison's co-writer, staying with us. I thought, "How wonderful. We've got the writer of 'It's Over' and 'Oh! Pretty Woman' in our house" but it was a nightmare as he never stopped singing. He was used to peddling his wares around Nashville and he did it all the time. We would get into a cab and he would say to the driver, "Hey, do you want to hear a song?" and off he would go. He was a great bloke with a kind nature, but we could see why Roy didn't take him on tour.

I did meet Orbison himself at Southport Theatre and he was with his brother, Sam, who acted as his road manager and looked like him. For some reason, the Big O showed me the scar from his heart surgery, a remarkable thing to show to a stranger. My friend Tony Marsh, who played with Chick Graham and the Coasters, had a private chat with him about Buddy Holly and he said that Holly had a great trick: he would play a riff backwards and come up with a new tune, thus Little Richard's 'Lucille' inspired the Crickets' 'Maybe Baby'. I wonder if the big O passed that tip onto the Beatles as they sometimes did that too.

On The Beat had a varied collection of guests and fortunately, the audience remained with it. In the course of a few months, the guests included Arlo Guthrie (a mesmerising speaking voice, just like 'Alice's Restaurant'), Tony Sheridan (an argumentative character who had recorded with the Beatles in Hamburg), Nana Mouskouri (delightful) and Eartha Kitt (bad-tempered - but I'm sure something had happened just before I arrived).

Stephane Grapelli was another unhappy subject. I met him on the first floor at the Southport Arts Centre and because the lift was broken the veteran jazz violinist had to climb the stairs. As his mobility was restricted, he was in an appalling mood but I thought if I just hang around, I may be okay in 20 minutes or so, and I was.

I went to an insurance meeting in London but managed to arrange an interview with the American singer/songwriter Mark Germino at his hotel. Not lacking in confidence, he sang a live version of 'Rex Bob Lowenstein' for me and for anyone else who happened to be in the lounge: it was a brilliant song about a DJ who refused to stick to the playlist.

I visited the BBC Written Archives in Caversham and became familiar with their wonderful files. They had amazingly good documentation on records that had been banned and the reasons why. I asked Mick Ord if I could broadcast my research and play the records. He said to steer clear of the Irish ones but otherwise okay, which was fair enough.

Peter Doggett, the editor of *Record Collector*, came to Merseyside for a couple of programmes in which listeners could bring in their records for valuation. Nothing fazed him: he could pass judgement on anything.

The Record Collectors was a fine programme broadcast across the Midlands and hosted by Mike Adams and Chris Savory. Although I did a programme with them, I never met Chris. Mike told me that Chris was on holiday that week, but he didn't want us to say so in case of burglars. Chris had taped an introduction which welcomed me and asked what my first record would be. The record was duly played and Mike then announced that Chris had had to go home because his wife wasn't well. We continued with the show and Chris was supposedly on the line saying that all was well and there was no cause for alarm. It was so bogus that I thought it might encourage burglars.

I did a few Saturday night programmes on Radio Merseyside when John Kennedy was ill. He had a rock'n'roll request programme and when I heard his show, I had wondered why there were so many requests from Walton. Once I received his mail, I realised these were from prisoners. Were there coded messages in the records they wanted?

As well as my weekly shows, I did a series about the Beatles' records, *Love Me Do,* and another about Elvis, *All Shook Up,* both featuring interviews I'd done over the years. There was also a series about other Merseybeat musicians, *Some Other Guys,* and one about country music, *Good Ol' Boys.* The old Tony Barrow maxim again: rework your catalogue.

I was the question-setter and presenter for a quiz series, *Beat It!,* which featured such teams as the Deadbeats, the Ageing Groovies and the Lubbock Light Infantry. A girl who worked with me in Royal Life, Tracey Cummins, kept the scores very efficiently and we made a couple of good series. It got replaced by a north-west series which was broadcast over several stations: Radio Cumbria, Radio Lancashire, Radio Manchester and Radio Merseyside, and I was part of the Merseyside team. The series was sponsored by the Post Office, and they might have been better off sorting out their computers.

Pete McGovern and others had written so many verses to

'In My Liverpool Home' that I thought it would be great to have as complete a recording of the song as possible and so I invited musicians one Saturday morning to a live recording for *On the Beat* with the recording being produced by Jenny Collins and Bill Holt.

Mickey Starke was the MC, making sure that the right performers got to the lead vocal microphone at the right time for the verses. There was a fantastic collection of musicians singing and playing and Hughie Jones, Count John McCormick and Billy Maher took it as a challenge as they were determined to play from start to finish.

The performers included Pete McGovern, Stan Ambrose, Bob Buckle, Billy Butler, Raphael Callaghan, Davy Edge, Johnny Gentle, Russ Hamilton, Adrian Henri Brian Jacques, Kenny Johnson. Billy Maher, Andrew Schofield, Gavin Stanley and two Spinners, two Merseybeats, a Mojo, a Hillsider, a Remo 4 and Sylvia Bawden from the Philharmonic Choir.

We started at 12.05 and finished just before the 1pm news. There was still half an hour to run so we had a few individual performances. However, Liverpool country singer Hank Walters had taken some performers across the road to the Holiday Inn and told the barmen that the drinks were on account to Spencer Leigh. On Monday morning, the hotel came over with a bill but I didn't mind as it was only £30. You had to be careful with Hank around! As well as being broadcast, the full 'In My Liverpool Home' was released as a cassette for Radio Merseyside's Charitable Trust. It was sponsored by Royal Insurance and I had asked Pete to write and sing a new verse for the occasion:

"*Royal Insurance, a firm of renown,*
Have built their head office, north end of town,
A fortress of steel and sandstone décor

There to protect them if the Pru declares war."

In 2018 Gerry Jones and John Haines compiled a book of all the known verses up to that time – and they had 163. It is more a labour of love than a commercial enterprise and it is on sale at the Museum of Liverpool.

When the Tall Ships returned to the Mersey, we recorded another live *On the Beat,* this time from Vittoria Dock in Birkenhead. We had Hank Walters with the Arcadian Ladies (his three daughters), Jerry Devine, Johnny Gentle, the songwriting duo Lennon and Higham, Pete McGovern (with a new verse) and Chris While. It was released as another charity cassette, *On the Beat at the Tall Ships.*

The country singer Jerry Devine would dress up smartly and go to the Grand National each year. He would talk his way into the winner's enclosure and every year on TV, he would be seen alongside the winning horse. It took about 15 years before the BBC realised that this white-haired man was a constant feature but they didn't know he was. Well, I did – and everybody else who attended his pub gigs.

I had, and still have, the strongest admiration for Cavern City Tours, a company primarily operated by a schoolteacher Bill Heckle and a cabdriver Dave Jones, who realised that the city should take Beatles tourism seriously. They built up their business in the 1980s, establishing the annual Merseybeatle convention and creating a Beatles tour bus which did very good business. They started the Mathew Street Festival in 1993, but even though it brought business into the city, it met with opposition and what I thought was an event for life was an event for just a few years. I thought the same too about the excellent Summer Pops in the big tent.

I loved the fact that John Lennon's Uncle Charlie would go

down his street every day and the tour guide on the Magical Mystery Tour bus would say, with surprise, "Look, there's John Lennon's Uncle Charlie" and Charlie would wave. He had little else in his life to keep him motivated and though he had only a few John Lennon stories, he was at least a Lennon who lived in Liverpool. Everybody loved him.

In 1991 Cavern City Tours published a book of my interviews, *Speaking Words of Wisdom*, which followed *Let's Go Down the Cavern* and featured 200 celebrities talking about the Beatles. Their opinions were so wide-ranging that I loved compiling this book and deciding what worked with what. Furthermore, Bill Heckle is a brilliant proofreader (indeed, one of the best) and the book looks fine even 30 years on.

I hoped to get a few new McCartney quotes in 1990 when he appeared at the King's Dock in Liverpool but the press conference was disappointing. It was full of foreign journalists who asked, "When are you going to play Brazil, Paul?" and 'When are you going to play Australia?" Okay, they need something for home consumption, but it made the conference boring as one similar question followed another, each being given a hopeful but vague reply. I asked if he ever felt like Bob Dylan who often revised old lyrics. "Not at all," said, Paul, "I'd rather be writing new songs."

CHAPTER 47

Dr. Heckle And Mr. Snide

You can watch TV all you want but nothing beats live theatre with the possibility of great heckles, although personally I think the best Heckle is Bill.

In the 1970s Jack Jones was going out with the actress Susan George and at the Liverpool Empire he said that Susan's parents were in the audience and would they take a bow. Jack remarked, "You're quite a way back. Couldn't they find you better seats?" "We paid for our seats," shouted someone at the front.

In the 1980s Peter Duncan and Linda Lusardi were starring in a sex comedy *Funny Peculiar* at the Neptune Theatre. Peter Duncan jumped out of bed when her husband came home. "What shall I do? What shall I do?" he panicked and someone in the audience shouted, "Stick a Blue Peter badge over it!"

When Dennis Locorriere of Dr Hook was at the Neptune, somebody from the balcony shouted, "I love you, Dennis!" He looked up and said, "Who's that?" Some wag shouted, "It's Sylvia's mother!"

Colin McCourt never had the finance to stage his excellent musical, *The Devil Rides Out* properly. It was based on the Dennis Wheatley novel in which the main characters stand inside a circle to avoid the Devil, riding in on horseback. I was sitting behind Carl Chase, the *Brookside* actor, at the Neptune. When they reached this crucial scene, the shocking moment was no more threatening than a pantomime horse. "It's Muffin the bloody Mule," muttered Carl Chase. I had to stuff a hanky in my mouth to stop laughing.

In 2010 Alexei Sayle attended a signing for his autobiography, *Stalin Ate My Homework,* at the News From Nowhere bookshop in Liverpool. He had brought his mother Molly to the event and as he described his Communist childhood she shouted, "It's all lies. He's made it all up." Fancy being heckled by your own mother.

The Geordie actor Jimmy Nail had had a couple of hit records and he agreed to sing with the Royal Liverpool Philharmonic Orchestra at the Summer Pops, one of the city's best initiatives. He came on stage and was well out of his comfort zone, asking the orchestra if they could start again. A Scouser shouted out, "Don't worry, Jimmy mate, you're among friends", which broke the ice and the concert went fine.

In 2004 Mark McGann never stepped out of character when giving a John Lennon concert at the Philharmonic Hall. He even replied to hecklers as John Lennon. When he said that he hadn't passed any exams at Quarry Bank, someone shouted "Same as me". Mark responded, "But I got into art school – and you didn't." And that is it. The artist has the microphone and if he is quick enough, he can get the final word.

Wreckless Eric was at the Philharmonic Hall in a support spot. He broke a string but said he would continue. He broke another string and said he could continue with four. Someone shouted, "We paid for six strings, you fucker, and we want six strings." Wreckless Eric responded, "It's Mr Fucker to you."

In 2009 a lady heckled comedian Andy Parsons and said that he should be doing more for the working class and he replied, "This is a comedy show: are you sure you've come to the right place?" Then someone heckled her to which he replied, "See, even the hecklers are heckled in Liverpool."

In 1964 Spike Milligan starred in a revival of a serious Russian play, *Oblomov,* in the West End. It didn't go well on the opening night and rather than cut costs and close, the producers let Milligan run riot. The other actors, mostly seasoned professionals, behaved normally and kept the play on the road, but Milligan could do whatever he liked. It was hilarious and a different show every night. When I saw it, he was in a scene alone on stage: he left the set and sat in the stalls and looked up, saying, "Haven't seen this bit myself, folks." I was watching a comic genius at work.

The Lord Chamberlain's rules were still in force at the time so how had the producers managed to get a licence for such a spontaneous production, now renamed *Son of Oblomov?*

When Spike Milligan and Jeremy Taylor were at the Royal Court, Liverpool in the 1970s, I went three times in one week to judge how spontaneous Milligan was. The answer is "Very". No one could outsmart him, but best of all, he came on stage one night holding a *Daily Telegraph* with a huge hole in it. He sat down and started reading and then looked up, "Not much in the paper today." I felt sorry for Jeremy Taylor who would often start a song and be interrupted – one night Milligan walked across the stage with a ladder while he was singing. It was a total disregard for another artist's talent but on the other hand, Taylor wouldn't have got the gig without Milligan so I suppose, he was taking the rough with the smooth.

Taylor, incidentally, made his name in the South African revue, *Wait a Minim,* and his song, 'Ag Pleez Daddy', could have been the inspiration for Mike Hart's 'Son, Son'.

The Europa in Belfast was the most bombed hotel in Ireland as it wouldn't pay protection money and had trouble from both sides. When Billy Connolly was in Belfast for one-nighters, the manager thanked him for staying at the Europa and asked, "How did you hear of us?" Connolly replied, "*News At Ten*".

Comedian Rich Hall came on stage at the ornate concert room in St George's Hall in Liverpool and said, "I feel like I'm performing in Liberace's intestines." You have to know that hall to get the joke, but it's a brilliant observation.

Alan Davies was heckled when he was filming part of *The Great Britons* in Menlove Avenue. "What are you doing here? said a passer-by, "You put Liverpool in *Room 101?*" "That's seven years ago." said Alan Davies, "and I thought you Scousers appreciated humour."

CHAPTER 48

Days In The Life: 1992-1994

We can never say that the world is good or bad as so many things happen at the same time and it takes years to put them into perspective. Certainly, the release of Nelson Mandela from prison in early 1990 and his subsequent role as President of South Africa was very positive and Bill Clinton was an effective American President until his private life got the better of him. The years of discord with Margaret Thatcher's premiership were being repaired by the more compassionate John Major. There was talk of the worldwide web and the information superhighway, but nobody knew if this would be a force for good or for bad. Even now in 2024, nobody really knows how it is going to play out in the future, especially now that AI is in the frame.

In terms of *On the Beat*, one of my favourite programmes was with Connie Atkinson, an American writer from New Orleans, who was doing a postgrad at the Institute of Popular Music at Liverpool University. She gave a wonderful account of the city, a cosmopolitan port like Liverpool and how all those influences created a musical gumbo.

There was talk of Liverpool being twinned with New Orleans but it didn't happen. A few years later it was suggested that Liverpool should twin with Nashville and then it was Memphis. Recently, a councillor thought Liverpool should twin with New

Jersey, the sole reason being that it might bring Bruce Springsteen to Liverpool. Even in 2024, Springsteen has yet to play Liverpool, Now in 2025 Bruce will be playing two nights at Anfield. He will be 75 and why has it taken him so long? He stills youthful and looks like Bruce Springsteen and yet when I saw Marlene Dietrich at the Royal Court, she was only 61 and yet seemed like an old lady.

Regular guests on my programme included Peter Doggett (editor of *Record Collector*), Mark Lewisohn and Chas White (Dr Rock), the owner of the most contagious laugh in the music industry. Roughly, they would appear once a year and there would always be a different theme.

We had concerts from the Merseybeats, Ian Whitcomb (with his love for pre-war novelties), Dennis Locorriere (freed from Dr Hook and a wonderful solo artist where his conversation was as good as his songs), Sonny Curtis of the Crickets (who worked with a scratch band from the audience) and Kelvin Henderson (Bristol-based country singer with a very deep voice). Kelvin died a couple of years later: he had lived his life in the same house in Bristol, dying in the very bed in which he had been born.

Keith Skues from Radio Caroline talked about pirate radio, and as the shanty group Stormalong John were in the next studio, I invited them to sing for Keith. Tom Robinson and TV Smith did a session together, while Carl Chase and Davy Edge worked as Wear Two Hats (We're Twats).

One day I went into Radio Merseyside after work and found Terry Waite, the Archbishop of Canterbury's envoy, in reception. He had been tied to a radiator and kept in solitary confinement in Lebanon. He was here to talk with Bob Azurdia about his book. A book with local connections, I might add, as the Archbishop had been Robert Runcie, a Merchant Taylors' boy. I went to the main office where Bob was talking 19 to the dozen as usual. I said, "Bob, do you know Terry Waite is downstairs?" He said, "That's okay, he's used to waiting."

When Gilbert O'Sullivan agreed to be a guest he said he wouldn't allow the lyric of 'Alone Again (Naturally)' to be changed as the song meant so much to some people. Like Tom Russell, he was great for a summer series I did called *Songwriter*. A few years later, Gilbert refused Nina Simone permission to change 'Alone Again (Naturally)' but she went ahead and did it anyway – who's going to sue Nina Simone?

I found Joe Fagin of the Strangers living on a houseboat in the Thames: he had sung 'That's Livin' Alright', the theme for *Auf Wiedersehen, Pet*.

That's the great thing about doing interviews: you can end up in the most unlikely places.

Sometimes, I interviewed fan clubs - Frank Sinatra's, Guy Mitchell's and Cliff Richard's. The one thing that made those interviews interesting was that true fans would invariably pick the most unlikely tracks.

On a rock'n'roll package show at Southport, I spoke to Jack Scott, Johnny Preston, Frankie Ford (wearing a scarf with piano keys), Charlie Gracie, D J Fontana (Elvis' drummer) and Freddie 'Fingers' Lee in quick succession. This was the greatest rock'n'roll package to ever hit Southport and I loved every moment of it.

Charlie Gracie was a small man with a big guitar and a very warm personality, and he thanked me for taking such an interest in him. He was of Italian heritage and he pinched my cheeks just like they do in *The Godfather*. Charlie had toured the UK in the summer of 1957 and spent a week at the Liverpool Empire.

That tour had almost been cancelled because the star name, the feisty Dorother Squires, had pulled out: she didn't want to share the limelight with some upstart playing rock'n'roll music.

The tour went ahead anyway and Charlie had a longer spot in which he could impress with his singing and guitar mastery. Indeed George Harrison had been so impressed with 'Guitar Boogie' that he wanted to be a musician himself. I felt sorry for Charlie: he knew he had been too young when he made it and he had been exploited.

Johnny Preston had had a UK No.1 with the Big Bopper's song' Running Bear' and the whole audience was going "oompah, oompah" along with him. The Canadian Jack Scott was a much underrated singer/songwriter, setting the path for Roy Orbison with his ballad 'My True Love' and he had the show's showstopper with 'What In The World's Come Over You'. Frankie Ford was a gay rock 'n' roll singer from New Orleans with a wonderful scarf with piano keys on. He told me that his car number plate said "OOO-EE" - the key phrase from 'Sea Cruise'. When the 10 minute call was announced, he grabbed me and said, "Don't you just love show business?" Add to that, Elvis Presley's original drummer D J Fontana and the UK rock'n'roll wild man, Freddie 'Fingers' Lee and you have one marvellous rock'n'roll package - and in Southport of all places.

On another trip to Southport Theatre, this time to interview Foster and Allen, I found Matthew Corbett putting Sooty and Sweep to bed after the afternoon show. I wondered if he'd been right for the job when he spoke, years later, at Gerry Marsden's memorial service at Liverpool Cathedral. Matthew could have been the first person to say 'fuck' in Liverpool Cathedral – and he said it twice in case we weren't sure what we heard the first time.

My quiz series was now called *Rockscore* and we had a team from *Brookside*. Even now I feel I cheated them by asking them to identify a song from just these words: "If I feel edgy". It was too hard – it's half a line in 'Don't Let Me Be Misunderstood'.

In 1994 I did a Saturday evening show with Jon Anderson of Yes and after logging the records, I took a shortcut across waste ground to Central Station. I was jumped by two lads, one with a knife. They took me to a cashpoint and told me to get out the maximum, which was £100. I did but fortunately they didn't take my card or my pin. I reported it to the police and went along to the police station to create an identikit. The sketch maker said, "I've only been asked to do one", which was pointless: surely it would have been easier to identify two friends. After that, I never heard from the police again.

A few days later the Bronx crime writer Evan Hunter came to Radio Merseyside for an interview with the presenter Bob Azurdia. He saw a warning on the noticeboard to be careful when leaving by the back door as I had been mugged. He said to Bob, "What did this guy do?" "Gave them £100," said Bob. He replied, "In New York you fight back as they're gonna kill you anyway."

Around this time, I began writing entries for an encyclopedia created by Colin Larkin. Colin, who was born in Dagenham in 1949, had studied printing and graphic design. He had designed art books and in the late 1980s, he wanted to publish music books. In 1990, his company Square 1 published an outstanding history of the Byrds, *Timeless Flight*, by Johnny Rogan. Johnny had studied classical poetry and he brought forensic detail to rock journalism. Johnny was a secretive, maybe paranoid, writer, always feeling that somebody was out to get him. Indeed, Morrissey didn't thank Johnny for his biography and hoped he would die in a car crash. He also had a run-in with Van Morrison, but Johnny felt that if the subjects objected to his books, he must be doing something right.

Because he had friends on Merseyside, Johnny came to Liverpool to promote *Timeless Flight* and I devoted an *On The Beat* to the Byrds. He told me that Colin Larkin was undertaking a giant encyclopaedia of popular music and that I might like to be involved. Colin wanted specimen entries. The first ones I wrote were Charles Aznavour and Gerry and the Pacemakers because I could draw upon my interviews. I wrote a couple of hundred entries, sometimes checking facts with the performers. The folk singer Richard Digance told me that he never wanted to appear in an encyclopedia, which was backed up by a letter from his agent. When it was published, Colin cheekily wrote, "At the request of International Artists Limited, Richard Digance's entry is not listed."

In 1992 Colin Larkin published the gargantuan *Guinness Encyclopedia of Popular Music*, four volumes in a box, although the fourth volume was mostly a marathon index. Colin Larkin must be praised for his phenomenal effort, not least in getting the financial backing to publish it and in organising his writers.

As well as the box set, Colin wanted spin-offs on specific subjects, one being country music. Some of the rock-based country entries had already been written by that seasoned journalist, John Tobler. Colin knew I wrote for *Country Music People* and wanted the traditional artists to be covered. I brought in another *CMP* writer, Hugh Wilson from Lincoln, who was older than me and had a vast knowledge of the pre-war acts.

Hugh wrote to Hank Snow and asked him, amongst other things, if he wore a hairpiece. He got the most incredulous reply from Hank saying he never wore anything like that. Of course he did, but as if it mattered.

The original sponsor was replaced by Virgin and when the text was reprinted, the new company wanted album ratings. This seemed too vague to have any specific purpose. For example, *Johnny Cash at San Quentin* is a brilliant and important album but I deducted a star because of the laziness of following the song about San Quentin with a second version of the same song. However, readers would not know why I marked it down. Another Virgin spinoff was the *All-Time Top 1,000 Albums* with votes from musicians, critics, and the general public. In 1994 the top album was *Sgt Pepper* but in a second edition in 1998, it had been replaced by another Beatles' album, *Revolver*.

Having contributed to the encyclopedia and spin-offs, I had an idea for *Aspects of Elvis* in which various writers would share their views on Elvis Presley: this was going to be with Colin Larkin and he himself planned an assessment of Elvis' album sleeves. I coordinated the contributions but because of other commitments, Colin had to drop out. I told writer Alan Clayson of my dilemma, and he arranged a deal with Sedgwick and Jackson and added some other contributors. The book was published in 1994 and had good reviews but the one I remember was from *The Guardian*, which was a demolition of Elvis rather than the book: it was along the lines of *why is this guy worth writing about?* In a completely surprising moment, one character in *Neighbours* received *Aspects of Elvis* as a present, on one of the episodes. How's that for product placement? The book did have a very distinctive cover, so I imagine that was the reason it appeared.

Full of pertinent details and shrewd observations, my favourite contribution was Tim Whitnall's visit to the Sun Studios in Memphis. Pete Frame created a real family tree and traced Elvis back to a Cherokee Indian, Morning Dove White. Bob Groom wrote movingly on Elvis and the blues; Patrick Humphries told us why he *Never Loved Elvis* (although he has since changed his mind) and Bryan Biggs considered the art around Presley in *Kitsch Elvis*

Has Surely Come. Mort Shuman was writing about songwriting for Elvis when he died, so how sad is that. I wish that we had used the subtitle, *Tryin' to Get to You*, as the main title. Did I pick *Aspects of Elvis* because *Aspects of Love* was in the West End? Don't remember, but it wasn't a good idea.

In 1994 we had a two-hour Saturday evening *On the Beat* where we got Hank Walters into the studio under false pretences and did a *This Is Your Life* with the Arcadian Ladies (his three daughters), some Dusty Road Ramblers, Pete McGovern, the Miller Brothers, Sam Hardie and Davy Edge. It couldn't have gone better as Hank was the perfect subject. Ironically, Hank had tried to call Pete McGovern an hour or so earlier and had wondered where he was.

I attended the premiere of *Backbeat* at the Odeon, Liverpool. It was about the Beatles' art school years and their time in Hamburg. One of the characters portrayed in the film was Arthur Ballard, who taught both John Lennon and Stuart Sutcliffe. I walked out of the cinema with Adrian Henri, once a lecturer at the art school. He said, "That's the worst impersonation of Arthur Ballard I've ever seen."

CHAPTER 49

Comic Genius

I saw Ken Dodd many, many times – on stage and at social occasions, at BBC Radio Merseyside and also in the street or in the shops. He was fantastic company and was not someone who told the same jokes over and over. His last words to me were "Young man," (he always called me 'young man'), "how old is Willie Nelson?" Me: "82." "Ah, a mere stripling." If he mentioned my name, he would say, "Spencer, why are you named after a woman's undergarment?"

Once he told me of a pre-war comic, Billy Bennett. I'd never heard of him and right there in the centre of Liverpool, Ken Dodd gave me a five-minute rundown of his material. I'm sure he had an appointment but that was Ken Dodd: he was late for everything.

Ken wrote many of his own jokes but some early scripts were written by Eddie Braben. He, like Ken, had a joke for every occasion, but Eddie had a compulsion to tell jokes, any jokes, to make you laugh. I could imagine him making jokes on the operating table.

Apparently, Ken gave Eddie tips for avoiding tax and he could be the only person who took tax advice from Ken Dodd. The authorities came after him and he lost his second home. He switched to writing for Morecambe and Wise, but when Ken himself was charged with tax evasion, Eddie was a character witness. He then wrote Ken's comeback special.

When Eddie was writing for Des O'Connor's TV show, he had to fashion gags to fit in with his guests. One day Bob Azurdia and I were talking to Eddie in a corridor at Radio Merseyside. He came out with a brilliant observation about being creative, "Sometimes I have my breakfast and go into my room and it is like Jack Elam is waiting behind the door for me." And, if you don't know who Jack Elam is, just Google him and you'll know exactly what Eddie Braben meant.

Ken Dodd made hit records in the 1960s and had a No. 1 with 'Tears' in 1965. It was the height of the beat group era and I asked him if he felt uncomfortable on *Top of the Pops*. "No, it didn't bother me at all," he said, "I'd loved 'Tears' by Rudy Vallée from the 1930s and I thought it was the best song on the charts."

In 1971 Ken Dodd had a straight role in *Twelfth Night* at the Liverpool Playhouse but he was allowed a few jokes at curtain call. He said, "Please come to our next production, *The Merchant of Widnes*." I've no idea why that is so funny, but it has entertained me ever since. This title may have prompted the witty plays that we now see at the Royal Court like *The Hitch Hikers' Guide to Fazakerley* and *The Scousetrap*. They should write *The Merchant of Widnes*.

At a charity show at the Empire, also in 1971, Ken Dodd said that a second Mersey Tunnel would enable dockers to get to their strikes more quickly. A brilliant joke, partly because it's so visual, but also, if anyone other than Dodd had said it, they would have been blackballed on Merseyside. Indeed, the dockers were a constant source of humour: "This docker went to a carol concert and they were singing 'I saw three ships come sailin' in'. He said, 'Not in Liverpool you don't.'"

For all that, Ken was very positive about the city and hated anybody knocking it. He believed that Scousers were full of humour. "You can get a lot of enjoyment just by walking around. I always have a notebook with me so that I can write funny names or anything I hear. I've dozens of notebooks at home, although I only keep three going at any one time."

I was backstage with Ken at a charity show at the Liverpool Empire. The comic on stage was swearing. Ken said, "I wish he wouldn't do that." I said, "But Ken, you love Billy Connolly and he swears all the time." "Yes," said Ken, "but Billy Connolly knows what he's doing."

In 1989 Dodd was charged with tax evasion and the prosecutors did not want the trial in Liverpool. What Liverpool jury would convict Ken Dodd? The trial lasted several weeks, making headlines on most days. His quirky lifestyle kept us amused throughout the summer, and his appearance in the dock was his greatest performance.

Roy Hudd described how Ken had come to see him after a show and wanted to buy him a drink. This was out of character but he wanted Roy as a character witness.

Ken was found not guilty but had to pay millions in back taxes. He had avoided jail although he would have got on fine in Walton and could have given comedy classes.

There were jokes everywhere: there were two new Diddymen, Diddy Pay and Diddy Heck. Doddy's own joke about self-assessment – "I invented that" – was brilliant. As was, "I got a letter from the Inland Revenue. I thought it didn't apply to me – I live by the sea."

There was also Ken's wonderful ability to top a joke as Ricky Tomlinson recalls, "I was in a bar with some other acts and one of them said, 'What's the difference between Ken Dodd and a coconut?' and the answer was, 'You can get a drink out of a coconut.' It turned out that Doddy had come into the bar and the comic said, 'Oh, I'm sorry, Ken.' 'No offence,' said Ken Dodd, 'Would you like a drink?' 'Oh, thanks very much, Ken.' 'Okay, then you'd better go find yourself a bloody coconut.'"

Bob Azurdia told me that Ken had hoped to be the first comedian to be knighted since Sir Harry Lauder. He felt slighted when Norman Wisdom was knighted in 2000. Ken was eventually knighted in the 2017 New Years Honours. Being at the BBC, I saw the list a few days before publication and when I walked in the station the next morning, I saw Ken Dodd, Sir Ken Dodd, at reception. Should I congratulate him or should I not know about it? Ken resolved this for me because as soon as he saw me, he said, "Arise, Sir Spencer".

In 2011 a new artwork was unveiled by Ken Dodd outside Blackpool Tower. It features scores of comedians and their catchphrases. Ken Dodd said, "This is not up to date, no, not at all. I've got a new catchphrase, 'Happy Christmas', and in a couple of months' time, I think everybody will be saying it."

Ken died in 2018 at his home in Knotty Ash. He had married his partner, Anne Jones, shortly before his death and she is preserving his legacy, which is a full-time job. An exhibition, *Happiness!*, was launched at the Museum of Liverpool in 2023 and on display were some of the notebooks in which Ken had written jokes, assessments of his performances, and comments on life in general. Hopefully these notebooks can be the backbone of a full biography and form part of a permanent archive devoted to his comedy and remarkable personality.

Most of all, Ken will be remembered for a host of silly jokes. Whenever I have gravy, I think of Ken Dodd going, "I like good gravy, oh yes, I'm the Count of Monte Bisto."

80@80

CHAPTER 50

Days In The Life: 1994

When you go to interview someone, you're never quite sure what is going to happen, and sometimes it would have been impossible to predict.

Take Billy Eckstine, He was a jazz vocalist of the 40s/50s with a distinctive baritone and such successes as 'I Apologise', 'Passing Strangers' (with Sarah Vaughan) and 'Prisoner of Love'. I was told to be at Southport Theatre at 3pm. After the interview, he asked, "Is there a Marks and Spencer store in town?" "Yes," I said. "Can you take me to it?" "Certainly," I said, agreeing to take him there. He had bought M&S underwear on a previous visit to the UK and he declared it was the best in the world. So, there I was in Marks and Spencer buying underwear with one of the greatest singers in popular music.

When I interviewed P J Proby, he told me that his peculiar vocal on 'I Apologise' was not intended as a joke but as a tribute to Billy Eckstine. Jim - everyone called PJ Jim - had been in a charity show the previous evening at the Liverpool Empire and he was being paid £3,000. If his money didn't come, he had his gun and he was going to kneecap the promoter. This was flawed logic as surely if he wasn't going to be paid, the promoter wouldn't show up. I spoke to him for an hour for *Record Collector* magazine and no one appeared. Jim was ready to shoot him, no matter what. I said, trying to make light of it, "Well, never mind, if it all goes wrong, you can get a job with the IRA." Proby said, "Are you making fun of me, boy?" There followed a fearful moment when I didn't know what might happen next.

Proby had an incredible memory. He had known everyone in Hollywood. He had played in Rick Nelson's football team and he made demo recordings for songs being given to Elvis. He sang them as much like Presley as he could so that Presley wouldn't have to make key changes or whatever.

Another firearms story: I spoke with Tony Jackson who had been managing a golf club and was now returning to the music business. There were two bands doing Searchers material – the original Searchers and Mike Pender's Searchers. He planned Tony Jackson's Researchers, but it didn't get far. One day he wanted to use a phone box and a girl was making a long call. He pulled a gun on her, got arrested and went to Walton. He wrote to me from prison, which is some unlikely memorabilia in my possession.

I went to talk to the Three Degrees at Southport Theatre and had been given a 4pm time slot. They were running late and three of us were waiting for interviews including Johnny Kennedy from Radio City and we had all been given the same time. He was thoroughly impatient whereas I always took a book so it didn't bother me. The first bloke went in, ostensibly for brief 'get well soon' messages for hospital radio but it dragged on. Johnny Kennedy felt that the whole world revolved around him and I said, "I can wait, you go first." Anway, he went for a pee, the previous bloke came out, and the Three Degrees' road manager said, "Your turn." I said, "Johnny's first. I'll get him." He said, "No, you're here, come on." Johnny was seething when I got out and whenever I saw him subsequently, he cut me dead.

I met the pint-sized comedian Charlie Drake when he was in

a sexy pantomime, *Sinderella,* in the West End. They're the rage now, but it was new back then. He offered me a drink in the smallest cup I'd seen outside of a dolls' house. In the middle of the interview, the star Jim Davidson popped in to see if Charlie was okay and had everything he needed. I'd no time for Jim Davidson's humour but this was an insight into his caring nature.

We took my in-laws on a short trip on the QE2 which was magical, but there was too much food. Jimmy Savile was on board, always in his tracksuit, and he was given free passage so long as he engaged with the passengers. I spoke to him for 20 minutes and I did wonder what was going on inside his head, and now of course we know.

After *Cavern of Dreams* and *Be-Bop-A-Lula*, I suggested a third musical that Bill Morrison and I could work on, *Save the Last Dance for Me*, the story of New York songwriters, Doc Pomus and Mort Shuman, both of whom I'd interviewed. Doc was a big man in a wheelchair and this might suit Mickey Starke or if the money were right, Robbie Coltrane. At his wedding, Doc Pomus couldn't dance with his bride and on the menu, he scribbled the lyric for 'Save the Last Dance for Me'. Bill decided it would work better as a radio play for Radio 4 and somehow my name got left off. Ho hum.

Motivated by all the advice in my *Songwriter* series, I wanted to try lyric writing and came up with *Up in the Air,* a radio musical about the Liver Birds leaving the city. I wrote the songs with Davy Edge and there were sessions to record them, produced by Caroline Adams: first the backing with Davy Edge, Ritchie Galvin, Kenny Johnson and Northwind and then the vocals with Hank Walters, the Arcadian Ladies, Billy Butler, Brian Jacques, Pete McGovern, Billy Maher, Eithne Browne, Pauline Daniels, Al Kossy, and Mick Groves (Spinners). It was an all-Liverpool production. The songs included 'Birds of a Feather' (Davy Edge), 'Sea Fever' (my favourite, for Hank Walters) and 'Someone Must Be Missing You Tonight' (the big ballad with Billy Maher and Eithne Brown). I was very glad that the station had taken this and felt proud.

CHAPTER 51

Don't You Want To Apologize For That Awful Review?

In 1998, the singer-pianist Leon Russell released a third album under his country music pseudonym of Hank Wilson, and Craig Baguley asked me to review it for *Country Music People*. The review of *Legend In My Time - Hank Wilson Vol. III* appeared in May's edition and although I like Leon Russell a lot, the album only received one-and-a-half stars out of five. A mediocre review but not a terrible one.

A few days after publication, Leon Russell came to London for *Later with Jools Holland* on BBC-2. He was available for an interview and I hoped he hadn't seen my review. He'd only just arrived and anyway, an artist of his stature must see scores of press cuttings, so mine would hardly stand out.

I went to his agent's office and Leon came through from the back. He said, "I only got here yesterday and already I have seen one of the worst reviews I've ever had."

The penny didn't drop. I thought, "It can't be my review as it wasn't that bad." But it was. Leon told me, "This guy says, 'Leon Russell sounds like he's been strangled as he sings.' I'm not Michael Bolton but I do my best, and to read that is devastating. I told my wife that it's reviews like this that make me want to quit the business."

Before I got the scoop, *Leon Russell Retires*, I thought I'd better confess to writing the review. "You!" said Leon Russell, "You wrote that hideous review. You seem to be a nice guy, so it's hard to imagine how you could say those things."

"I wasn't being malicious," I told him, "I normally love your albums and your voice which is very distinctive."

"I accept it's not malicious but that makes it all the worse. You're so offended by my work that you think I should become a plumber." Who's exaggerating now? Leon added, "You'd better get out of here!"

I couldn't see Leon's eyes because of his dark glasses, but he didn't sound too angry and after all, it wasn't my fault that he'd made a bad album - it was his.

"It wasn't a hideous review," I said, "I must defend myself. I simply asked why someone as creative as yourself should make another album of covers?" "It was requested by the President of Mercury Records when we started out," said Leon, "he wanted another Hank Wilson album and it turned into an Ark 21 release." I was going to get my interview after all.

At the end, I thanked Leon Russell for his time. He said, "Don't you want to apologise for that awful review?" Not really, but had I known I was going to meet Leon Russell, I wouldn't have written it in the first place.

When I got out, I looked at how he had signed my copy of *One For The Road*. He had written "Don't choke me, Leon Russell."

Perhaps brevity is the best option when struggling to write a glowing review. When *Country Music People* asked me to review a show featuring John Rex Reeves, Jim Reeves' nephew, I just wrote, "He'll have to go", which I thought was funny, but the editor insisted on "a proper review". Indeed, Paul Gambaccini once reviewed a Yes album for *Rolling Stone* with the single word, "No".

CHAPTER 52

Days In The Life: 1995-1997

The key thing for a writer, a broadcaster or researcher is to rework your catalogue. Once you've been going a few years, it isn't often that you start on a new project with nothing useful to hand.

The interviews I had done for the radio series *Shakin' All Over* became a book *Halfway to Paradise* which had the subtitle *Britpop 1955-1962*. With that subtitle, I was noting a similarity as those early UK acts were establishing their own scene without relying too much on the Americans.

The book was published by Finbarr International in Folkestone, a mail order company for rock'n'roll CDs run by James Cullinan, a doowop enthusiast. It looked good although the text itself was small and it sold 2,000 copies. It had good publicity through Bob Harris (Radio 2), Gary Crowley (Radio 6) and a joint review by Joe Brown and Marty Wilde, also on Radio 2. James' mail order business had a profitable strand of black magic books. I'd never seen such rubbish but a black magic reader might have said the same about the rock'n'roll catalogue, so to each his own.

Some of my interviews were used in *Memories of Buddy Holly*, which I compiled with the American author, Jim Dawson. He wanted my interviews rather than my opinions and there isn't much of me in there.

I was pleased when the budget label MCI (Music Club International) allowed me to choose tracks as well as writing CD booklets. I put together compilations for Pat Boone, Jim Croce, the Everly Brothers, Brenda Lee, Mungo Jerry, Leo Sayer, the Searchers and the Tremeloes. I've done so many sleeve notes for the Searchers that dedicated collectors must have been thinking, "Oh no, not him again!" – not to mention what the Searchers themselves must have thought.

I enjoyed writing notes for See For Miles, a label owned by Colin Miles and clearly a nod to the Who's 'I Can See for Miles'. They were well-considered compilations and one was of little-known Merseybeat tracks and called *Liverpool 1963-1968*. Unfortunately, his design skills went adrift on that cover which was of four real mop-tops, a feeble joke which turned the album into a novelty.

I did a Stanley Unwin collection for Sequel and got to know the eccentric comedian with his unique wordplay. A couple of years later, he wrote the foreword to my book on the Merseysippi Jazz Band and I was delighted to have a page of his gobbledegook.

Writing the notes *The Complete No.1's of Country*, a 5CD set for Reader's Digest confirmed how country music had changed so much over the years and I wondered how many people would buy a compilation that spanned so many years. I wrote booklets (or anglicised American ones) for the UK market for 15 years including a series of *You Must Remember These*, which effectively was a licence to include anything. Reader's Digest took great care in finding the original hit versions and mastering them correctly They unfortunately followed a box-set of No.1 records with a box of No.2s.

Reader's Digest paid well but doing CD booklets for Columbia was great as they paid £500 a time when mostly I was getting

£50 from See For Miles or MCI. I did *The Ultimate Rock'n'Roll Collection* for Columbia, a 2CD collection of 42 key tracks, but omitting Elvis Presley who, at that time, couldn't be licensed for compilations.

This was followed by a real winner, a double-CD of 60s tracks with plenty of TV advertising called *The Best of Heartbeat*. This ITV series, about a Yorkshire copper played by Nick Berry, was set in the 1960s and they used the hits of the day. *The Best of Heartbeat* became the UK's No.1 album and I felt proud, although nobody bought it for my notes. However, for about a month after its release, people at work were asking me to sign the booklet.

The TV series was popular around the world and Les Chadwick saw it in Australia and wondered why he was getting no royalties as a former member of Gerry and the Pacemakers. Indeed, the three former Pacemakers told Gerry that he wasn't entitled to the lot. Gerry hadn't even passed royalties to his brother, Fred. I miss Fred as he ran the Pacemaker Driving School and he would often have his clients reverse around our corner.

I did an interview with Keith Emerson of Emerson, Lake and Palmer in Radio Merseyside in 1990 and I walked him over to the Cavern. He had to call someone and I offered him a phone in the studio. No, no, he told me, he would make the call as we were walking along. I'd heard of mobile phones, but I'd never seen one before. Once in Paradise Street, he got it working. It was impressive but it was like walking around with a brick.

Then a lad in our office, a filing clerk, had a mobile phone. Again, it seemed a very immobile phone as it was so heavy. Occasionally, it would ring dramatically. It was only a call or two a day so it wasn't disruptive and it intrigued me. Was this the future? I wasn't sure.

David Parry, a dynamic salesman from Leicester, was the

new head of the life department and he enjoyed having actuaries report to him, a non-academic. He liked change for change's sake, but he could reverse turn tomorrow. He didn't like opposition, especially when it was his idea. He had a large mirror in his office and if you sat in front of it, you had his attention or at least he looked your way and saw his reflection. Vanity, Vanity.

Once, early in the morning I was walking down a corridor and he was coming from the other direction. He thrust a complaint into my hand. "Find out who is responsible for this and kick them," he said, "and if you haven't kicked them by four o'clock, I'll kick you!" Generally, there is no point in kicking anyone. Someone can see what has gone wrong and they know not to make the same mistake again. I saw Parry at 4pm and said, "All sorted" and he said, "What are you talking about?" He had forgotten he'd given anything to me.

Parry was arrogant and rude, but he was a magnificent salesman. Directors looked at the amount of new business he could generate. His impatience could be reinterpreted as a virtue as he was encouraging everyone to work flat out. There was one wonderful day where the reassurer, Mercantile and General, treated a few of us to the Old Trafford test match. Parry was out of his depth as his idea of sport was the 100 metres run.

His impatience made him a figure of fun: Once a phone rang at a branch and a lad picked it up.

"Parry here. I want blah, blah, blah."
Lad: "Who?"
Parry: "Parry."
Lad: "Harry Who?"
Parry: "Parry, you idiot. Don't you know who I am?"
Lad: "No. Do you know who I am?"
Parry: "Of course not!"

Lad: "Well, bugger off then!"

(Lad puts phone down.)

David Parry was a human dynamo but much more of a comic turn than authoritative, although he would hate me for saying that. One morning he read an article in the *Insurance Post* which was critical of Royal Life. "I'll break them," he said, "Cancel all the subscriptions. No one is to read the *Insurance Post* anymore." Well, we wouldn't have known what was going on elsewhere without it. There were about 100 copies in the Life departments at Head Office and perhaps 200 in the branches. Cancelling them all would hardly break them. "We're only the life department. What about general insurance," I said, "They've got no axe to grind." He'd have a word with someone at lunch. This magazine was going to go under.

Absolute bollocks, of course, and I knew that if all the magazines were cancelled, he would say the next week, "Where's the *Post* magazine?" and I'd be in trouble for cancelling the subscriptions.

When I was writing for the insurance press, I tried not to make my articles too starchy and get a few jokes in there, however feeble. A feature I wrote about genetic testing for *Planned Savings* was called *Genes to an End*. I had some fun with Peter Elson of the *Liverpool Daily Post*, with a double page spread on how long a reader might live, set out like snakes and ladders. Take off eight years because you are smoking and another two because you are drinking but add four because you are taking exercise and so on. I hope no one took it too seriously.

When I look at my *On the Beat* programmes, there was a wide variety of guests but not the really big names. Because I had my day job, I couldn't be making endless calls trying to get someone big to talk to me. Nearly all my interviews were through me making a written request and then doing the interviews if they said yes. I remember going to interview Gene Vincent's Bluecaps in London one Saturday afternoon. They were very enthusiastic and very funny. The drummer, Dickie Harrell, told me that he was only 16 when he made 'Be Bop A Lula' and he let out a yell to show his mother that he was on the record.

Another time I went to London to interview Marshall Chess about his family's company, Chess Records, and passed a theatre where David Soul was appearing. He was doing a matinee performance in an Alan Ayckbourn play, so I left a note asking if he had half an hour when the play was over. I spoke to Marshall Chess and then walked back to the theatre and David Soul had said yes. Later on, he rang me a couple of times about the tracks that should appear on *The Best Of David Soul* and I was surprised how seriously he took his work: he wasn't an actor who had made a few records for fun.

I had a fabulous lunch-hour with Emmylou Harris in the bar at the Holiday Inn. She had never heard of a ploughman's lunch before and was fascinated. I had a pleasant chat with Paul Rodgers of Free and he asked me to show him the Cavern. I took him around and right on the spot, they offered him a gig in a few weeks' time, which he accepted.

The academics Clinton Heylin and Martin Cloonan talked about Bob Dylan and banned records, respectively. The horror writer, Ramsey Campbell, was Radio Merseyside's film critic and we did a programme about Oscars for film music.

The American instrumental band, the Hellecasters, performed a marvellous show at New Brighton which was recorded by Bill Holt. It was broadcast as a one-hour special, but Bill omitted an 18-minute rave-up based around 'Orange Blossom Special'. He gave it to me for *On the Beat,* knowing it was a maverick show.

I was glad to broadcast the first radio interview with the brothers Pete and Roag Best together and to have Beatles stories from Tony Bramwell (who said John Lennon had tried to burn down a church hall) and the Hamburg photographer, Astrid Kirchherr. Johnnie Hamp talked about producing the Beatles for GranadaTV and recording that famous conversation between Ken Dodd and the Beatles in 1963 when George Harrison managed to top Ken Dodd's joke.

On the whole, Liverpool musicians are known for their good humour and if you can get two or three together in a studio, you will get some good jokes. I enjoyed when the group members came together every few years for a Class of 64 CD. In essence, Frankie Connor (Hideaways), Alan Crowley (Tuxedos) and Billy Kinsley (Merseybeats) wrote and produced four albums as the Class of 64 with a succession of guest singers from Liverpool groups. They're all good but the first one was the best with 'Poor Boy from Liverpool' (Tony Crane and Billy Kinsley), 'Falling Apart at the Seams' (Mike Pender) and 'Looking for a Girl like You' (the underrated Kenny Parry).

Like me, Pete Frame loved the Liverpool humour and the interplay between the musicians. He was on my programme from time to time as he was researching his Merseybeat Family Trees. They were displayed at the Bluecoat Chambers alongside an exhibition of Stuart Sutcliffe's work, a *tour de force* curated by Bryan Biggs.

Live music was going through a downturn, prompted by Billy Ray Cyrus with 'Achy Breaky Heart' in 1992, which brought line dancing to the UK. You could argue that it brought a new audience to country music but not really. Both Kenny Johnson and Phil Brady were working in line dance clubs with backing tapes, and there were fewer country bands on Merseyside, whereas it had been a county stronghold. If Pete Frame took his Merseybeat family trees to its sad conclusion, it would end up with solo musicians and backing tapes.

One of my more unlikely interviews was with Issac Hayes who was making a film in the UK with some scenes to be shot in Liverpool. What a magnificent rich, deep voice, perfect for radio, right down to his boots. Having quite a bland voice myself, it made him sound really, really good.

I had interviewed Clifford T Ward at his home in Kidderminster in 1987. He had multiple sclerosis and spoke with difficulty but he told me that he was still working in the studio, although that was hard to believe. I went back in 1996 and he still had his humour although his illness had no respite. I enjoyed the Englishness of his work like "How are things in Worcestershire?" and in 'Home Thoughts From Abroad'. He said, "It wasn't something I contrived, it was something that just happened. It's the way I was. It seemed very natural and normal."

Anne was with me and he remarked how well suited we were to each other. What a lovely man; He died in 2001 at age of 57 but 'Gaye', 'Scullery' and 'Home Thoughts from Abroad' still have a magic to them that is very much a British form of songwriting. His songs were often about home life and watching television. I enjoyed the fact that he once wrote a song to the newscaster, 'Julia' (Julia Somerville), begging her not to go into celebrity shows.

CHAPTER 53

A Not So Sunny Alliance

Royal Insurance was founded in 1835 and so in 1985, was 150 years old. It made a strong point of its history when advertising, although the public often thought it was the same as Royal Liver, which had the advantage of owning one of the most recognisable buildings in the world. Its Liver Birds are the very symbol for Liverpool.

In the early 1970s the chief actuary Tony Baker was fascinated by the opportunities offered by computerisation, and Royal Life was established as a separate financial institution within Royal Insurance. When there was a court hearing about this, the judge said that he might have to step aside as "I have a Royal Insurance policy". The counsel wittily responded, "Your Honour, it would be difficult to find a High Court judge who does not have a Royal Insurance policy." The company issued coasters saying "Royal Life – Judge for yourself" with a cartoon of a happy judge.

A beautifully produced hardback history of the company called *Absolute Integrity* was published for its anniversary and a copy given to each member of staff.

At the end of 1995, the company was doing well across the board with a fine reputation, good products and a highly motivated sales force, but rather than grow gradually, the hierarchy decided it would be better to merge with Sun Alliance, whose head office was in Bristol. Expenses could be reduced through economies of scale, and one giant company might place the company well ahead of the opposition.

On the other hand, it would take time to merge the companies; staff motivation would suffer with redundancies and staff reapplying for their own jobs; and rebranding would be very expensive.

The rebranding was difficult from the start as the new company was called Royal Sunalliance (sic) and was managed jointly by Richard Gamble (Royal) and Roger Taylor (Sun Alliance). Neither wanted to give up the top job and when there isn't one man in control, you can expect trouble. Both of them had left RSA by 1998, so make what you will of that.

There have been problems over the years: historical claims for asbestosis (Royal) and the insurance of Sheffield Wednesday's football ground (Sun Alliance), which had a bearing on the aftermath of Hillsborough. RSA is now under Danish and Canadian ownership.

Proposed mergers are determined in private as information can affect share prices and staff morale. I know this because in the 1980s, Royal Life nearly bought a troubled company. I was travelling on a London train with one of our executives and he had determined code words so that if we discussed anything, no one would know what it was about. Therefore, the proposed merger of Royal and Sun Alliance took me by surprise but it couldn't be any other way.

I was keeping a journal and it's worth looking at the entries in the light of what happened.

1 February 1995: I'm 50. I thought my birthday was going to fall on John Ford's centenary, but his birth certificate was recently discovered and he was a year older than he had stated. However,

Stanley Matthews is 80, Peter Sallis 74 and Boris Yeltsin 64. I haven't wanted to wish my life away but at least if I'm bipped now I would get an immediate pension.

(The casual reference to bipping is the Royal's Business Improvement Plan, and reorganisation was in place sometime before the merger. Management consultants were asked to time what we were doing. They never allowed for thinking time.

2 February 1995: David Parry (58) told me that there is only one person in the company older than he is. Andrew Gilchrist said, "Wonder if he's got a high profile." I said, "I doubt it. Parry can't stand being second in anything. He'll be keeping his head below the parapet." I suppose I'm in the Top 10. This notion of getting rid of the age - and the wisdom(?) - of a company is surely untried and untested.

10 February 1995: Owen Oyston has been arrested on four charges of rape and several other offences. To think that he is one of the Royal's largest private shareholders and that I am, therefore, working for him! John Parker worked alongside him for three months over the Shipways deal and says he was a complete rogue and "a total adulterer and fornicator". No character references from the Royal then.

22 July 1995: All this lunacy at work - Activity Based Costing, Zero Outstanding Daily (Daily Outstanding Zero Yardstick might be a better acronym), Risk Profiling, Survival Plans, Self-Appraisal Documentation - one scheme after another is introduced. It is time someone coordinated the lot. I am on an internet committee tomorrow to see how it will affect Royal Life. In time, maybe only a year away, clients will communicate with us via e-mail.

27 August 1995: Unlike previous years, the Royal is not sponsoring the Mathew Street Festival. It's a big event now.

It started with £10,000, last year it was £33,000 and now it's £101,000.

14 September 1995: How many Royal staff does it take to change a lightbulb? We don't know, but we'll employ a firm of consultants to find out.

15 January 1996: When *The Independent on Sunday* asked me to write an article on life assurance, I asked, "What's the payment?". They replied, "No cash, but we'll give you some good furniture." I expected a three-piece suite but they meant they would give Royal Life a mention in the byline.

23 February 1996: Had an excellent meal in Jenny's Seafood Restaurant in Brunswick Street, courtesy of Skandia Re. Peter Noall was in there - he has been retired from Royal UK for 12 years. He was a master of the Expense Form and once included a geisha girl when he was in Japan. Wouldn't get it through now as you get a call from Finance if you have a second cup of coffee on a train to London.

7 June 1996: Chairing a conference on Critical Illness at the Royal Lancaster Hotel. Not too difficult as no-one finished early, so there was no blank spaces to fill. Phil Wolski took 52 minutes when he was only allocated 30 – this on a Friday afternoon on the hottest day of the year. Several were leaving before he finished, which was hard on the final speakers. I thought of cutting him off, but he was in full flow. He apologised afterwards but said that when he had timed his talk at home, it was only half an hour.

25 June 1996: Been hectic at work - as if it wasn't busy enough. Mel White told me that the report I have to do was my top priority - taking priority over day-to-day work and also my home life. I didn't want to tell him that seeing Bob Dylan was my top priority on Thursday night.

Graham Spittles of Sun Alliance came to Liverpool and we

spent one and a half days compiling and writing a report about our similarities and differences on underwriting matters. We are close, which is what management will like to hear. Been given a report about the future – roughly speaking, there are 2,000 jobs in Royal and Sun Alliance but by 1999, it will be down to 1,000. Effectively, the staff of one company will be doing the work of two.

12 July 1996: When the managers at Commercial Union came into work a fortnight ago, they learnt that 1 in 6 of them had been sacked. I'm not sure if it's better that way or the protracted way it is at the Royal. Probably the Royal's way is best as we can talk about it and prepare for it.

18 July 1996: We were shown the new logo today - the famous red shield has gone but in its place is a partial compass - I say 'partial' because the North-West is missing. The company is now called Royal and Sunalliance (all one word). Whoever thought of the name may have thought Hereford and Worcester was a good name for a county.

Don Shore told me that I could appear on *The Money Programme* answering questions about genetics and life assurance. Mike Kipling at Sun Alliance then decided it was too dicey and I was to turn it down. The BBC has sent what can only be a threatening letter to the Royal saying that they plan to quote from my paper and will say that I've been gagged! (Before I did media appearances, I used to discuss them with the Royal's press offer, Roy Sully. He was brilliant at spotting beartraps.)

13 September 1996: Last week I thought I would taking the early bath, but Graham Spittles has sent such silly memos to his superiors that he's clearing the way for me. We shall see. Earlier today, I gathered the underwriters around, who thought I was going to announce that I had got the job and started applauding -

it turned out that I was giving Sue McNulty a recognition award. Rather encouraging that they would like me to stay - the devil they know, I suppose.

17 September 1996: Graham Harrison chaired the meeting to decide who would be Chief Underwriter of Royal Sunalliance. He asked me why I wanted the job. I said, "I don't really. I only filled in the form because you asked me to. In my view, nobody can do this job well as he or she will invariably be in the wrong place when they are wanted. There's too much travelling involved."

26 September 1996: I'm getting a pension of 38/60 of my salary with no discounting payable immediately (Wow! I'm 51.) and a cash sum that will pay off my mortgage: it's very generous. Under government rulings, I can't do any work for Royal Sunalliance for two years as it would jeopardise my benefits. Jolly good, I have a feeling that things might go wrong and legally, they can't ask me to help out.

30 September 1996: Today I was deselected and Graham Spittles took the job of Chief Underwriter of the new group - I feel a weight off my shoulders: how I would have hated all that travelling to Bristol, especially in the winter. Indeed, all the toing and froing is going to be very unproductive - and the managers may have accidents on the motorway through being so tired. Graham Harrison will ask Sun Alliance when I can be released and I said that I would prefer it as soon as possible. Trevor Rogers was deselected, cleared his desk and went, just like that. Anne said she would be going to bed with a pensioner, and I said, "Who is he?"

3 October 1996: Sam Laughlin was dismissing a salesman and got into an argument with him. Sam said, "I've had enough of this. Just give me your fucking car keys!" The salesman said, "Here they fucking are! Now you find out where the fucking fucker is fucking parked!" In all my years in Royal Life, I have never heard such language and I haven't heard it now, but Sam's secretary told me about it. Top marks for the salesman for using 'fuck' as an adjective, a noun and a verb in the same sentence.

16 November 1996: The Royal has a 'Lest We Forget' plaque and permanent wreath in New Hall Place - trouble is, the names of all the people that we mustn't forget have been lost in the move to the new building.

17 November 1996: Graham Spittles thinks we should talk to various affinity groups about the Disability Discrimination Act. I showed him an invitation I'd had from the British Colostomy Association and told him he was welcome to it.

18 November 1996: I try to ration myself to one hour's television a day - Anne asked me how video conferences comes into this: they could mess up the average as I talk to people in Sun Alliance. We see jerky pictures because pictures cannot be transferred as fast as sound, but couldn't we just put a photograph of the person up on the screen?

13 December 1996: Chris O'Brien says that the airline flights between Horsham and Manchester have a worse performance standard than Merseyrail, and yet they are not obliged to publish anything. Yesterday he got the 7.30pm back, which got diverted and got into Birmingham at 9.30. He had to wait for a coach to take them all to Manchester where he got a taxi to home, arriving at 2.15am. Almost in time to get up for work the next morning. I'm glad I'm going. Also, no more budget meetings and no more management reports, which are time consuming and don't allow us to get on with the main job, which is accepting business.

16 December 1996: My last day at work. I was told to arrive at 10am with a sensible tie and when I got there, my area had a huge sign above it wishing me good luck. So much effort has been put into making this a memorable day for me: if half that effort is put into the harmonisation, the new company will be very successful. The presents included a gold disc thanking me for my 33 years. Best of all was a visit to the gym at 11.15 for a group photograph, hence the sensible tie. About 70 people were there and it was a tremendous idea. I don't know of it being done for anyone else but it could set a trend. The best years of my adult life were spent in the Royal - heck, all my adult life has been spent in the Royal. I have done 33 1/3 years which is appropriate for me - 400 months exactly. And I've not left anything since I left school!

In my speech, I said I would miss them all, but I know I would miss the photocopier more. I ended on a knock, knock joke. "Knock, knock." "Who's there?" "Spencer." "Spencer who?", "You see, you've forgotten me already."

And today, I haven't forgotten them and I treasure the photograph I was given. The farewell photograph could be my personal Alzheimer's test but whoever is conducting the test would have no idea as to whether I am giving the right names or not.

80@80

CHAPTER 54

Days In The Life: 1997-1999

I had taken early retirement but Anne was still working at the library, though had moved from Southport to Ormskirk. I was not intending to do any more insurance work and I set up Spencer Leigh Limited as I could claim expenses for interviews and rent myself an office (actually, a room in my house). I was planning to make a go of it as a full time writer and was excited by the challenge.

As it happens, some insurance work from other companies came along and that money also went into Spencer Leigh Limited. *Financial Times* wanted me to write a feature, *Who Is Being Unfair?* about the relationship between the person wanting life assurance and the office.

I spoke at some conferences and was even given a trip to Toronto to deliver a paper. Whilst there, I went to interview Gordon Lightfoot on Yonge Street. It was impressively long and it took me half an hour to walk to his office. I asked Gordon how long Yonge Street was and he replied, "About 60 miles." It was the longest street in the world.

I did some work for Royal Liver (head office in the Liver Buildings), Swiss Life (head office at the Albert Dock) and Marks and Spencer (insurance arm in Chester). Royal Liver had hired a management consultant to change their image and hence, obtain more business. His first recommendation was to drop the association with Liverpool: how bonkers is that?

Then Worldwide Reassurance in Windsor offered me a place on their board and I was a director for five years but I felt too far away from the action to make a substantial contribution.

Generally speaking, I was available in the daytime which meant that I could attend different events in Liverpool such as the Yellow Submarine Day at Liverpool Town Hall. Some of the animators and voice artists associated with the *Yellow Submarine* film had come to Liverpool for the launch of a postage stamp to celebrate the film and the showing of a digitally enhanced print at the Philharmonic Hall. At first, the Beatles thought that the cartoon film would be their way out of a film contract but they came to realise that this was an extraordinary project.

The promoter Sid Bernstein who had put the Beatles on at Shea Stadium came to Liverpool. I never understood why he was here and he was always promising things that didn't happen.

For example, I heard him talk at a meeting with Liverpool councillors. We had previously had Michael Jackson at Aintree Racecourse and Sid said that he could promote even bigger concerts there. He said, "I can't tell you who they are at the moment." Pause. Sid seemed to have lost the thread and then he sang a snatch of 'Second Hand Rose'. "Oh," said Sid, "whatever made me do that?" It was ham off the bone but it was great to watch him at work and the city elders lapped it up. The concerts would never happen, nor his so-called Millennium Festival, nor his *Robin Hood* musical, but I didn't know what Sid himself was getting out of his visits. His man on the ground was Joe Flannery, a charming man but Flannery will get you nowhere.

Sid was wonderful to meet one-on-one. At a guess, he was five foot seven and 23 stone. I went to see him at the Moat

House (the former Holiday Inn) and he was tired and alone in the restaurant with the largest bowl of ice cream I had ever seen. I didn't even know it was possible to eat that much ice cream. He was exhausted because he had been forced to exit the plane he had arrived in earlier at Manchester Airport via a chute, but he had been given flight vouchers to compensate. We walked across the road to Radio Merseyside and I recorded an interview but he went to sleep.

A few days later we met again and he suggested Thornton's, the ice-cream parlour on Whitechapel "as it doesn't matter if you're late". This was roughly on the site of NEMS, which fascinated him, and as we walked to Radio Merseyside, he already knew every hot dog seller..

Sid was a soft-spoken, kindly man but there was a steelier resolve. He told me of a show where his client Bobby Darin got top billing over Sam Cooke, who was managed by Allen Klein. Someone who got the better of Allen Klein must be tougher than he appears.

I befriended Paul Murphy, a Liverpool singer who had gone to Hamburg and was working for Polydor Records when the Beatles were on the label. He was in possession of the infamous Star-Club tapes, recorded on New Year's Eve, 1962. The quality was abysmal but that wasn't the point: they were historic.

Their performance had been recorded by Kingsize Taylor who has passed the tapes to Allan Williams who in turn gave them to Paul. Their release in 1977 had been blocked by Apple, although bootleg versions appeared. Paul had cleaned them up and they were about to be released 'officially'. He received an injunction and George Harrison told the court, "The Star-Club recording was the crummiest recording ever made in our name." The Beatles won the action, and the tapes could not be released.

Now that technology has advanced, it begs the question as to whether they could be released in enhanced form today. Peter Jackson, the director of *The Beatles: Get Back*, has bought the tapes and is determining what he can do with them.

Chris Farlowe was still a great 60s singer who performed on oldies shows. He had invited me to come to his theatrical shop in Euston when I was in London. In the 1960s, when he had gone to Hamburg, he discovered that former German soldiers were not allowed to sell their collectables. He met them, bought their uniforms and brought them back to the UK, where his mother repaired them. He opened a theatrical store and would loan clothes for productions. Those are Chris Farlowe's uniforms in *'Allo! 'Allo!* The shop had hundreds of costumes and Chris let me wear a German uniform (only in the shop, I hasten to add.) When he did 60s tours, he would get into town early and go round the vintage shops to see what he could find. He'd bring back the spoils for his mum to sort out. Chris was great on stage and I loved seeing him but I also loved the fact that he had this second life.

A Liverpool singer, David Garrick, had made records in the early 60s without much success in the UK but he had topped the German charts with 'Dear Mrs Applebee' in 1967. Now he was back in Bootle, looking after his mother, and Joe Flannery was getting him gigs. I saw him on Merseyrail, a medallion man like Barry Gibb, talking in a loud voice in German on a mobile phone. I introduced him to Mal Jefferson who had a studio in Birkdale and he made an album of Italian arias, *Apassionata*, his tribute to Mario Lanza. Other guests included Nils Lofgren and Clarence Clemons, both associated with Bruce Springsteen. I encouraged acoustic performances and guests included Chris While and Julie Matthews, Gary McGuinness, Dean Johnson and Ethan Allen.

80@80

Dianne Oxberry, a presenter at *Look North West* had an interview with Elvis Costello arranged at the Royal Court, but couldn't get to Liverpool and could I do it? More than that, I got an expanded interview for *On the Beat*. His dad, Ross McManus, had sung with jazz bands on Merseyside and his mother had worked on the record counter at Rushworth and Dreaper, so it was good to have him talking about that.

By luck, Billy J Kramer was at Radio Merseyside talking to Billy Butler at the same time as I was with Licorice Locking, the bass player from the Shadows. Billy agreed to do a radio concert with the Dakotas as they were back together and he invited Licorice to join them. He did Shadows' hits and played harmonica on an R&B rave-up, 'Sugar Babe'. At the end, there was a great photo op with Billy J Kramer, Mike Maxfield and Tony Bookbinder (Dakotas), Licorice Locking (Shadows) and Les Maguire and Freddie Marsden (Pacemakers), who were in the audience. They had all had three Number 1s.

Another concert was with Chip Taylor, who had written 'Wild Thing' 'Angel of the Morning' and now sang highly personal songs. Pete Wylie gave a fine concert but had said we could ask listeners for songs he could cover. He did 'Alone Again Naturally' and ignored the rest.

I loved seeing Joan Baez and the Buena Vista Social Club at the Phil. The Five Blind Boys of Alabama at the Everyman were led on single file by their one sighted member and they each had their hand on the other's left shoulder, a very memorable image.

My friend Michael Heatley wrote for several music papers and compiled and wrote the notes for back catalogue CDs. He had a contract for *Behind the Song* with publishers Blandford, an illustrated book telling the stories of "100 great pop and rock classics" and going from Elvis to Oasis. I was happy to do it but I'd no idea who was going to read it. If you spread your net too wide, you don't catch anything at all and this book lacked direction.

It wasn't difficult work and it was a good-looking book. However, the proofreader changed the title of Gerry's song to 'Ferry Across the Mersey' and Gerry rang me annoyed that I had put an extra syllable into his title. Nothing to do with me, guv. What he really objected to was us saying that its notes were similar to 'Venus in Blue Jeans'. I had Gerry on the phone singing 'Venus in Blue Jeans' and saying, "That's nothing like 'Ferry Cross the Mersey'." Sorry, Gerry, but it is. However, perhaps the inspiration was the Tornados' 'Globe Trotter'.

I didn't write about any Oasis song for the book. I always felt that their sound was a variation of a Beatles' B-side, 'Rain'. The Beatles did so many things, but Oasis rewrote 'Rain' time and again. There was a busker in Mathew Street who sang 'Wonderwall', which was sacrilege. There was something unbalanced about him as he was the man who then attacked George Harrison.

I also wrote a book for Michael Heatley's Northdown called *Drummed Out*, about the sacking of Pete Best from The Beatles. There was not one reason why Pete Best was sacked but several. John, Paul, George, George Martin and Brian Epstein had reasons for wanting Pete to go but they were not the same. Pete always said that he was never given a reason, but at that fateful meeting, Brian did tell him that his drumming wasn't good enough. Pete chose not to believe it.

I was working with Bob Wooler on a feature for *Record Collector*, which would lead to us working on his biography. He had this revealing quote, "The Beatles used to play the Cavern at lunchtimes and sometimes they would stay behind and rehearse, and just myself and the cleaners would hear them. One day I came back from the Grapes about ten past three and the Beatles were rehearsing. Paul was showing Pete Best how he wanted the drums to be played for a certain tune and I thought, 'That's pushing it a bit.' At times Pete would be like a zombie on the drums: it was though he was saying, 'Do I have to do this?', and that went against him with Paul McCartney, who was all for communication. Pete had no show about him - he always looked bored - but he certainly came alive for photo sessions as he was very photogenic."

The jazz critic Steve Voce lived in Crosby and wrote obituaries for *The Independent*. I knew him through his *Jazz Panorama* for BBC Radio Merseyside. I thought that he didn't have much time for me, but shortly after I retired, *The Independent* called me as Steve had told them I was available. It was 11am and they asked me if I would write 1,000 words on LaVern Baker and get it to them for 2pm. This was a test, so I got to work and it was in the next day's paper. After that, I did hundreds of obituaries and it was a good exercise to determine the important facts of someone's life in a couple of hours.

Getting family details was the most difficult part. When I was writing about Les Braid, the bass player of the Swinging Blue Jeans, I rang the family and to my embarrassment (and shame) found that they were still at the hospital by his bedside. These obituaries led to appearances on Radio 4's obituary programme, *Brief Lives*.

Sometimes I had personal knowledge to add. When Frankie Laine came to Merseyside, Allan Williams took the sculptor Brian Burgess to meet him with a statue of a bull. It was presented to Frankie by the fan club. Unfortunately, there were crossed wires as Frankie wasn't Taurus. He accepted the gift with gratitude but it was enormously heavy and I wondered what happened when he got to Customs.

CHAPTER 55

Run Devil Run

On the 15th of December 1999, Paul McCartney returned to Liverpool to play the Cavern, a gig that was broadcast around the world. Bill Heckle at the Cavern had promised me a ticket for the event as he was being allocated 90 of the 300 tickets available. He only received 55, but I was fortunate enough to receive No.55.

Around the time of the soundcheck, Paul McCartney heard that Bob Wooler was in the Grapes and he asked somebody to bring him over. When he saw Bob, now in ailing health but still with his faculties, he said, "Would you like to introduce me?". It was a nice thought but Bob thought it would be too demanding.

On the way out after the concert, I passed Neil Aspinall, standing at the back. "Good show, Neil," I said. He replied laconically, "I've seen better." Of course he had – he'd seen the Beatles at the Cavern.

This is the review I completed for BBC online:

"I'm a little mixed-up but I'm feeling fine," sang Paul McCartney in his homage to Elvis Presley, 'All Shook Up'. I too am a little mixed-up but I'm feeling fine as I have seen Paul play what has been dubbed 'the gig of the century', that is, his return to the Cavern.

I could be cynical and say that Paul did this gig to promote his album of obscure rock'n'roll covers, *Run Devil Run*, but if he did, good luck to him. It was a tremendous night and Sir Paul and Sir Cliff can teach the young Turks a thing or two about marketing, promotion and presentation.

For years, Paul has been lamenting the loss of the Cavern and now he accepts that the new building at the same address is the Cavern and that this was around his 293rd gig there. In that sense, it was a pity that he chose to play in the larger back room rather than in the arched area which so closely resembles the original. That stage was too small for the band's hi-tech equipment and the modern lighting effects.

Not to worry as Paul was in brilliant form playing 12 songs in 40 minutes, mostly from *Run Devil Run*. Someone shouted for 'Satisfaction', but he said he didn't do requests and impersonated Mick Jagger's lips. In a lovely nostalgic moment, he thanked the Cavern's original DJ, Bob Wooler.

In any other circumstance, it would be a major boost for Pink Floyd's Dave Gilmour to be playing Liverpool. Here he was one of the twin electric lead guitarists with Mick Green from the Pirates.

I am sure that Mick Green's contribution to Paul's CD has been understated as so much of the CD sounds like the Pirates reviving old rock'n'roll songs and indeed, Paul has plundered their powerhouse arrangement of 'Honey Hush'.

Paul limited himself to short, pertinent introductions. He said that 'Lonesome Town' was "for lovers, past, present and future", so make what you will of that.

He remembered that John Lennon was impressed that he knew the words of 'Twenty Flight Rock' and he stuck to Chuck Berry's original lyric for 'Brown Eyed Handsome Man' in that he repeated Chuck's reference to the 'Milo de Venus' (sic). He contorted his face like Gene Vincent when he sang 'Bluejean Bop': maybe that's the only way to sing the song.

Paul's current single revives the skiffle song, 'No Other Baby'. I thought that this single was inconsequential, but it sounded so much better live and it was good to hear him slow down both tempo and volume for one number.

Paul did a couple of new songs, 'What It Is' and 'Try Not To Cry', but the biggest applause was when he did a song from the 60s, 'I Saw Her Standing There', quintessential Beatles, quintessential McCartney and total magic. Although the large man in front of me did his best to obscure my view by waving his hands. This was the best moment I've seen on stage anywhere. No doubt about it, Paul got back to where he once belonged.

80@80

CHAPTER 56

Days In The Life: 2000-2001

At five minutes to midnight on New Year's Eve 1999, I said to Anne that I must start the Millennium by playing something that was joyous, optimistic and full of life, and she said, "Well, that rules out Leonard Cohen." I began with the war cry of rock'n'roll – Little Richard's 'Tutti Frutti', released in the UK in 1956 and a record that told you that life would never be the same again.

We watched the fireworks lighting up the sky and then with some trepidation, we switched on our computers. Would we be hit by the Millennium bug? This had been in the newspapers over the past weeks. In the past, there may have been coding shortcuts and so only the last two digits changed, that is 85 to 86. Why nobody anticipated that the problem with 1999 clicking over to 2000 baffled me. Did they think computers weren't built to last? We feared the worst but fortunately there was no Y2K bug, for us anyway, and all was well. Loudon Wainwright had written a song about it, a rare example of a song suddenly having no application at all.

In the years up to the Millennium, I had been trying to find a publisher for a book about songwriting throughout the century called *Brother, Can You Spare a Rhyme?* The title paid tribute to lyricists and was a nod to a song from the Depression, 'Brother, Can You Spare a Dime?', made famous by Bing Crosby in 1932.

It still had relevance and it kickstarted modern day protest songs.

In a few short lines, the song describes how people are laid off: "Once I built a railroad, now it's done, Brother, can you spare a dime?" It's not "Mister, can you spare a dime?" as "Buddy" gives us a kinship and shows that we are part of the family of man (to quote another song). The lyricist Yip Harburg had lost money in the Depression but fortunately he could write songs – this one.

Harburg later wrote songs for *The Wizard of Oz,* and 'Over the Rainbow' had veiled comments about social justice: "Birds fly over the rainbow, Why then, or why, can't I?"

A book about songwriting seemed a good idea but publishers weren't interested. The proposed book was seen as too wide in its application, although that was my point. Omnibus told me that a book had to be in the A to Z shelving as otherwise they got lost in 'Miscellaneous', and this was Grade A Miscellaneous. I was also aware that I mustn't make the mistake of *Behind The Song* and I should consider just who was going to buy it. Judging by the comments I got, it was a book about songwriters for songwriters.

Undeterred and ignoring sound advice, I determined to do it myself and asked a good friend and excellent artist, Tony Brown, to design the book. The book dealt with the songs from each year of the Twentieth Century, together with long interviews with key songwriters: Sammy Cahn, Gordon Lightfoot, Tim Rice, Jimmy Webb and Elvis Costello. Dennis Locorriere from Dr Hook wrote a kind foreword. Six songwriters were illustrated on the cover but perhaps we shouldn't have had George Gershwin as nobody recognised him.

It's frustrating doing a book yourself and I should have had an outsider checking the text for typos. An author tends to read what he thinks is on the page and not what is there. Fortunately, there are no real clangers.

As I was compiling the index, I realised that a few names were missing – Robert Johnson, Randy Newman, Tom Waits – and I wondered how I could have overlooked them. By then, the text was locked in with the photographs and so no new paragraphs could be added but I did add an Afterword to give them credit. It's annoying but it illustrates the immense amount of songwriting talent during the century and how popular music developed so radically.

The book had good reviews, particularly from Billy Maher who featured it on his weekend show at BBC Radio Merseyside for years. He said it was the best thing I ever did.

A firm in Lancaster distributed the book but they didn't get behind it. It was reasonably priced at £17 and although I sold most of the 1,000 copies that were printed, it could have done better. Some shops take books on sale or return, but the ones they return are well thumbed and have no commercial value. I lost £10,000 but in return, I learnt about book production and it was worth doing. *Brother* still lives on as an ebook on Kindle.

Maybe I should update it but where are the great songs from the last 20 years? There's a vast number of new songs, but how many will endure? I love the singer/songwriter from Liverpool, Jamie Webster, but his songs often sound like early drafts. Why doesn't he learn from the masters and tidy up his lyrics? The sad fact is that his fan base, like any other singer's fan base, doesn't really care: a half-rhyme is good enough for anybody nowadays.

Once things are out there, they can sometimes have a life of their own. An unexpected spin-off from *Brother* was being picked up by BBC-2 when they were making a series about popular music, *Walk On By*. That led to me making notes about the featured songs for *Radio Times*.

Bob Wooler was encouraging when I was writing *Brother, Can*

You Spare a Rhyme? He loved the old songwriters himself and we would talk about them. He had suggested to John Lennon that the Beatles could do a very good version of 'I Only Have Eyes for You', but the Beatles could have turned their hands to pretty much anything.

Bob was wary about a biography, largely because he wanted to write an autobiography without the personal stuff. He felt, I think, that his own personality had held him back and for example, he had not gone to London with NEMS although Brian Epstein had offered him a job and then, in 1967, he had turned up drunk for a possible job at the new BBC Radio 1. He had no wish to discuss his own sexuality nor the circumstances of his beating from John Lennon.

But Bob knew that he should write an autobiography because so many of those associated with the Beatles were making up stories. The former NEMS and Apple employee, Alistair Taylor became his *betê noire.*

In 1961, 18-year-old Raymond Jones went into NEMS and asked Brian Epstein to order the single that the Beatles had made with Tony Sheridan in Germany, 'My Bonnie'. The local impresario Sam Leach had said he himself had ordered the record from NEMS but used a false name because he knew Epstein didn't like him and would cancel the order.

Decades later, Bob and I went to the Penny Lane Festival where Raymond Jones was said to be appearing alongside Alistair Taylor. We were intrigued. Alistair talked about his management experiences with the Beatles and left the stage to warm applause. The host said, "And now we have the moment you've been waiting for. We are going to meet Raymond Jones, who went into NEMS to order 'My Bonnie'."

Out of the wings stepped Alistair again. He said, "I am Raymond

Jones. I worked for NEMS and I wanted to hear this record by the Beatles. I made up a name for the order book". I don't know why he couldn't have ordered it without the subterfuge.

Bob whispered to me, "Let's do a Spartacus. You stand up and say, 'I am Raymond Jones' and I will follow you." It was tempting. From that moment on, whenever anybody said something ridiculous, Bob would say, "He's doing an Alistair."

Bob did have a photo of Raymond Jones, admittedly in 1962, and I tracked him down to a printers in Burscough. His son and daughter ran the company and he had retired to Spain. As proof that he was the right man, I was shown a letter that Brian Epstein had written to him. I talked to Raymond Jones in *On The Beat* and Alistair said that I was broadcasting fake interviews. He still insisted that he was Raymond Jones, while the real Raymond Jones was appalled that both Alistair and Sam were claiming to be him. Don't you just love Beatle world?

My great-great-great-great-great-great-great-grandfather, Samuel Leigh

80@80

My brother Chris, Mum, Dad and me at a family wedding, 1960.

Opposite, top right: Willie and me.
In his right hand and out of sight is a large spliff.
Right: Guest appearance with Scaffold at the Cavern, 1968.

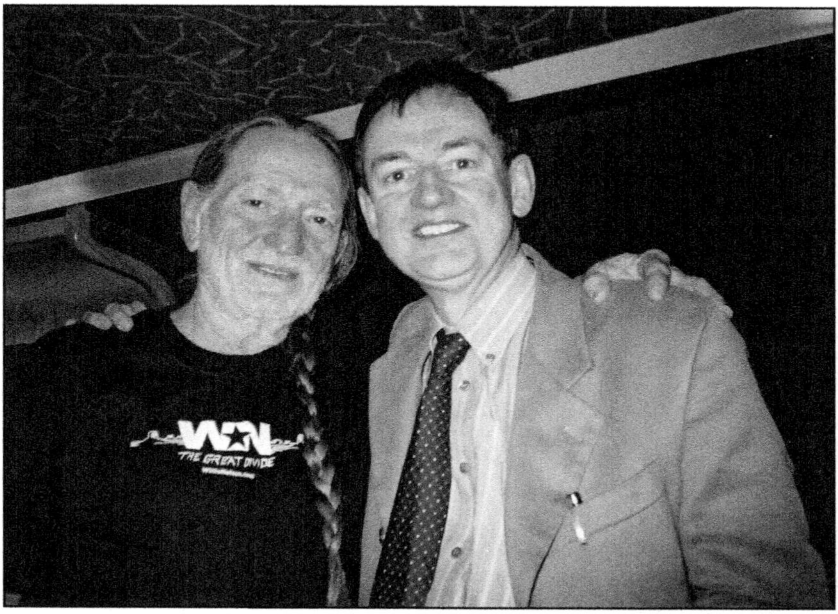
THE GREAT DIVIDE

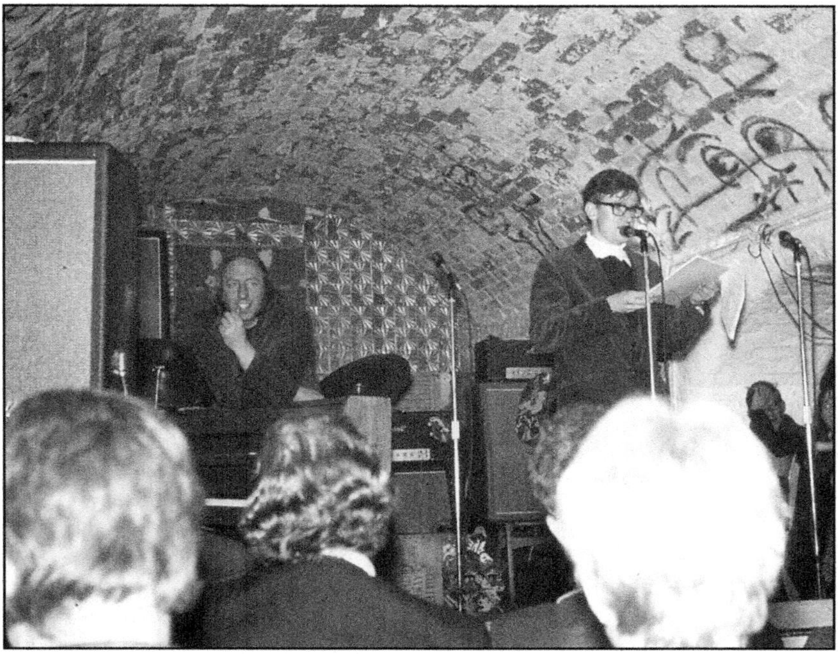

80@80

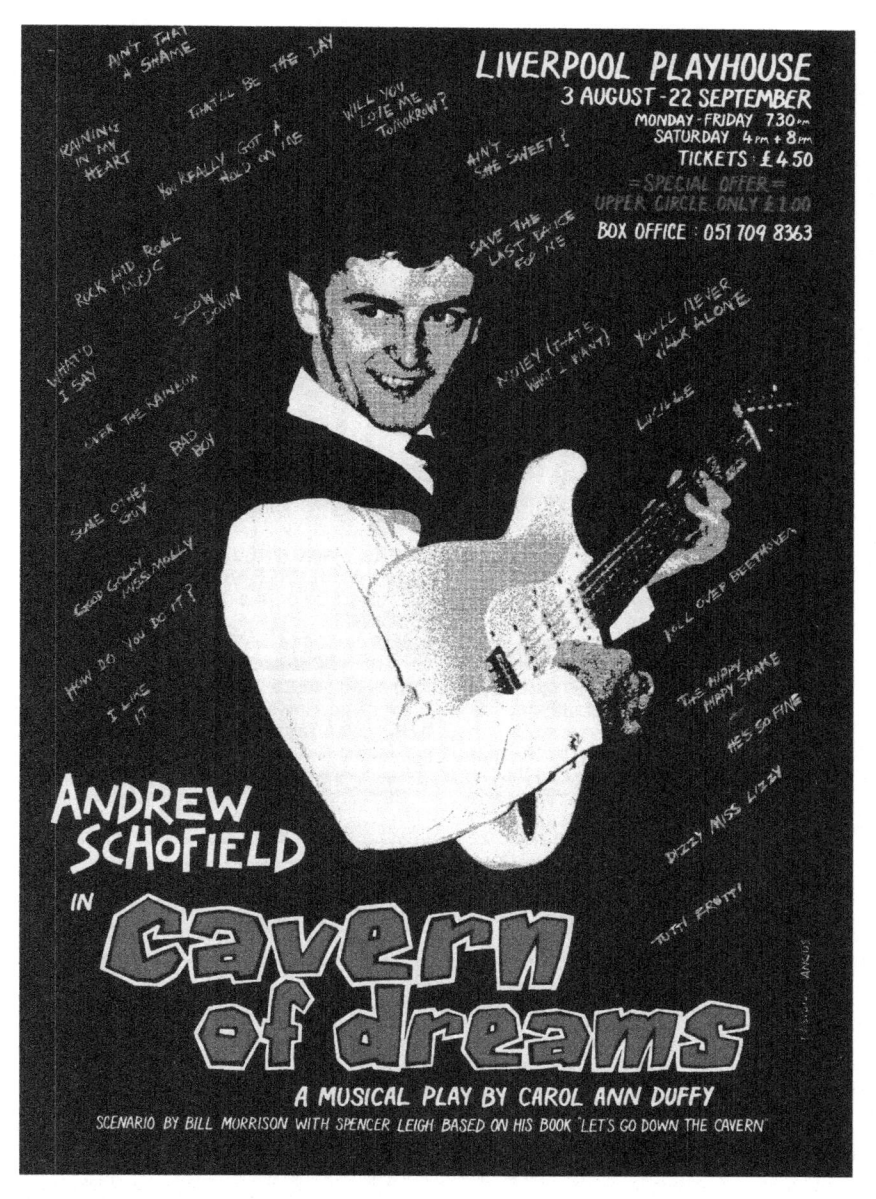

Top left: Gerry Marsden given the Freedom of the Ferries by Lord Mayor Steve Rotheram.
Left: Spencer Leigh and bluesman Eric Bibb.

Spencer Leigh and bluesman Eric Bibb

Above: Paul McCartney installs me as an Honoured Friend at LIPA, 2011.
Left: Two iconic Liverpool record shops.

80@80

Below: Scaffold reunion at Everyman Theatre, 2022! (Spencer in background). **Bottom:** Actor John Gregson takes his Uncle Paddy to see the Beatles in Southport, 1963

Opposite, top: *On The Beat* at BBC Radio Merseyside with Brian O'Connell, Mick O'Toole, Tim Adams, Chas (Dr Rock) White, Norman Killon and Ron Ellis. Their combined pop knowledge is enormous. **Right:** Merseyside artist Anthony Brown found a new way of portraiture by inviting sitters to bring items related to their lives.

SPENCER LEIGH

80@80

Above: Andrew Doble and Spencer Leigh at Andy's wedding in 1969.
Opposite: Gene Vincent with Gerry and the Pacemakers at the Star-Club, Hamburg, 1962 and Ken Dodd with Spencer Leigh (note the Klopp sweatshirt).

80@80

Above: Which one's Cliff?

Below: Andrew and Rosemary Doble at Brian Epstein's statue in Whitechapel, 2022. They're not small – it's the statue that's large!

Above: Merseybeat musicians gather for the reopening of the Cavern in 1984. **Below:** Producers Tony Macaulay and John MacLeod of Pye Records with Timon (later Tymon Dogg).

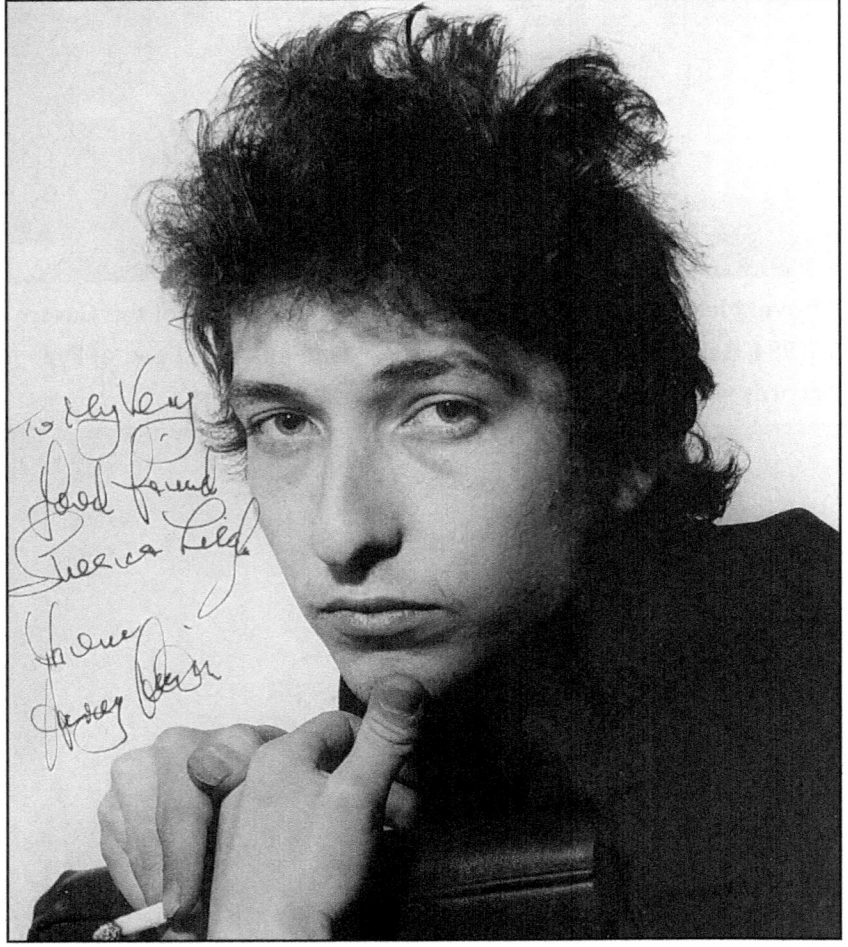

80@80

Opposite: Boxing Day at the Sparrowhawk with Anne, sister Pam and husband Digby, niece Clare and husband Dave. **Opposite left:** Bob Dylan in Sheffield 1965, photographed by Harry Goodwin.
Below: George Melly and Spencer Leigh and Father Tom McKenzie and Uncle Charlie Lennon at a Beatle Convention.

80@80

Above: With Anne on the balcony at Liverpool Town Hall where the Beatles stood in 1964.
Left: A long-haired lover from Liverpool meets a man sporting a Yellow Submarine tie.

CHAPTER 57

Where Have You Been All The Day, Billy Bob?

Talk about a surreal day: try this. *Wednesday 3 April 2002.* The day before the hugely popular American star Billy Bob Thornton appeared at the Cavern, I was told that my interview would be at 3pm and that he would be going on stage at 8.15pm. Sounded fine to me, but the next morning there was a change of plan. The Cavern Club interview had been moved to 5pm and when I got to the Cavern, Billy Bob said, "Sorry to mess you around. I've been taking a ferry cross the Mersey with Gerry Marsden. He even sang the song for me – and I've got it on video!" I knew Billy Bob was wild, but Gerry and the Pacemakers – wow!

"I'm doing some sixties songs tonight and starting off with one of Gerry's," said Billy Bob, "He's going to see Liverpool play football and he can't get down until ten o'clock. We'll start the show then."

Was I hearing things right? Showtime was being delayed for nearly two hours because one solitary member of the audience couldn't get there. This is taking audience participation too far and, in any event, if Gerry were to miss the start, surely Billy Bob could repeat his song for an encore. "No, no, this is a football town," said Billy Bob, totally indoctrinated by Gerry Marsden, "It's better to start late. The audience will like it more."

"Not if they've bought tickets saying 8 o'clock, they won't," I argued, but my reasoning fell on deaf ears and my hopes for an early night faded away. Just one thing though, Billy Bob, why Liverpool, what did it say to a boy in Arkansas? "Well, I love Liverpool. Those records got me through my childhood. I disappeared into that world. When the Beatles came out, I wanted to rebel and be in a band. My brother and I were fans of the Beatles as well as the Dave Clark Five, Gerry and the Pacemakers, the Animals, the Kinks and all of the British Invasion Groups. I am a huge fan of Gerry and the Pacemakers and it's been a fantastic day sailing the ferry cross the Mersey with Gerry himself. It's the dream of my life to be here in Liverpool and playing the Cavern because this music got me through my childhood."

In case there had been a change of plan, I returned to the Cavern at eight o'clock. The door to the stage where Billy Bob would appear was shut and his audience of 250 was watching a talented duo, Feelin' Groovy, working through folk-rock classics.

Fortunately, the match didn't go into overtime. Liverpool won, and once King Gerry had arrived, we were allowed into the back room. Billy Bob's band came out at 10pm and established a funky riff. After a couple of minutes, Billy Bob appeared, wearing a headscarf, and singing a minor hit for the Pacemakers, 'It's Gonna Be Alright'. The new arrangement had more depth that Gerry's single, but Wayne Fontana's 'Game Of Love' was more predictable. Several covers followed – 'Green Tambourine' (with Billy Bob calling the sitar 'an Indian banjo'), 'California Dreamin'', 'Hang On Sloopy' (an audience singalong) and 'I Still Miss Someone' (Johnny Cash meets Nick Cave).

With the broadest of smiles, the Arkansas boy told the audience, "I thought my family came from Ireland but now I've found out that my mom's people come from Cheshire and my dad's from Yorkshire. I'm a hillbilly but I come from here." The audience cheered, not caring that the wannabe Scouser's geography was a little wayward.

When he began his litany of favourite Liverpool groups (Beatles, Gerry, Searchers), some wag shouted "What about A Flock Of Seagulls?"

As we climbed the stairs out of the Cavern, everyone was saying how good the show had been and what a wonderful band it was. The other comment was that Billy Bob did not appear to be a wild man at all. "He could be the guy next door," someone said to me. Well, not quite. My neighbours won't be showing home movies of Gerry Marsden singing 'Ferry Cross the Mersey'.

Billy Bob Thornton

CHAPTER 58

The Best Of Fellas

Every Saturday morning I would head to Keith's Wine Bar in Lark Lane and meet Bob Wooler. I'd be ready to work on his biography but I never knew which Bob Wooler I was going to meet. He might say, "I don't want to talk about the book today". This would have been infuriating if I'd come from London, but as I was only on the other side of Liverpool, it didn't matter much. On other days, Bob might plonk down a file and say, "Let's talk about the Dennisons."

I never went into his flat, which was 200 yards away, but it was full of files. Bob slept in an armchair: the bedroom was packed with papers and as for the bathroom, it was impossible to take a bath. It was the living embodiment of *Krapp's Last Tape*. I had suggested to Councillor Robbie Quinn, that Bob might give his memorabilia to the city, but nothing came of it.

Bob was in poor health. When I accompanied him to the chemist, I was astonished by his large bag of medication. When I visited him in the Royal Liverpool Hospital in 2001, he said, "Can you come tomorrow with some weedkiller?"

I said, "I love you, Bob. and I'll do anything for you, but I'm not doing time."

Despite his prevarication, he did want to chronicle his time at the Cavern, but he was intensely private. He had always been that way. Paul McCartney said that in the 1960s, the Beatles would speculate about what Bob had in his flat.

In January 2002 Bob was being awkward and I returned the photos he had given me (including one of Raymond Jones) and suggested he found somebody else to ghost his book. I was half-serious: one, I wanted to move on, and two, someone more skilled in diplomacy might persuade him to continue. I sometimes met the Beatles' first manager Allan Williams in Keith's. Allan was living with Bob's former wife, Beryl Adams, although their marriage in the 1960s had been short lived. Allan's first wife was also a Beryl and when Allan and Bob were talking, they would refer to 'Beryl 1' and 'Beryl 2'.

Allan said, "I know what you're doing, Spencer. You're keeping all this until Bob dies and then you can keep all the royalties for yourself." That hadn't crossed my mind and I suspect that Allan judged everyone by his own standards.

When I had Terry Sylvester of the Hollies and Escorts on my programme in 2000, I arranged for Bob to meet him in the Moat House afterwards, Bob said, "Don't tell Allan. He'll spoil it for everyone."

During this impasse in February 2002, Bob Wooler died. Bill Heckle said Bob had no money for a decent burial, so would I contribute. Several of us put money forward. Beryl 2 asked me to say a few words at Liverpool Parish Church and I felt that they should be Bob's words. I looked at my draft copy of his autobiography and I found myself laughing at the sharpness of his wit: this is terrific stuff, I thought, it should be published. I chose a few paragraphs near the end of the book where Bob is talking about *Desert Island Discs, Room 101* and becoming the Ghost of Merseybeat Past.

Here's Bob on *Room 101*: "I would put Bob Dylan in *Room*

101: he is the musical con-man of the century. However, my pet hate for *Room 101* is closer to home. Nothing could be worse than being closeted in a room for days on end listening to someone endlessly fabricating stories about his days with the Beatles."

His words were packed tight with Woolerisms, many of which would have been new to the mourners, and his pointed observations were aimed at some of them. "More than anything, I hate people who do not tell the truth about the past. People take liberties as they think, 'No-one will remember: I can say what the hell I like.' I told Allan Williams, 'You'll be glad when I'm dead. There'll be no-one to correct you when you come out with your ridiculous statements.' He said, 'Well, I won't be the only one.' Allan is by no means the worst culprit. He embroiders his tales to make them more entertaining, but others do it to make themselves seem more important. Well, I have news for them all. This is my o-bitch-uary: I am coming back to haunt them. I am the Ghost of Mersey Beat Past. My demise will end the lies."

After the service, Bill Heckle said, "I could imagine Bob in his coffin rocking with laughter as you read that." it seemed like the entire congregation was saying, "You must publish this book."

Jim Turner, a Liverpool club manager and agent from the 1960s, offered to publish it and it was fitting that Bob's book should be published in his hometown. *The Best Of Fellas* (He hated Americanisms) is the story of ghosting Bob Wooler's autobiography and I can imagine Bob saying, "Revenge, Spencer, you're getting your revenge." I wouldn't deny it, but you can imagine him saying every word. As indeed he did.

In keeping with his shambolic life, Bob died intestate but not impoverished - he usually wore the same herring-bone jacket and he called Oxfam his tailors - but he had £25,000 in an Irish bank account.

CHAPTER 59

Days In The Life: 2002-2004

For some years, the University of Liverpool held out against the academic study of popular music but in 1988 it established the Institute of Popular Music under its director, David Horn. Since then, there has been an uneasy alliance with the Music Department as a whole and there have been similar issues at Liverpool Hope University. It is staggering that academics question what is blindingly obvious to everybody else, namely, that on musical, cultural and historical grounds, there should be academic studies of the Beatles and what is a better and more apt location than Liverpool? Students from around the world want to study the Beatles in Liverpool and should be encouraged to do so, not least as a boost to our local economy.

Unlike the great classical composers, the Beatles had no academic training but that is not an argument for saying they are not as worthy of study as Bach and Beethoven. Indeed, that could be precisely why they are worth studying. How did they do it without that training? Where did their originality come from? Why does their impact continue to this day and, if we localise it, what have been the benefits to the local economy?

Over the years I have got to know the staff at IPM including its first director, David Horn, its current director Sara Cohen, and lecturers Mike Jones (also the lyricist for Latin Quarter),

Marion Leonard, Rob Strachan, Holly Tessler and many of the students. Mike Brocken, a lecturer who has also been at Hope, is the most stimulating speaker I've ever met with well-argued views on everything. I used his great gift in two one hour *On the Beat* programmes sub-titled *One Man's Meat Loaf Is Another Man's Poison*. I had Mike, Tim Adams and Andrew Doble stating what they disliked in popular music and they were hilarious programmes, particularly Mike's demolition of Paul McCartney's solo work.

I did consider studying at the IPM when I left Royal Life but such a torrent of work came in that I thought it better to write about popular music professionally. However, I did suggest to the IPM that I should chronicle the history of the Merseysippi Jazz Band. They had been playing continuously on Merseyside since 1949 and four of the members – John Lawrence (cornet), Don Lydiatt (clarinet), Frank Robinson (piano) and Ken Baldwin, known as Nob (banjo, guitar) – had been there since the start.

This was the opposite of punk where the bands came out of unemployment; these were musicians with day jobs and I was sure the balance between working and playing would be an hilarious story, which indeed it was. I could see too that it had some bearing on my own life.

The Merseys were part of music history as they had opened the Cavern on 16 January 1957. John Lennon referred to them as the 'old buggers' who were keeping the beat groups off the stage. At the time, those old buggers were around 35 years old.

Plus, and this was a great boost to the story, they had a guest vocalist in Clinton Ford. Clinton was a national personality, steeped in music hall and novelty songs. I was with Clint when he arrived for a jazz festival at the Crowne Plaza in 2000. He said to the receptionist, "I have a reservation". Asked for the name, he replied, "Geronimo".

When Elvis didn't release 'Old Shep 'as a single, Clinton stepped in for Oriole. Clint's manager said, "We'll get publicity if you give your royalties to the Battersea Dogs Home." Clint agreed – it was his biggest hit and he never made a penny from it. In the 1970s, after playing summer seasons in the Isle of Man, he bought a guest house. However, this was when holidaymakers were starting to go to Spain, so again Clint lost out.

I told the Merseysippis' story both as a series for Radio Merseyside and as a book published by the IPM, *Sweeping the Blues Away*. It's history that would otherwise have been lost. The IPM launched it at the View One Gallery in Hanover Street with the MJB and Clinton performing. In the book, Clinton comes along every 20 pages or so and when he does, something crazy happens. The book reads well because, irrespective of the music, you warm to the characters.

John Higham, their trumpet player since 1970, had a more challenging time than most as he had to juggle his Merseysippi bookings alongside being a GP. Naturally, everybody calls him Doctor John.

I met up with the original Doctor John at Bridgewater Hall in Manchester in 2002. I knew he'd be wonderful from the instant I met him with his fabulous walking stick that could tell its own mojo stories. His speech was full of patois and his pronunciation straight out of New Orleans.

I got a wonderful interview but I asked listeners not to switch off immediately because after a minute or so, they would get the gist of what he was saying.

Dr John had written Lloyd Price's 1960 hit 'Lady Luck' but Price had listed himself as composer. "I was going to shoot him over it," he told me. "Really? Have you seen him since?" "No, I don't want to shoot him and go to jail."

Seeing Dr John perform in both Manchester and Liverpool, I loved the atmosphere he created. One of his songs had the great title, 'How Come My Dog Don't Bark When You Come Around'.

Solomon Burke was a mountain of a man with a fabulous memory. He recalled that at the opening of the Cavern in 1966, the Coca-Cola had not been put on ice: what an extraordinary thing to recall. Solomon had 21 children, 64 grandchildren and eight great-grandchildren. He stressed the importance of family life and asked me, "When did you last tell your lady that you loved her?" I said, "Maybe a month ago, but she knows that anyway." Solomon Burke was horrified, "You go back home and tell her now."

Willie Nelson was more serene. He was in his Winnebago, parked at the side of the Philharmonic Hall. He sat in front of a pile of weed. When I asked Willie, for his favourite Beatles song, he said, 'Yesterday'. Playing Devil's Advocate, I said, "Is it a great song because you don't find out what happened yesterday?" Willie said, "That's what makes it a great song." I was delighted to pass that remark to Paul McCartney. He thanked me profusely and said Willie was a great songwriter. Willie's few words are like a masterclass in songwriting.

Stuart Colman was a rock'n'roll country producer known for his work with Shakin' Stevens and Cliff Richard. In 2002, when he was seeing a few Beatle sites in Liverpool, he asked me what the Searchers were like on stage and would it be a good idea to record a new album with them. I said that they had been bitten by their Sire experience around 1980 as they thought nobody wanted their new songs and it created friction within the group, but if we had a good plan, maybe they would go for it. Stu said, "Let's have some guest artists but not like Lulu's *Together*. There are so many names on that album like Paul McCartney and Elton

John that it's like Lulu is the guest artist. We'll only have five or six guests."

We came up with *In Our Tracks* in which the Searchers would perform songs that had been influenced by them, alongside new versions of their hits with guest artists. It was a strong list including the Byrds' *Mr Tambourine Man*, Richard Thompson's *Wall of Death*, the La's *There She Goes* and Tom Petty's *I Won't Back Down*. The Searchers were keen and a few months went by and Stu said that Bruce Springsteen would record *Needles and Pins* with them.

Universal got really interested. They wanted the tracks to be recorded live with the guests so that they could be filmed for a documentary. They envisaged a one-hour TV documentary with plenty of advertising and some big gigs with guest appearances.

The Searchers' management thought that the deal wasn't right and backed out, but whatever the pros and cons, they should have done it. It would have been a great way for the Searchers to show that it wasn't over yet and that, had it not been for the Beatles, they would have been Liverpool's top group.

I wish that Searchers album had come off because it would have been a fabulous end to their career., although they did have such a fabulous farewell tour in 2023 that they repeated it in 2024.

The Searchers had a fabulous run of hits but some groups lose their mojo shortly after they've started. River City People is a case in point as they had great potential and they cut a fine revival of 'California Dreamin''. Billy Maher's daughter, Siobhan, had sung with River City People and had moved to Nashville, now married to the producer Ray Kennedy. I had a fine interview with them and I was amused that they lived by Emmylou Harris. How great it must be to have Emmylou for your neighbour, I said, but maybe not as she looked after stray dogs and there was plenty of noise. Siobhan said that when Ray Davies came to make an album, he brought a bag of dirty washing and handed it to her.

Another Scouser living in Nashville, Michael Snow, wrote 'Rosetta' for Georgie Fame and Alan Price. He was part of a Nanci Griffith tour and some of the musicians came in for a session. I had concerts from the underrated folk-based rock band Magna Carta and the Dylan Project, which was an offshoot of Fairport Convention. I was impressed with the Liverpool blues singer Connie Lush and her vibrant stage personality. She could have gone global with the right song but she was a little too specialist.

On the other hand, Nasher of Frankie Goes To Hollywood had had enough of the big time and told me he was content to play clubs. Eventually, a huge demand built up to see Frankie Goes To Hollywood again. Such a demand can be illustrated with the difference between China Crisis and Orchestral Manoeuvres in The Dark (OMD), both big in the early 1980s. OMD split up and the demand grew for them to return and then they played arenas. China Crisis kept going and could command 500 people a night, but they never had the brand name for arenas. I did enjoy ringing Gary Daly of China Crisis one morning in 2014 and saying, "Congratulations!". He said, "What for?" and I said, "We went to the flicks last night and one of your songs is in *Gone Girl*." He said, "I'll go tonight!"

While OMD were off the road, Andy McCluskey discovered and produced Atomic Kitten. When he came into *On The Beat* early in 1981, he brought an acetate of his new song with Atomic Kitten, 'Whole Again' and we got the first airplay of a record that went to the top. It sounded like the Shirelles being brought up to date.

Over the years I'd collected around 100 unissued tracks by Merseybeat bands. Paul Hemmings (Lightning Seeds) and Mike

Badget (La's) had started their own oldies label, Viper, and they put out three volumes of *Unearthed Merseybeat,* a very worthwhile project. One band escaped the net. I wish I could have found tracks by the infamous band Them Grimbles.

Jim Turner, now a landlord and property developer, had run the Odd Spot club and managed Them Grimbles in the 60s. As nobody knew what they looked like, he thought he could have any number of bands called Them Grimbles. Both David Crosby, who owned Rox Records in Birkenhead, and Mike Byrne had been in Them Grimbles, and Ron Ellis had booked them. I had all four in to talk about the experience. The band came unstuck when a girl went to see Them Grimbles with her father because one of the band had got her into trouble. She didn't recognise any of them and so they were exposed by the *News of the World* as charlatans, Them Grimbles led to them grumbles.

I had met Bobby Vee on a few occasions and he always recognised me and was friendly. I assumed he had filing cards relating to the towns he visited. This time I visited his tour in Leeds and I had asked to interview Freddy Cannon and Little Eva. However, when I went to the theatre, the first person I saw was Bobby Vee who said, "Hello, Spencer, how are you?" How did he do it? I've no idea. I told him I had come to see Freddy Cannon. He said, "I'll introduce you. He's like a Duracell bunny."

Around this time I began working for the record label Chrome Dreams. The Dixie Chicks were hot sellers and Chrome Dreams wanted to put out a Dixie Chicks album that didn't include any songs and just told their story. I was asked to write their story which was narrated over bland backing music and marketed as *The Complete Dixie Chicks.* My next project for them was *Songs That Elvis Loved,* which was the original versions of songs he'd covered and was perfectly fine and then Hugh Wilson and I compiled an excellent boxset of vintage country tracks called *Maverick Country* for Chrome Dreams. As *Chrome Dreams* was an album title by Neil Young, that may be where their interests lay but they didn't have the finance to record and produce contemporary rock. It was hard to get them to pay me but fair enough, it's hard being a small publisher. I remember sending a note, "May your chrome dreams turn to rusty nightmares."

I did a compilation for Sanctuary of Pye's jazz recordings called *Trad Mad!,* and a 6CD set of Chris Barber's work. I wanted to get Steve Voce in on the Pye Jazz catalogue as he had got me into *The Independent*. However, I once held up a Chris Barber record at Radio Merseyside and he said, "Spencer, that's like holding up a crucifix to Dracula."

Luckily, Sanctuary wanted a compilation of Pye's modern jazz recordings and Steve did *Red Hot,* a definitive collection of UK modern jazz. I also did a double-CD of Lita Roza's Pye recordings which was immaculately presented and called *But Beautiful*. Lita, rang me delighted, and said, "Wasn't I beautiful then?" Then and now, Lita.

CHAPTER 60

Germany Calling

For the summer of 2002, I wanted to make a comprehensive documentary series about the Liverpool groups in Hamburg in the early 1960s. Nobody including myself had come to grips with how tawdry and sex-driven the St Pauli area of Hamburg was and how these boys became men overnight. It would be as honest as I could make it.

The station manager Mick Ord liked the idea and *Germany Calling* was scheduled for Sunday afternoons in June 2002 in eight one-hour episodes. I was unsure of the timing as years earlier there had been complaints when I played Peter Sarstedt's light-hearted 'Take Off Your Clothes' as some listeners were preparing for church.

Nevertheless, Mick wanted to fill that time spot and didn't want a tense warning beforehand. My opening introduction made it clear what the series (or at least some episodes) contained and listeners could switch off if they chose. I wasn't going out of my way to be raunchy, but I did have Merseybeat musicians, now aged around 60, talking about their time with prostitutes with, it must be said, some delight. I did toy with the title, *From Sexy to Sixty,* for the final episode but decided against it.

Although Liverpool is famed for Maggie May marketing herself around Lime Street, there were scarcely any striptease or sex shows in the city in the early 1960s. Hence, St Pauli was a revelation to the young musicians. The series had serious intent as I wanted to discover how much of that Merseybeat sound was down to Hamburg. There is a tendency for Scousers to say they invented everything, but what did the Beatles owe to Hamburg? In November 2001, I spent a week in Hamburg recording interviews and collecting information. The news of George Harrison's death came through as I was returning home.

Situated on the Elbe River in northern Germany, Hamburg is Germany's second city and largest port, now a container port like Liverpool. The director of the Museum of Hamburg History, Dr Ortwin Pelc told me, "The people in Hamburg feel separate from Germany and also from Saxony or Bavaria. They won't say, 'We are German, we are Bavarians.' The Hamburgers say, 'We are from Hamburg.' It has been that way for hundreds of years." I could sense the pride that links the people of Hamburg and Liverpool. Dr Pelc also warned me, "If you are in St Pauli at night, you may meet people that you would prefer not to meet."

Hamburg champions freedom, and all manner of unsocial behaviour is tolerated in St Pauli. There are elegant department stores and beautiful town houses elsewhere, but St Pauli is a working-class district down by the docks. The thoroughfare is Die Reeperbahn, which means 'Rope-making Street' and provides another link to the ships, and the Star-Club was in Die Grosse Freiheit, which means The Great Freedom. Some centuries ago, the Reeperbahn was divided from the rest of the city by a wall, and the prostitutes, gypsies and beggars lived there. St Pauli is cosmopolitan, created for sailors (and we all know what sailors want), and hence, there is nothing especially German about it.

Henry Heggen, a blues singer based in Hamburg, told me: "The Reeperbahn is where they let it all hang out. They made the ropes for the ships and then they established the dives, so it became the place to get drunk and be with a woman. The equivalent would be Las Vegas where prostitution is legal, but it doesn't have the tradition the Reeperbahn has. It is 100 yards from the harbour, so over the centuries sailors have been going there for a good time."

Oh yes, there is culture in St. Pauli. When I was walking round the Reeperbahn, I came across a museum – a museum devoted to erotica. The entrance looked supremely unerotic. What was in it? Inflatable dolls from the 30s, sex aids from the 19th century? If you didn't get a hard-on, could you ask for your money back?

It was 7pm and ten girls propositioned me within a hour – if I had said yes to them all, I would have been worn out. A blonde with pigtails put my hand on her breasts to assure me that they were real. I didn't doubt it but I wondered about the rest of her as she wore a red miniskirt and fishnet stockings, which appears *de rigueur* for a Hamburg prossie. Still, I liked the idea of a free sample from a good-looking girl, but who would want to shag someone who had already been shagged six times that day? Not to mention the possibility of theft as the best time to steal your wallet must be when your trousers are round your ankles. Most of the prostitutes were good-looking: you'd have to be to compete for the business, but a couple did look as though they had been around at the time of the Beatles. Perhaps I should have asked for an interview.

There appeared to be no regulations regarding what sex shops can show in their windows and all manners of dildos and condoms were on open display. One shop's centrepiece was a gigantic, erect penis. Who on earth buys inflatable dolls, especially the ones with three orifices: would a purchaser ever admit to owning one and wouldn't you feel like Benny Hill as you cuddled it? I found the answer at the Tate Gallery at the Albert Dock in 2004. One artist had two sex dolls on display, and I asked if he had made them himself or had simply purchased them. He bought them at a German airport and it is an example of Found Art. I think I will become a Found Artist.

I walked past sex shows, scores of them, some of them offering nude photographs of artists who definitely won't be appearing there – Demi Moore and Madonna – but you might be intrigued to discover what was inside. Others had such unappetizing pictures out front that you would have to be desperate to go in and even then, you might prefer to take a chance on Demi Moore. It would be the equivalent of Liverpool groups appearing in St. Pauli with a photograph of Elvis outside.

In Liverpool, such posters would have been riddled with comments, but there was surprisingly little graffiti in St. Pauli. I didn't feel intimidated when I was walking around. I didn't come across anyone begging, nor anyone selling the German equivalent of *The Big Issue*. Walking round St. Pauli at night is less menacing than the centre of Liverpool. You do have to be wary of cyclists in Hamburg though: cycles are everywhere and often ridden on the pavements.

As well as being accosted by prostitutes on the Reeperbahn, there is a whole street of them 100 yards away in the Herbertstrasse. Walls have been built at each end of the street to hide it from public view. You walk through the entrance and there are 14 terraced houses on either side. They have large front windows where the girls wait for business. You knock on the door and go in.

Lee Curtis, whose band included Pete Best after he'd left the Beatles, told me, "I have sat in those houses." *What?* I remember asking, *Offering yourself for sale?* "No, I have been backstage in those houses. The girls became great friends of the bands. They loved the musicians and they came into the Star-Club in their free time. The girls around the Star-Club would spoil you bloody rotten. They bought you everything - meals, drinks - if you didn't have it, you got it. If you didn't have a woman, they gave you one. They tried to make you happy." Very happy, it would seem.

In the middle of an all-purpose store, Aladdin's Cave, I came across a gangster's paradise selling guns, knives and handcuffs - opposite the children's videos as it happens. I hung around for a few minutes looking at postcards but hoping I might witness some exciting purchase: just how did thugs choose their knives, but nothing happened. Isn't there a danger that a customer may say, "Yes, I'll take this gun. Don't bother to wrap it and, by the way, hand over your takings." The store was close to the police station – the very police station in which Paul McCartney and Pete Best were charged with burning down the Bambi Kini club, but this was just Bruno Koschmider extracting revenge after an argument.

The radio series, *Germany Calling*, was broadcast in 2002 and, almost a decade later, my friend Mike Evans introduced me to the Elephant Book Company run by Will Steeds and Laura Ward. Happily, a good deal of my Hamburg research ended up in a book I completed for them in 2011 (*The Beatles in Hamburg*).

CHAPTER 61

The 1,000 UK Number One Hits

Jon Kutner, a compiler of chart books and a professional quiz organiser around London, asked me to join him on the book *The 1,000 UK Number One Hits*. We would have to find something informative and sensible to say about every No.1 from 1952 to 2005, an intriguing exercise.

We shared the writing: we each drafted 500 entries and shared our entries with each other and it worked out well. Jon had more facts than me and I had more opinions, Spencerisms if you like. The first thing I did was draft all of the Elvis No.1's, little knowing he was going to have reissues of original singles in 2005, which Elvis fans lapped up. Sales of singles were flagging and 20,000 Elvis fans made all the difference. Elvis and the Beatles had been level-pegging with their No.1's but now Elvis leapt ahead with 'Jailhouse Rock' (999), 'One Night' (1,000) and 'It's Now or Never' (1002).

The book itself was exceptionally well designed by Chloë Alexander. The editing came from Chris Charlesworth, a Yorkshire Jack Dee, making valid and pertinent recommendations as well as having very funny stories. The book was some months in the writing so we had no idea when the 1,000th No.1 would be or what it would be. We're so glad it was Elvis and what a sensational track. Here's what I wrote:

Elvis Presley – One Night
RCA 82876666682
Producer Steve Sholes
Writers: Dave Bartholomew / Pearl King
Weeks at No.1: 1

In 1958 'Jailhouse Rock' was the first record to enter the chart at No.1 and in 2005 it became the first record to enter the chart for the second time at the top. This time, however, its stay was limited as it was replaced by Elvis's third UK No.1, 'One Night'. Elvis beat off new material from the Manic Street Preachers and the Killers and a reissue from Iron Maiden as well as some poor distribution as many potential purchasers found the Elvis singles weren't in stock. Elvis became the first third act to replace himself at No.1, following the Beatles (1963) and John Lennon (1980).

Although Elvis was at his peak in the 1950s, his records did not automatically go to No,1. His follow-up to 'Jailhouse Rock', 'Don't' was a No.2, and 'Hard Headed Woman' and 'King Creole', also failed to reach the top. He secured his third No.1 with 'One Night' in 1959.

The new CD single was enhanced by Elvis' original recording of Smiley Lewis' 'One Night Of Sin', cut in January 1957 while he was making the *Loving You* soundtrack. It had been too raunchy for a clean-living teen idol and Elvis must have known that. Both Colonel Parker and RCA told Elvis that it was unacceptable, but Elvis liked the song so much that they negotiated a revised lyric with the publisher.

A month later Elvis returned to the studios with an amended lyric and this version with Scotty Moore (guitar), Bill Black (bass), Dudley Brooks (piano) and D.J. Fontana (drums) is the version that has made the top – twice. However, because Elvis had been recording a treasure-trove of riches, its initial release was held back until he was in the army.

The majority of purchasers of 'Jailhouse Rock' already had the track in their collection and were buying the single to support Elvis. 'One Night' is less iconic and so possibly some fans were hearing it (and loving it) for the first time.

So, Elvis' twentieth chart-topper was also the 1,000th No.1 and few will dispute the merit of his achievement. It rekindled interest in the singles chart and there was speculation as to whether Elvis could continue hitting the top with his former No.1s ('Wooden Heart' anyone?) or if normality would return to the charts.

*****

It's likely that we will reach 1,500 Number 1's in 2025 and we have discussed with Omnibus whether to expand and update the book. Unfortunately, it seems that, outside of the industry, nobody is interested in the charts anymore. The public enjoy seeing a song about sausage rolls or by Wham! at the top at Christmas or learning that the Beatles topped the chart with 'Now and Then', but other than that, does anybody care? Nobody physically buys singles and we have lost something now that everything is available without charge at the click of a button.

CHAPTER 62

Days In The Life: 2004-2005

I knew the Voice of Anfield, George Sephton, because he was a computer specialist with a contract at Royal Life. I told him that Louise Cordet would be on my show on Saturday. She was a dolly bird from the early 60s and had success with Jerry Lordan's wistful song, 'I'm just a Baby', although the title has unfortunate overtones today. She recorded Gerry Marsden's 'Don't Let the Sun Catch You Cryin'' before he did. As she was one of George's favourite artists, he joined me for the programme, which turned out fine. George was, and is, a terrific guy who knows how to get the Kop singing.

When the singer/songwriter Lee Hazlewood played his first UK concert at the Royal Festival Hall, I had the opportunity to interview him the previous day. I went to the rehearsal room and as they were running late, I was the only person to hear a whole Lee Hazlewood concert and then see it for real the following day. Like Leonard Cohen, he had a dark rich voice which was utterly compelling, although Lee did say to me, "Compared to my dad, I'm a soprano." He was fascinated by our fish and chip shops.

We had a fine concert with Jerry Lee Lewis' sister, Linda Gail Lewis and her daughters at Radio Merseyside. She could attack a piano just like the Killer and was enormous fun. Eddie Braddock was her eighth husband, and they seemed happy together.

I wrote booklets for a couple of CDs for Shirley Bassey, *Contemporary Classics* (Recall) and *Live At Carnegie Hall* (BGO). The Carnegie Hall concert was from 1973 but Shirley had played there first in 1964. She had been booked by Sid Bernstein who told me that the hall had frowned upon rock music. He had booked Tony Bennett, Shirley Bassey and the Beatles as a package and all three nights had gone well. Shirely returned in triumph in 1973, hence the contents of the CD.

I did another book for Finbarr, this time about Billy Fury, and Harry Goodwin gave me unseen photographs of Billy at the BBC for *Top of the Pops*. I wasn't sure what to call the book as I had used *Halfway to Paradise* elsewhere, but Anne suggested we change 'Wondrous Place' to *Wondrous Face* and that was perfect.

On 25 October 2004, the news came through at lunchtime that John Peel had died on holiday in Peru. *The Independent* asked if I could write 2,000 words for 5pm. I couldn't let them down as every paper would be publishing a large obituary the next day. Anne was out but her sister, Lynda, came round immediately and she went through my files and rock books for references to John Peel and pointing out anything significant. I drew up a timeline and checked my own interviews for comments. By 3.30pm, I knew where I was going and most importantly, how I would start.

You never start an obit, "John Peel was born in Heswall, Cheshire on 30 August 1939", as it is dull, although in his case he was born only hours before the Second World War began. So, my opening was: "For over 35 years, the BBC disc jockey John Peel was committed both to the music he played and to promoting new talent. He disliked the cult of the DJ whereby the DJ becomes more important than the records he plays, but his idiosyncratic personality and his deep, deadpan tones were copied by numerous broadcasters and impersonators."

From that set up, it was plain sailing and the obituary was published the next day. I read the other obits (*Times, Telegraph, Guardian*), hoping that there was nothing significant I had missed. Mine was okay but I didn't get to grips with him marrying a 15-year-old girl, albeit legally, when he was in America in 1965. He had spoken openly about casual sex with teenage girls, who might have been equally young. In the years since his death, we know that his behaviour was, at the very least, questionable.

A Liverpool Wall of Hits outside the Cavern was unveiled with Lita Roza, the Real Thing, the Christians and Scaffold attending. I felt that it should have been Merseyside and hence, could have had more contenders. Marc Almond, from Southport, is a good example. He agreed with me and, as an aside, told me he was once beaten up on a Merseyrail train when he dressed appropriately to see David Bowie at the Liverpool Empire.

For Christmas 2004, I was asked by Capsica Books to compile a Liverpool pop quiz book. The art of a good quiz book is knowing your audience and how the book might be used. As a general rule, you want a reader to get 50% of the questions right. When I'd finished, it looked neat and I covered the decades, but the editor chose to amend it.

Okay, the Jude Law remake of *Alfie* was partly shot in Liverpool but what has that to do with Liverpool pop? It looked like I was filling up space when I wasn't.

The songwriter Mitch Murray had established a dining club for top songwriters, which he called the Society of Distinguished Songwriters (SODS). It did charity work, but mostly it was for good meals and friendship. They had been going ten years or so, and the President, Bill Martin, who wrote 'Puppet on a String', 'Congratulations' and 'Back Home', thought that I was the right person to write a history of SODS. I had interviewed several of them including Barry Mason, Don Black, Justin Hayward, Tim Rice and Mike Batt.

First of all, there wasn't much story in SODS itself: this was a group of songwriters who mostly had their successes in the 60s and 70s. I could write about their hits but I couldn't write a history of British songwriting as so many composers were missing: no Lennon and McCartney, no Jagger and Richards, no Ray Davies, no Elton John, no Paul Weller and no Mark Knopfler. And no females!

Some key songwriters had died (Lionel Bart, Jerry Lordan) and Andrew Lloyd Webber had only joined SODS briefly, Andrew deciding a dining club wasn't for him. Gary Glitter was a member but *persona non grata*. Björn Ulvaeus from Abba had joined but not his songwriting partner, Benny Andersson.

The SODS felt that members should be treated equally, but how would that work? Eddie Seago had written hits for Tom Jones ('A Boy from Nowhere') and Vanity Fare ('Early in the Mornin''), but how could he justify equal space with Mike Batt or Justin Hayward?

Instead, I persuaded *Reader's Digest* to issue *The Best of British Songwriters*, with a byline, "The undiscovered heroes of British pop." There were 89 tracks over five CDs. When it was about to be released, I told the membership about it. They were delighted when I said it would be on a shopping channel. I thought that was naffness in the extreme, but quite the reverse: many of their wives were viewers.

Further down the line, the SODS had individual photos taken professionally and a book of British songwriters was published, although I am not sure there was much market for their full-page portraits.

CHAPTER 63

Sam The Sham

Over the years there have been several attempts to twin Liverpool with another city that has a cultural or commercial alliance. The ones that I know of are Cologne (1952), Odesa (1957), Dublin (1997), Shanghai (1999) and Rio de Janeiro (2003). As far as I know, nobody has suggested Hamburg, which is the obvious one. The twinning is symbolic, but it can boost tourism. The Metro Mayor Steve Rotheram has said we will help Odesa restore its cultural heritage once the war is over. An obvious twinning would be with a musical city. The Merseysippi Jazz Band pushed hard for Liverpool to be twinned with New Orleans. The aforementioned were cosmopolitan cities that led to innovations in music. Wouldn't it have been neat to have direct flights from John Lennon Airport to Louis Armstrong Airport? Whatever, it didn't happen.

Both Nashville and New Jersey and have also been suggested as possible twins and just before Christmas 2024, two markers were placed in Mathew Street showing our connection to the blues heritage of Memphis. The link between these cities is being presented as something new but it isn't.

In 2004 and on the fiftieth anniversary of Elvis Presley recording 'That's All Right, Mama' in Sun Studios, it was suggested that Liverpool should twin with Memphis. It could have worked but the planning was bonkers or at least, what I saw of it. There would be a free concert at the Pier Head to celebrate the connection. Memphis would send over a star for the event: Sam the Sham. Okay, he was born in Dallas but he lived in Memphis.

In 1965 Sam the Sham and the Pharaohs reached No.11 on the UK charts with 'Wooly Bully', a fabulous dance record. Sam was coming with Rachel (not his wife, but his guitar) and would be backed by the Beat Generation, also from Memphis. The rest of the bill would be tribute acts and so ironically, the only genuine act was a guy called Sam the Sham. Sam came all this way to sing 'Ring Dang Doo', 'Lil' Red Riding Hood,' 'Cross Road Blues', a gospel number, and 'Wooly Bully (twice).

I'd arranged to interview Sam. I went with my friend, Tim Adams, and Sam suggested we went for a meal. Sam's family name is Zamudio, but one of his relations was a bad guy who was killed by Texas Rangers and so they changed it to Samudio, hence Sam the Sham. "I saw my first killing when I was ten," said Sam. First? "I've never been scared to ask for my money, and I've always got it," he added.

The Olympics from Athens was on the TV while we chatted. The athletes did nothing for him. "Those times don't impress me. How fast I run depends on the calibre of the pistol pointing at me. And I have to zig zag too."

Sam had amazing tales of his fellow Pharaohs. "Ronnie had a pet lamb and his father slaughtered it when he was 10. Ronnie went into the woods and wept and when he came back, he said, 'I'm never going to cry again', and he became a hard, hard man."

On the train home, my mind was in overdrive. We would pick Sam up at the Holiday Inn at 11am. What could we show to somebody interested in voodoo? In Liverpool? And then I had it - McKenzie's grave in Rodney Street.

Towards the end of the nineteenth century, Mr McKenzie was playing cards and losing badly. His opponent said, "I'll give you a chance to win everything back, but if you lose, I will take your soul." Mr McKenzie lost and the man left: he was sure he had been playing with the Devil. He went to the church in Rodney Street and asked if he could be seated at a card table when he died, holding a winning hand. A pyramid could be built around him, and that is, apparently, what happened.

The next morning Tim and I went to see Sam and drove him to Rodney Street. He said of Tim's parking: "Man, you're as good as *The French Connection*." We couldn't have shown him anything better. He took photographs and said, "This cat should have realised that the Devil was a liar. He wasn't gonna come back for his soul. Anyway, God might have got to him first. Most musicians say that there is no God, but I know there is. I spoke to him this morning. (Laughs)"

We went into Liverpool Cathedral and Sam was entranced by both the building and the view from the tower – the QE2 looked so small from that distance. Two Americans recognised him and we talked about 'Wooly Bully': "I counted it off in Tex-Mex to encourage the guys, to wake them up, and I never intended for the countdown to stay on there. I said, 'Put a label on that and watch it go.'"

And what did Wooly Bully mean? "It's kudos. When somebody does something well, it's wooly bully for you, big deal, great. Everybody was doing protest songs or the British thing but it sounded right to me. The rhythm is so driving on 'Wooly Bully'. To pull that off, you need a certain type of organ. We travelled in a hearse and we put the organ in the back." Did you have to go slowly in a hearse? "No, no, but people had regard for the deceased and they'd get out of our way."

Back on the ground floor, Sam bought a pen in the cathedral shop. "This is a good one. There'll be a lot of poems and lyrics in this. I was born to sing and I'll always be singing. Only God can silence my singing, and the only thing sham about me is my name."

Sam the Sham with his Pharoahs, long before political correctness

CHAPTER 64

Days In The Life: 2006-2007

I loved presenting *On the Beat* for BBC Radio Merseyside as it wasn't tied to a genre and I could do whatever I liked. I strayed outside the boundaries with the classical violinist Nigel Kennedy, but the listeners stayed with me. When I held a competition for Jane Birkin's *Arabesque,* French songs with Middle East influences, I only had nine responses, so I knew I had gone too far.

From time to time, I had a guitar pull. There are guitar pulls in Nashville, especially at the Bluebird, and we have had several in Liverpool. Three or four performers on stools with their guitars and it goes song by song from one singer to another. When they've all done five songs, the show's over. Mostly everybody chips in on everybody else's song. One particular guitar pull was with Ethan Allen, Ian Prowse, and Kevin Littlewood from the Bothy Folk Club. Kevin performed 'On Morecambe Bay' about the Chinese cockle pickers who had died in 2004. The song had been covered by Christy Moore and was up for Folk Song of the Year. Neither Ethan nor Ian had heard the song before, and they were visibly shaken: they could appreciate outstanding songwriting. Kevin doesn't write many songs but they are all exceptional.

It didn't matter if the guest was unknown if they had a good story. Who in the UK had heard of the Fireballs, led by George Tomsco? Only Buddy Holly fanatics, as the group had added backing to Buddy's demos for commercial release, notably 'Brown-Eyed Handsome Man' and 'Bo Diddley'. George played the Cavern to a handful of fans, but hopefully, his radio appearance made his visit viable.

Marcel Stellman had worked at Decca, producing 'The Ying Tong Song' for the Goons and writing English lyrics for Charles Aznavour. He was the most urbane interviewee and his wife Jean insisted that I stay for lunch. When he was in France, he saw a TV show, *Des Chiffres et des Lettres*, and he bought the rights and screened it here as *Countdown*.

Similarly sophisticated, I met Leslie Bricusse in his luxury flat facing the Thames. He said, "Do you like the view?" and pulled a little curtain to his left to reveal a painting by Whistler, who had been standing on the same spot. He told me that tomorrow Tommy Steele would be sitting where I was "because he wants a new song for *Scrooge*". Tommy made the valid point that the songs had been written for a non-singer, Albert Finney, who half-sings, half-narrates them in the film. Tommy could sing so Leslie had written a couple of belters and he could choose which he wanted.

Kevin Roach, an archivist at Liverpool Central Library, found the Lord Mayor's papers for the Beatles reception at Liverpool Town Hall in 1964. This was to celebrate their homecoming and to attend the premiere of *A Hard Day's Night*. Wilfrid Brambell (old man Steptoe) who appeared in *A Hard Day's Night*, sent a bitter letter: nobody took any notice of him at the Town Hall and he hadn't expected to be upstaged.

The two-hour programme, which contained interviews as well as the correspondence, was scheduled for Christmas Day. The only person on the station was Marc Gaier, who read the news at noon and realised that the next programme hadn't started. It took him a few minutes to find it so it started 10 minutes late and had to be faded out because something else was automatically scheduled for 2pm. What I didn't like about Radio Merseyside was that you never got an official apology when things went wrong.

2007 marked the 800th anniversary of King John signing the charter to establish Liverpool. I liked the historical events but professionally I was celebrating the 50th anniversary of the Cavern. It was a chance to revisit my old interviews (of course!) but I did several new ones. Mark Lewisohn suggested I talk to the family that ran the snack bar and I got terrific stuff. Indeed, the series was called *Soup & Sweat & Rock & Roll*. Although my first series was called *Let's Go Down the Cavern*, not much of it was about the Cavern. In this series, you never left the basement club.

My mother-in-law Lil had introduced me to Jim Rimmer, a retired sanitary inspector from Liverpool, and he had told Ray McFall that the Cavern must be improved or shut down. The sanitation was so bad that one area of the Cavern was called the deep end. It's surprising that there wasn't food poisoning, so well done those ladies who ran the snack bar.

Monty Lister presented Radio Merseyside's *Tune Tonic* but during the fifties and sixties, he had interviewed celebrities visiting Liverpool for hospital radio in the Wirral. He was the first broadcaster to record an interview with the Beatles, which was in October 1962 and, in the interview, Paul calls John the leader of the group.

His other interviews had been unheard since first broadcast and then only been heard if you were in hospital in the Wirral. I heard his encounters with Bill Haley, Gene Vincent, Eddie Cochran, Little Richard, Mitchell Torok, Lonnie Donegan and Marvin Rainwater. We put together a two-hour special, *Monty Lister's Rock & Roll Tapes*. The interviews were troublesome as

Monty had had to plug his heavy tape machine into electric light sockets in the dressing-rooms. The tapes made great listening as Monty was super-polite and even retained his cool when Little Richad was flirting. As Bill Haley was from Chester, Pennsylvania, Monty gave him a guidebook to Chester, England.

Because Billy Fury had been so ill, he had empathy with the hospital patients. Monty took Billy and Joe Brown to Port Sunlight so that they could entertain the workforce at Lever Brothers. Billy Fury loved Port Sunlight and wanted to buy a house there. Monty said, "You'll have to work for Lever Brothers first." Doesn't that contrast with today's pop stars who have such grandiose objectives? When they had a meal afterwards, Joe Brown fired a starting pistol to get attention.

CHAPTER 65

After Bathing At The Adelphi

On Tuesday 23 March 2004 it was expected that both Paul Kantner and Marty Balin would be part of Jefferson Airplane/Jefferson Starship/Starship or whatever they were calling themselves that week, but only Kantner turned up. Their tour manager wondered why the Cavern management was bothered: "What does it matter? We've already done some gigs and nobody's complained?"

Kantner had requested hotel rooms with open windows. He didn't want smoke alarms going off while he was smoking weed. The Adelphi had sealed windows and his 'transcendental vision' couldn't operate without it.

This was the grumpiest band to arrive at the Cavern and things were little better when the show started. Paul Kantner sat throughout the two hour performance and smoked non-stop – in-between songs, in instrumental breaks and while singing, this was a *tour de force* in itself.

He looked round the Cavern: "So this is where western civilisation got fucked up. It didn't get fucked up in London, man: it didn't get fucked up in San Francisco, man: it got fucked up in Liverpool, man. And hey, man, we're by the sea. How far are we from the fucking North Sea?"

This was a valid question and I wasn't sure that I knew the

answer – probably 100 miles if he did mean the North Sea: three miles if he meant the Irish Sea – but the audience took it as a reference to the Mersey and someone shouted, "500 fucking yards, mate."

Whatever, we then got 'Wooden Ships', so at least a little programming was going on.

CHAPTER 66

Days In The Life: 2008-2010

Long before Americana, there was John Stewart with his potent mix of folk, country and rock, usually writing about America and all bound up with a remarkable voice and its surprising vibrato.

When John Stewart died on 19 January 2008, I persuaded *The Independent* that he deserved a full obituary. That Sunday morning, I laid out 72 albums of John Stewart in the hall and was working my way through them as I wrote my piece. The last time I interviewed him, he had said, "I've been very successful if you view my career as a quest for anonymity." Almost everything he said was quotable. He had died in the same San Diego hospital as he was born and I wonder what he would have said about that; well, maybe he did when he wrote 'California Bloodlines'.

I felt a responsibility as no other obituarist in the UK had my background knowledge – or 72 of his albums. It was my finest obituary and Bob Harris mentioned it on Radio 2. I wish though that it had created more interest in his work. There are so many wonderful songs ('Lost Her in the Sun', 'Runaway Train', 'The Pirates of Stone Country Road', 'Armstrong'), yet hardly anybody knows them.

When Richard Dreyfuss was on *Desert Island Discs*, he chose 'Mother Country'. I saw him in a Neil Simon play in the West

End and I went to the stage door. I said, "I love the play but I've really come round to thank you for playing John Stewart on *Desert Island Discs*." He said, "Come here" and hugged me and added, "There aren't many of us." What I've noticed is that everybody who likes John Stewart is a really nice person, so when you meet a John Stewart fan, you meet a friend.

In 2012 John's widow Buffy Ford was on Merseyside and I invited her to the BBC for an afternoon of reminiscences. We had Andy Fergus (who promoted John in Scotland), Brian O'Connell, Andrew Doble and Geoff Davies (from Probe who promoted him four times in Liverpool). Buffy told us John was an amateur dentist who would travel with a drill, which led to some hilarious stories.

The internet was abuzz with the news that Slim Whitman had died. He had been 84 the previous Saturday so maybe blowing out those candles had been too exhausting. I started to write an obituary although there was no official confirmation, but I had got his telephone number in Florida.

I thought I'd call him. Slim answered the phone. He said that Tommy Overstreet had paid tribute to him by mistake on *The Ralph Emery Show*, "but no, I'm alive and well." He was fitter than ever and back to the weight he was when he pitched baseball. Slim lived until he was 90 – and I finished his obituary then.

That has happened before, and I'm surprised it doesn't happen more often. The Royals are at risk as newspapers and broadcasters have prepared pieces ready to go and something could get out unintentionally as happened with the Queen Mother in Australia. Radio stations record obituary items in advance and one for the Queen Mother was broadcast inadvertently when she was very much alive.

In 1999 the *Daily Telegraph* ran an obit of the fiddler Dave

Swarbrick, known for his work with Fairport Convention. He was, however, in hospital in Coventry and he commented, "This isn't the first time I've died in Coventry". A few years later I interviewed Dave in Birkenhead and asked him to sign and date his obituary. Fortunately for the *Telegraph,* he had a good sense of humour and he named his new band Lazarus.

When the music manager Allen Klein died in 2009, the obituaries were unkind but accurate in calling him a gangster. His clients included the Beatles and the Rolling Stones but there were few good words about him. Alarmed by this, the British manager Jeff Kruger wanted to assist me with his own obituary. Really, he didn't want to be portrayed in a bad light. *The Independent* agreed that this was OK so long as I didn't commit to the obituary being published as it was.

I got to know Midge Ure when he was making a documentary about Liverpool for BBC Radio Scotland. He told me that 'Vienna' by Ultraxox had been kept off the top by 'Shaddap You Face' by Joe Dolce and then 'Imagine' by John Lennon "so we were beaten by one of the worst records ever made and then by one of the best. We can't complain as we had a long run at No.2." Funny how your mind plays tracks: 'Imagine' was going down as Ultravox came into the Top 10 and it was beaten by 'Shaddap You Face' and then by another John Lennon song, 'Jealous Guy', performed by Roxy Music.

Paul Du Noyer was going to write an official day-to-day history of the Cavern with the publishers SAF. The book was set up by Bob Young, Status Quo's road manager (and harmonica player) who organised special projects for the Cavern. It would be published for the club's fiftieth anniversary in 2007 with a foreword from Paul McCartney. However, Paul Du Noyer had other commitments and couldn't write it. The Cavern asked me to step in and because of the delays, the book couldn't be published until 2008. I had access to their papers and press cuttings and also had my own interviews and cuttings.

I brought in John Firminger to help with the illustrations and we had a good book, *The Cavern - The Most Famous Club in theWorld*. They printed 5,000, and 3,000 of them went to America. In the credits, I had been generous about Phil Thompson's 1994 book, *The Best of Cellars,* with its day-to-day listings for the Cavern. I described it as an 'invaluable source', which Phil took to mean that I had pinched everything from him. I had looked at his listings, true, but I had found many things wrong with them. He had used the *Liverpool Echo* microfiche at Central Library and yet the billings were often changed on the night, especially with supporting acts. Phil said it was not his fault as his brother had done the research. Well, I ask you! You can't be proprietorial over facts. They are what they are. People take stuff from my books all the time and it doesn't bother me one jot. I just hope I have given them correct information.

I had told SAF about the Buddy Holly book I had written with Jim Dawson and that I wanted to write a Buddy Holly book of my own. That became *Everyday: Getting Closer to Buddy Holly* and I liked the way I did it. Buddy Holly was born 7 September 1936 and he lived just 8,184 days. Therefore, I presented his life as a countdown: we know how many days Buddy has got left but he doesn't know, so it adds poignancy to both his life and career. When his first hit single was released, he had only 617 days left; when he came to the UK, 348 and when he married Maria Elena, 172.

When this book was repackaged as *Buddy Holly: Learning the Game* in 2019, I added an analysis of Don McLean's 'American Pie'. I have interviewed Don McLean, but he never explains

'American Pie'. I took Anne to see him and, unfortunately, she thought all his songs, not just this one, were interminable.

My *On the Beat* show continued to be a source for interesting guests and stories. Here's a few random memories:

I was very impressed with a singer/songwriter from Nashville, Alyssa Bonagura, who was studying record production at LIPA. Her parents were two-thirds of the hit-making country group Baillie and the Boys. She wrote good songs and had a lot of heartache for someone so vibrant and beautiful. Later, she formed a duo with Rod Stewart's daughter and they often toured with him.

John Pearson was a superb blues guitarist who had been a resident at the Bothy Folk Club in Southport. He moved to Portugal but his house burned down during a heatwave. He was surprisingly sanguine but then he knew of all the hardships that American blues musicians had been through.

Michael Gray from Birkenhead is a leading authority on Bob Dylan. Dylan wrote a brilliant song around Blind Willie McTell, but little was known about him. Michael spent months in the Deep South researching McTell's life and he wrote the remarkable *Hand Me My Travelin' Shoes*. The book works well as Michael is a stranger in a strange land and his quest is part of the story.

The *Daily Mirror* crime reporter, Howard Sounes had written excellent biographies of Bob Dylan and Paul McCartney and when I asked him what came next, he said it depended on who would give him a £20,000 advance. I thought, "I'll show him, I'll write a book for nothing."

I had a pensioner's pass on Merseytravel and Billy Kinsley of the Merseybeats lived on a direct bus route. I knew him well – he had introduced me to Alyssa Bonagura who was doing backing vocals for him on a radio concert – and I offered to write his life story. He had been involved with the Merseybeats, sessions at Apple Records, working with Jimmy Campbell, Liverpool Express and now had his own studio in Crosby. He was a family man and everybody liked him.

I laid down house rules: nothing off-limits and if anything was uncertain, he had to tell me now rather than later as it could affect the project. When he was 13 in 1959, Billy had given evidence against a thug who slashed his face. He wouldn't name him in case he still felt the same way. Similarly, Billy's wife Sandra gave me a rundown of their contraceptive habits. When 'You Are My Love' made the Top 20 for Liverpool Express in 1976, Billy told Sandra they could afford a third child and hence, Jonathan Kinsley owes his life to that record.

The Cavern published the book and Billy made a solo album, also called *It's Love that Really Counts*, issued at the same time and available for £5 to readers. This was too cumbersome, and we should have put the CD in a pocket at the back.

It's boring to start "Joe Smith was born on such-and-such" but Billy's birth certificate had the wrong date. He was born on 29 November 1946 but the doctor put it to the previous day to avoid the anniversary of the deaths of seven relatives in wartime bombing.

When Billy worked at Apple in the late 1960s, Paul McCartney interrupted a Jackie Lomax session and screamed a spontaneous song, 'Oh No!'. Years later, Billy realised it was 'Ono' and Paul must have had a tough meeting. He asked Paul if he could take what he remembered and finish the song. Paul had forgotten all about it and said, "It's yours." It went on a Liverpool Express album.

When Apple collapsed, Billy and Jimmy Campbell worked on cheapo-cheapo albums of hits of the day. They were issued anonymously at budget price. Billy disowned them and was embarrassed by them. The Institute of Popular Music has several and so I brought home a batch and invited Billy round. He was astonished to hear them and he had recorded 'My Sweet Lord', 'Without You', 'Alone Again (Naturally)' and several more.

Billy described an incident at De Lane Lea Studios where Paul McCartney was in the main studio and had asked the producer Bruce Baxter what he was working on: it was 'Mull of Kintyre' and he was adding the vocals the next day. "Who's going to do it?" asked Paul. "Billy Kinsley," said Bruce. "That's OK then," said Paul. Billy reckoned it was the best endorsement he's ever had.

I was getting the most out of the BBC written archive files at Caversham. Some of the banned records were put onto a 3CD boxed set with Acrobat, *This Record Is Not to Be Broadcast*, which got media attention, and this was followed by another 2CD set. I wrote a feature on the auditions for these albums for *The Independent* as it is fascinating to see who was spotted performing immediately and who wasn't.

I was involved with a box-set of Johnny Cash's Sun singles and did booklets for EMI sets of Herman's Hermits, Gerry and the Pacemakers and the Swinging Blue Jeans, all with unissued material. The real fans were having to pay for old favourites to access the few new tracks but that was par for the course.

I made a documentary for BBC Radio Lancashire about Eddie Calvert from Preston as his personal files had been given to the Institute of Popular Music. His telephone book had a page of sexy female singers and their numbers, I wonder why.

My Eddie Calvert memorial walk was frustrating as some of the locations had gone and there was no mention of him anywhere, not in the library nor the Museum of Lancashire. He had a US Number 1 in the early 1950s, even before rock'n'roll, and it should have been acknowledged. At the time his dad put his gold disc for 'Oh My Mein Papa' on his front door so that passers-by could see it. Of course that wouldn't last five minutes today.

CHAPTER 67

I'm This Close To Coming Back

When Liverpool received the honour of being European Capital of Culture in 2008, the humourist Alan Coren told BBC Radio 4, "Right, they now have four years to find some." It was funny but unfair and if he had visited the city, he would have seen its culture was thriving. Indeed, the city responded with a triumphant, full festival of events.

Ringo Starr was a guest at the first events, playing his drums on the roof of St George's Hall and appearing at the first concert at the new Echo Arena (capacity 11,000), *Liverpool – The Musical*, on 12 January 2008.

Publicly, the Liverpool Empire (capacity 2,400) was supportive as the Arena would be presenting major stars outside the Empire's range. They couldn't say anything else but I wondered if that was really so. Surely the public only had so much to spend on theatre tickets and they might now choose Arena events rather than the Empire.

Quite early on, the Echo Arena presented Steve Coogan and he didn't draw a big audience, and those who went didn't find him funny. He remarked, "You didn't like that but it's my show and I'll do what I want." Was he saying that as Alan Partridge or Steve Coogan? Whatever, his dispirited performance made national news which was hardly what the Arena wanted. The

Liverpool Echo review by Jade Wright — and bear in mind this was their own arena — was brilliantly titled, *Coogan's Duff*.

Fortunately, *Liverpool – The Musical* was excellent and made impressive use of the height of the stage. The musicians in the Royal Liverpool Philharmonic Orchestra were stacked six high and there were acrobatics and other visuals during most performances. Liverpool's story was told chronologically although the music for the early sections was a little odd - 'Rule Britannia' and 'Land of Hope and Glory' - but the connection of 'Amazing Grace' with the city was mentioned - (see Chapter 69 for the full story). Echo and the Bunnymen offered 'Nothing Lasts Forever', Connie Lush a very soulful 'I Put a Spell on You', and Pete Wylie, seemingly wrapped in Bacofoil, ended 'Heart as Big as Liverpool' with 'Ringo for President'.

Capital of Culture events were flashed up as Garry Christian sang 'Here Comes the Sun', and the RLPO's 'All You Need Is Love' with a massive choir was in *Cirque de Soleil* territory. The Farm had the audience on its feet with 'All Together Now'. Ringo Starr got tremendous applause for his new song, 'Liverpool 8' and his singalong 'With a Little Help from My Friends', the friends including the choir and the Philharmonic Orchestra. Ringo said, "I'm this close to coming back" to much applause and brought on everybody for 'Power to the People', although Pete Wylie sang lead. Indeed, I'd lost sight of Ringo by the end of the song. Among the iconic footage of Liverpool shown on the screen was me bandaging Yoko Ono at the Bluecoat in 1967 – and why not?

Much as I dislike arenas, this one is impressive but they should ban hot dogs and drink in the performance area although that is where profit lies. There was no interval in the two-hour show and the audience was drifting in and out, which was inconvenient because the rows of seats were so long.

And that should have been that. Ringo had successfully made his appearances and should have returned home. According to publicity, he was performing for free and that was true, sort of. At first, he had asked £30,000 for his appearances and when told that was out of the question, he said. "Okay, just pay my expenses", which was a bad mistake on the city's part. He brought over nine friends and they all stayed in the plush Hope Street Hotel. The bill for their expenses and accommodation came to £90,000. If there had been no other issues, such craftiness would have tarnished Ringo's reputation, but not by much and would have soon been forgotten. What sealed Ringo's fate was an appearance on *The Jonathan Ross Show*.

Ross quoted Ringo's positive remarks about the city and asked whether he'd like to move back. He replied, "Well, you have to say things like that." If your life revolves around LA and Monte Carlo, you might well think that – only he shouldn't have said it. Maybe it was a joke that went wrong. I don't know, but I always find it hard to tell what Ringo's thinking. He had been daft. He should have said, "Liverpool's great, go see Liverpool. I'm not moving back but I will return."

Liverpool Echo was bombarded with correspondence – 1,500 letters and emails, nearly all calling him an ungrateful bastard and saying he was only a passenger in the Beatles. Roger Phillips' Monday phone-in on BBC Radio Merseyside was wall-to-wall Ringo – and all negative: the gist being 'This city is picking itself up and we don't want Ringo saying things like that.'

The topiary of the Beatles at South Parkway railway station was vandalised as Ringo was beheaded. Billy Butler mocked his peace and love signs with variations of his original statement, "I'm this close to coming back."

Last Saturday, everybody had loved Ringo and now he'd had

it, and this was going to run and run. Jonathan Ross remarked, "You'd think he'd said that he was bigger than Jesus or that M&S underpants weren't any good."

The next arena show was to celebrate Liverpool Number 1s, and obviously, the Beatles' music would be prominent. As Billy Butler said, "56 Number Ones. Are you listening, Manchester?"

China Crisis did very well with Michael Holliday's 'Starry Eyed' and Ray Quinn was surprisingly well suited to the Real Thing's 'You To Me Are Everything'. Dr and the Medics had the audience on their feet with 'Two Tribes' and 'Spirit In The Sky' – the good doctor, Clive Jackson, comes from Knotty Ash. I liked Ian McNabb's 'Woman 'but it was a copy of the original: still, it's impressive that you can do that.

Scaffold, just Mike McCartney and John Gorman, did well with 'Lily The Pink' (John sang a new verse but I couldn't catch all the words: clearly a knob joke) and 'Three Shirts On The Line', a take on 'Three Lions'. Mike McCartney remarked to much laughter, "Our Kid was this close to coming here tonight."

Ringo's comments had mitigating circumstances as much of his childhood was spent in hospital. In a 1993 documentary for Disney, Ringo showed where he had been in hospital as a child with peritonitis and as a teenager with TB. His view of Liverpool was different from most Scousers.

In a *MOJO* interview in 2012, Ringo referred to Liverpool as 'my home'. Why couldn't he have said that to Jonathan Ross?

As another example of Ringo's lack of attention to detail, consider his TV ad he made to promote Norwich Union's new name, Aviva.

Over shots of Beatlemania Ringo said, "Would any of this have happened if I'd still been Richard Starkey?" What?! Beatlemania would have been exactly the same if you'd still been Richard

Starkey, mate. Ringo was probably reading a script, but he still shouldn't have done it.

Ringo was featured in Anthony Brown's wonderful portraits, *100 Heads Talking as 1* which featured 100 Liverpool personalities as they are now, but with a background of their history. In most cases, the subjects sat for the artist and supplied the memorabilia but in the Beatles' case, everything was out there anyway. The exhibition was in St George's Hall but the portraits appeared all over the city. My own portrait was in Lewis's window for some months, which was an amusing experience.

Although Ringo's remark was in 2008, there is a postscript for today.

Gary Astridge is Ringo's drum tech and he demonstrates his 60s kit at conventions. He is also promoting a large fibreglass mould of Ringo's right hand giving the 'peace and love' sign, which Ringo wants displayed in cities around the world. I hope Liverpool won't take it because it looks naff, and we should strive for superior artwork, especially as the statues of Beatles and Billy Fury at the Pier Head. Cilla Black in Mathew Street and Brian Epstein in Whitechapel are so good.

If you approach it from the back, it looks like Ringo is giving you a V-sign. One suggested location has been the Pier Head so that no one could walk behind it. That is even worse as it would look like Liverpool is giving a V-sign to Birkenhead or to the passengers on incoming cruise ships.

With time, Ringo's disastrous TV appearance will fade away. A good mural for Ringo has been created in the Dingle by the Welsh streets in which he was born.

Around 2012 Iris Caldwell, Rory Storm's sister, was surprised to find that she had a tape of Rory Storm and the Hurricanes, recorded professionally at the Jive Hive in Crosby in March 1960.

Although Rory had a speech impediment, it was not evident on stage and he narrated Bill Parsons' 'All American Boy' with local references. I wrote the CD booklet but we weren't sure if Ringo was playing drums. We knew from Johnny Guitar's diaries that Ringo had flu that week and this didn't sound like him. Ringo has now heard the album and confirmed it wasn't him. Ringo didn't recognise the drummer, so it's possible that Rory hired a club drummer for the night, who didn't really have the feel.

CHAPTER 68

LIPA

The Liverpool Institute for Performing Arts is in Mount Street, close to Liverpool Cathedral. It is in the Liverpool Institute building where Paul McCartney and George Harrison studied and next door to the art college, whose building is now also part of LIPA. LIPA's front entrance is opposite where Adrian Henri used to live, so I feel the area's cultural heritage whenever I'm there.

I've been going to LIPA's theatrical productions for 25 years and they are of a very high standard. They are also the best-kept secret in Liverpool as tickets are only £10. They choose demanding plays with large casts and there is a big musical every year. What could be more demanding than *Marat/Sade* and it was as good as any production in the commercial theatre.

There has been *Hair, Oh! What a Lovely War, Stop the World - I Want to Get Off, Cabaret, The Best Little Whorehouse in Texas, Little Shop of Horrors, A Chorus Line* and the premiere of an Andrew Lloyd Webber and Ben Elton musical, *The Boys in the Photograph*.

Stephen Sondheim was very supportive of LIPA performing his musicals and I have seen fine productions of *Into the Woods, A Little Night Music, Putting It Together* and best of all, the highly intricate *Sunday in the Park with George*.

The only time I've seen them pick the wrong play was with

Alan Ayckbourn's *A Small Family Business*. This was a play about the generations and there were too many 20-year-olds dressing up as old folk, which distracted from the plot.

In March 2024, I saw a remarkable production of the historical *Edward II*, which had started life as a play by Christopher Marlowe at the time of Shakespeare and had been reimagined by Bertolt Brecht. The writer and director Will Hammond had reworked it again so that it could involve contemporary fashion and rock music. God knows what year it was meant to be but it worked extremely well.

Edward II spent much of the play in his underpants, and his gruesome death was described in a voiceover, which may have been for the best. The play had themes of power, corruption, homophobia and a complete disregard by the monarch for what his subjects might need. A very thought-provoking evening indeed.

LIPA made me an Honoured Friend in 2011 as I had promoted their productions on BBC Radio Merseyside and in *Liverpool Echo* and I am proud to have supported them. LIPA is a huge boost to Liverpool's economy, both culturally and financially. It is known worldwide but how will it continue once Paul McCartney retires from public life as it will be harder to generate publicity?

At speech days, I have heard McCartney say that LIPA wouldn't be for everyone and that it wouldn't have been right for a maverick like Bob Dylan and perhaps, by implication, John Lennon.

LIPA is a wonderful use of an old building, bringing its remarkable history into line with the present.

CHAPTER 69

Days In The Life: 2011-2014

I was glad to interview Judy Collins at Radio Merseyside. She is famous for 'Amazing Grace' and I said, "Can I take you for a short walk?" Round the corner from Radio Merseyside is Manesty's Lane. John Manesty owned slave ships and one of his captains was John Newton. When his ship hit a storm, he prayed that all be spared and said he would devote his life to doing good. He became a clergyman and wrote 'Amazing Grace', which relates to his experience. Judy, I'm glad to say, was fascinated by this.

It was good to meet Stan Kelly who now lived in Oswestry. He had written 'Liverpool Lullaby' (Cilla Black, Judy Collins) and 'I Wish I Was in Liverpool' (Spinners, Dubliners) but he was also an academic who specialised in computer science. He emigrated to Silicon Valley in the 1960s and became an authority writing under his full name of, believe it or not, Stan Kelly-Bootle. He returned to Liverpool in 2011 for the tribute concert for Jacqui of Jacqui and Bridie at the Phil. This was promoted as the final night of Jacqui's folk club and one of her latter-day discoveries was Nathan Carter, who has become a major star in Ireland and had a hit record with a little-known Bob Dylan song, 'Wagon Wheel'.

Dire Straits' drummer Pick Withers and his wife Linda came

to Liverpool to be with their daughter and they got immersed in our cultural scene. Local musicians suddenly found they could have Pick Withers as their drummer, a very nice guy with no side to him at all.

The 50s rocker Vince Eager was often on Merseyside as his daughter and son-in-law lived here. I spent a fascinating hour walking around the *Wondrous Place* gallery at the Museum of Liverpool with Vince commenting on the stars he knew. In the gallery is a canary yellow Rockin' Cruisers stage jacket that I had loaned them: it had been given to me by Steve Fleming. I also arranged for Lita Roza to donate one of her beautiful stage dresses. When Liverpool Museum curator Paul Gallagher went to her home in Wandsworth, she was hoping he would take all twelve.

In May 2012, we hired the Palm House in Sefton Park for Anne's seventieth birthday and had a marvellous party in magnificent surroundings with Norman Killon as the DJ and the Christians playing an acoustic set, very much concentrating on their harmonies. They included the glorious 'Greenbank Drive' (a celebration of a Liverpool street), the poignant Cat Stevens song 'Where Do the Children Play?' and a great 'Harvest for the World'. They played as well as they would have done at the London Palladium – excellent. My aunt Eileen was thrilled – she had never heard a live rock band before, certainly not one that had topped the charts, and she thought they were great.

The Palm House had been in disrepair for many years but George Melly helped organise its restoration and one of the benefactors, although he kept it anonymous, was George Harrsion. The party was expensive but we didn't mind as the profits were going to a good cause.

My brother Chris was there with his wife Margaret and their

son Stephen. Chris met several people that he hadn't seen for years, like Joe Riley from the *Liverpool Echo* and Andy Doble because they were my friends rather than his. He'd had some cardiac trouble but he was very happy and it was the last time I would see him. He died in January 2013 when only 64. His wife Margaret had gone out for the evening and Chris was decorating. He was applying moisturiser to dry skin when he died, so presumably he died peacefully and I certainly hope so. Going to his funeral was a strange experience as it had never occurred to me that my younger brother might die first. He was a family man and I can see so much of Chris in his son Stephen – his unbound enthusiasm, his passion for public transport and his love of family life.

I think Chris' death was harder on my sister Pam who was closer to him than I was. This was nothing deliberate on my part but looking over my life for this book, I can see that I grooved along on my own and didn't pay too much attention to my parents or Chris and Pam.

Pam, who worked in a bank like my sister-in-law Lynda, married a Process Systems Engineer for Octel, Digby Wolff, who worked on oil rigs in the North Sea. Digby was a good friend of my good friend, Joe Riley from *Liverpool Echo*. Digby's aunt May Derome had been a commercial artist in London in the 1960s and she created the cover for the first Spinners' album and we asked her to paint a portrait of my dog-in-law Rufus, so you can see how everything goes round in circles, which is one of the great pleasures of life.

Another circle involves the art school student Rod Murray who shared a flat with Stuart Sutcliffe and John Lennon in Gambier Terrace, and in 1959 he was making his own guitar with a view to joining John's band. He and Stuart took Stuart's painting (or rather half of it) to the John Moores Exhibition at the Walker Art Gallery, which was then bought for £60. Stuart got a bass guitar from Frank Hessy's and joined the group, while Rod married Margaret Morris (known as Diz), sister of the motorbike riding Latin master, Sandy Morris, at Quarry Bank School. When they split up, Rod continued his friendship with her second brother Arthur, a photographer. Diz, Sandy and Arthur Morris are Anne's second cousins, so you can see how in a very roundabout way, I can get myself into the Beatles story. Eat your heart out, Mark Lewisohn! Rod, incidentally, is the living embodiment of Johnny Cash's 'One Piece at a Time' as he made his own car and he has a garage full of his extraordinary projects.

There is a plaque in Ye Cracke, a pub up by the art college, which acknowledges the Dissenters, a group of students who planned to change the world – Rod Murray, Bill Harry, John Lennon and Stuart Sutcliffe – and they did.

I enjoyed working on out of copyright albums because the full rein of tracks up to and including 1962 were available to a compiler. I suggested to Fantastic Voyage that we should look at Continental releases as most of these tracks had never appeared in the UK. They agreed to 3CD sets of 50 tracks apiece, and though I say it myself, the releases are wonderful. *Echoes of France* was first, followed by *Echoes of Italy* and then, although I had trepidation about the actual title, *Echoes of Germany*. The success of *Echoes of France* prompted a second volume.

The French collection was awesome with Django Reinhardt, Edith Piaf, Charles Aznavour, Juliette Gréco, Jacques Brel, Henri Salvador and Serge Gainsbourg. They had pioneered their own styles without owing much to the UK and America. On the other hand, the Italian collections showed how much American popular music owed to those warm romantic sounds. *Echoes of Germany* showed us what Hamburg youths were hearing before they went to St Pauli and heard the Beatles and Gerry and the Pacemakers. I loved Louis Armstrong recording a lullaby with an 11-year-old from Vienna and it reached the German Top 10. It was wonderful to hear Lotta Lenya doing the song that she introduced to the world, 'Mack the Knife'. All in all, 200 tracks that I'm glad I brought to the UK market.

From the 1990s onwards there was talk of cuts at the BBC, and local radio was an easy target. However, one six-part television drama costs more than the whole of local radio for the UK. Of course, dramas bring in revenue via sales abroad, but local radio is relatively cheap. I never got paid more than £100 for making *On the Beat* even when it was a two-hour show. A band might get £300 for a full one-hour concert but the week-to-week guest appearances were all done for free.

When Willie Nile, a New York rocker with associations to Bruce Springsteen, came into the station, he said, "Before I leave, can you take me to your manager and I will stand on the desk and say that nobody should touch your show." I said, "Willie, that's very kind of you but that's the one sure way of me losing my show."

I felt too that we were doing some good for the community. I was passing through Liverpool One at lunchtime and heard two excellent buskers, the Ragtag Misfits. I said, "Would you like to be on air at six o'clock tonight?" They made several appearances. A lot of their busking was for charity, and they were the first buskers to have a 'pay by card' facility, which got them on *Look North West*.

I met Southport's LibDem MP John Pugh on a London train and I asked him if I could have two tickets for Prime Minister's Questions. He said that MPs were given seats on a rota and he would put us down. He added that it wasn't worth it. He said, "I used to be a schoolteacher at Merchant Taylors' and when I go to PMQ, I always want to slap the lot of them into detention."

I was impressed when John Pugh rang a few days later and gave us a date for a Wednesday in December. There was stringent security at Parliament but tickets had been left for us. We watched the Serjeant at Arms with his mace and John Bercow march into the chamber at 11.30am. Everybody had to make way and the previous week Bercow had told Dennis Skinner to move out of the way. Skinner replied, "Oh shut up, you pompous twit."

We went up to the Visitors' Gallery where you can observe the proceedings through huge security sheets of bulletproof glass. As David Cameron was in China, we had the deputies, Nick Clegg and Harriet Harman. Clegg did a fair impression of Cameron baiting Labour with Harman replying in fashion. She said that their membership had been increasing because of deserting LibDems.

But we weren't only in London for that. Over the years I had spoken to 300 people about Frank Sinatra and this was a USP for a biography for his centenary at the end of 2015. At the time, I was working with Hunter Davies on a Beatles encyclopedia and when I told him I was going to HarperCollins, he said, "Remember this – all publishers are bastards."

HarperCollins thought it could tie in with the Martin Scorsese documentary scheduled for 2015. They later changed their minds because the Sinatra family was doing an official book in the US, which they would publish here.

To round off the day, Anne and I went to St George's Hotel, Langham Place for a *Top of the Pops* party. John Otway, Jona Lewie and Owen Paul performed and we met Pan's People and Legs and Co as of now. It was very friendly and we talked to

Patrick Humphries and Steve Blacknell, who had jointly written the *TOTP* book. I was the only person doing interviews, albeit for a local radio station in Liverpool. I spoke to the publisher, Andy Peden-Smith, and told him I was planning a Sinatra book. He said he would be interested, but I was pinning my hopes on HarperCollins.

When HarperCollins backed out, Andy suggested doing something with Sinatra on Pledge. Subscribers pay upfront for the book but get something extra like a book of lists and photocards. This plan to use Pledge was dropped but I wasn't told why.

Around October 2014, I had a working draft. It was a long book: 300,000 words. Andy published the crime writer, Tom Keenan, and his editor had pointed out a major flaw in his latest story. That had caused him to rewrite the whole book. That sounded ominous.

It reminds me of when I had the crime writer Ron Ellis on Radio Merseyside. I said that there was no tension in the book as I'd guessed who'd done it. "Clever you," he said sarcastically. "Not at all," I replied, "You call the book *Grave Mistake* so obviously somebody is in the wrong grave."

I thought the title, *Frank Sinatra: Call Me Irresponsible*, was spot on and that DJs would play that wonderful record when I was asked about the book. Andy wanted *Frank Sinatra: An Extraordinary Life* on the grounds that nobody (not just him) had heard of the song. (No, just you, Andy.) The new title was too obvious: it goes without saying that Sinatra had an extraordinary life.

However, the horse trainer Ginger McCain, who drove Sinatra around the north-west during his week in Liverpool in 1953, said, "I'll tell you something. Frank Sinatra hadn't got half the personality that Red Rum had."

Andy wrote to me, "I suggest that you drop what you are

doing this weekend and sort out the pictures. Send them to me for Monday and I will approve them and then we are ready to go on Tuesday."

This was good sense. When there is a major anniversary, members of the public are likely to say, "I'd like to read a book about so-and-so" but they will only want to read one. Therefore, you must be there from the start.

My Sinatra biography would be published as a quality paperback on 1 October 2015 and cost £15. It was relatively cheap and made a strong contrast with the official book.

I went into BBC Radio Merseyside and did interviews down the line to other local radio stations – Alfie Joey (a big Sinatra fan) at Newcastle, Tony Gillam at Radio Jersey, Kat Orman at Radio Oxford, Kate Justice at Hereford and Worcester, David Fitzgerald at Radio Devon, James Watt at Radio Stoke, Bob Harrison at Manx Radio, Paul Ross at Radio Berkshire and Simon Hoban for *Drivetime* on Radio Merseyside itself. A good day's work, methinks. I was telling the same stories but they got better with retelling. By the end, I was hoping that I hadn't repeated myself in the same interview.

But the day wasn't over yet. I crossed the Mersey to the Lauries, a community centre in Birkenhead where I spoke to the Sinatra Society.

The Society was to meet in the café and there were several young ladies there – my word, I thought, Frank has got the younger generation. No, it turned out that this was a women's night for the Labour Party, and the Sinatra Society had been moved to the bigger Function Room. So it's official, Frank Sinatra is more popular than Jeremy Corbyn: in Birkenhead at least. It was a lovely crowd and a lovely evening.

When Hunter Davies rang me about our Beatles encyclopedia,

he asked, "How's your Sinatra book going?" I said, "It's going OK but the publisher has dropped his publicist as she couldn't get enough interviews on a book about jewellery, which costs £75. He's determined to do the publicity himself, and now he has shingles."

Hunter Davies: "What did I tell you about publishers?"

My old friend Norman Killon with Billy Bragg and a copy of Lonnie Donegan's 'Rock Island Line'.

80@80

CHAPTER 70

Frankie And The Mob

Friday 27 June 2014: I got a message to call Gianni Rosso in Room 207 at the Hope Street Hotel. This was at 3.20pm and he said, "Can we do the interview at 4.30?" He was going to a Business Conference at 5.30 as an honoured guest. A member of the Mob speaking as an honoured guest to Liverpool businesses! What was he speaking on – how to eliminate your rivals?

I went into the Hope Street Hotel and into the bar. I looked around the room and knew who he was straight away.

If you wanted to meet a member of the Mob and you met Gianni Rosso, you would not be disappointed. He was spectacularly neat – an immaculate grey suit with white pinstripes. He was drinking red wine and I introduced myself. He had a wide smile and he said, "What would you like to drink?"

"I'm okay, thanks."

"I didn't hear that. Nobody says no to the Mob. What would you like to drink?"

"Tonic water please."

"Don't you drink?"

"No."

"I drink red wine. I am constantly drunk, but I can function on it."

Gianni told me that as he was in bed 11 hours a day, he needed to stand to maintain his gravity – he never sat down. He had a lot of jewellery, immaculate hair and the most brilliantly white teeth. He had an LA tan and he looked great for 72. He had nine children and he lived in Henry Mancini's old house in Beverly Hills.

He told me that his stepfather was Frank Costello, the union chief who had made it possible for Paramount to make *The Godfather*. As part of the deal, they were not to mention the Mafia or the Mob in the script.

Frank Costello had said to Coppola, 'You got a part for my boy?' Gianni Rossi was 27 and given the role of Carlo. He had known Frank Sinatra for eight years and he got a call from Frank who was opposed to the character, Johnny Fontane which was based on him. Frank said, "I hear you got a role in *The Godfather*. None of my friends are in that picture. You hear that, none of my friends." Frank slammed the phone down.

I said that I'd heard of Frank Costello and knew he was a union organiser like Jimmy Hoffa. "Bigger," said Gianni. He said it was no mystery how Jimmy Hoffa died. He was killed in a Buick and it was taken to a scrapyard and made into a rectangular slab. There is a coffee-table somewhere and its pedestal is where Jimmy Hoffa rests in peace.

Sometime after our meeting, I saw Dionne Warwicke's autobiography. She said that she lived with Gianni Russo for a couple of years and accused him of stealing $6m of her money.

A few weeks ago I caught the *Celebrity Masked Singer* and saw the Weather Girl being voted off. She took off her costume and oh, the indignity of it. It was Dionne Warwicke. I know she lost $6m through her relationship with Gianni Russo, but I didn't know things were that bad for her.

CHAPTER 71

Days In The Life: 2015

I was often asked, "Don't you run out of people to interview?" The answer was no: there are thousands of people I would like to interview and many, more than I would like to interview again. George Melly was an extreme example, a polymath, but every one of my six interviews was different and isn't it great to meet someone who uses words like 'avuncular' in normal conversation?

As well as the front men, the vocalists, I did enjoy meeting the producers, the songwriters and the backing musicians. I did toy with the idea of a book, *From The Drummer's Seat*, because they rarely get sufficient credit. All they see are the backside of the stars. The public assumes they are boisterous musicians with little to say, but it's not necessarily true.

All the members in the Bonzo Dog band were engaging and quirky and I loved catching up with Legs 'Larry' Smith in 2012 after 45 years of listening to him. He told me a wonderful tale about being out with a drummer, well, not just a drummer but Keith Moon of the Who. They went to the long-running whodunnit, *The Mousetrap*, which was even called 'long-running' in the late 1960s.

They were bored with the creaky plot and artificial acting and during the interval, Keith Moon told an usher that they were going home but they'd like to know who did it. "I'm sorry, sir, I can't tell you that," was the reply. "Go on," said Keith, slipping him a fiver. "Okay, sir, it was the detective."

Keith Moon walked to the front of the auditorium and announced, "Ladies and gentlemen, I can save you all a lot of time. The detective did it. You can all go home now." The theatre staff rushed up to remove him but by then he had scarpered and left the building.

Legs told me this story just before *The Mousetrap* was staged at Liverpool Empire. I thought "Do I?" or "Don't I?", knowing it would be hilarious to broadcast this before the production opened, but fearing that the manager of the Empire would complain to Radio Merseyside about such behaviour. After all, people have spent good money for their seats. I decided not to do it because I would be acting as badly as Keith Moon himself. And if you've just bought tickets to see *The Mousetrap,* bear in mind that the usher could have been lying.

I had known the singer/songwriter Michael Weston King for many years and even though he came from Southport, he had a real feel for Americana. He married a performance artist, Lou Dalgleish, and as a duo they were billed as My Darling Clementine. Together, they made a fantastic album of heartbreaking songs, *How Do You Plead*, which was up there with those of George Jones and Tammy Wynette. Lou would sometimes perform in her wedding dress.

The crime writer Mark Billingham included records that appealed to him in his novels and he met My Darling Clementine after giving them a shout out. They worked together on a show in 2015, which became the album, *The Other Half*. I caught up with them in the Music Room at the Phil and I asked Mark about the TV success of *Scandi Noir*.

He said that they had the one great image that the Brits hadn't got, namely, blood on snow.

I met the record producer Hugh Padgham in 2015 when he was receiving an honorary degree from LIPA. He had worked with Police, Kate Bush, David Bowie, Peter Gabriel and Genesis. He was known for his 'gated drum sound', which involved reverb and ambience, but how was I going to introduce such a technical subject to the radio audience? Listening back to my tape, I hear I asked him about the 'huge whack of drums" on his records, which is one way of doing it, I suppose. He commented, "I listened to the drums on Bruce Springsteen records in the 80s, and AMS in Burnley made a digital echo device and asked me to help with their programs. On the first Police record I made, *Ghost in the Machine*, the snare drum sounds too loud to me now but what do I know? People still really love that." Hugh was married to the fashion designer Cath Kidston so who knows if that could lead to some unusual collaboration.

I loved talking to Roger McGuinn about the Byrds as they had experimented with so many different things. Anne loved his song about catching a wild horse, 'Chestnut Mare', those jangly guitars and horses, two of her favourite things. However, I was never overstruck with Roger McGuinn in concert as he would talk about his songs and sing half of each one. If a song's worth doing, it's worth doing well and only doing snatches is frustrating for most audience members and, I suspect, for him as well.

One of the thrills of my life was seeing Gary Brooker fronting Procol Harum at the Philharmonic Hall, admittedly with no other original members but they did their successes so well. It was a magical moment when Gary Brooker played 'When a Man Loves a Woman' and said, "If I change a few notes, we have this" and he turned the song into 'A Whiter Shade of Pale'.

One of the great fun gigs was seeing John Otway at the Cavern. He sang 'The House of the Rising Sun' with audience participation. When he sang, "The only thing a gambler needs is a suitcase and a trunk", we all responded, "That's two things!"

I did a two-hour show where I played long records, nothing shorter than seven minutes, including Arlo Guthrie's 18-minute 'Alice's Restaurant'. I had a Valentine's Day show where I started with one duet, Kenny Rogers and Dolly Parton, and then moved onto Dolly Parton and someone else, and then that someone else with someone else, and so on for two hours until I got back with Dolly Parton and Kenny Rogers again. I thought it would be easy as Elton John, Diana Ross, Willie Nelson, Lulu, Frank Sinatra, Barbra Streisand and Tony Bennett had recorded so many duets, but it took me a day to work it out. Try it sometime: it's great fun.

CHAPTER 72

Paperback Writers

Writing Beatle books is a growth industry and there are over 5,000 books on the them. Do they say the same things or are there significant variations? Indeed, is there anything new left to be said about the Beatles?

I'm wary about the word 'research'. When a new Beatles book is published, the author often says he has undertaken a lot of research. What he usually means is that he has read six books on the subject and taken the best bits from each. If you see a new book on George Harrison, you might see an acknowledgment to previous books on George Harrison and of course to Mark Lewisohn, the supreme researcher and writer of the Beatles. Nothing wrong with that and indeed, researchers have got to see what's in those books, but they should also be looking for new avenues to explore.

Although a big seller, I felt Craig Brown's *One Two Three Four: The Beatles in Time* (2020) was an example of that. He had read many existing accounts of the Beatles, taken what he wanted and then put his own humorous take on top of it. It made for a very lively story, but it didn't honour what the original researchers had written.

Although there are 5,000 books, only two were written while the Beatles were still active as a group, that is up to 1970.

The first was *Love Me Do - The Beatles' Progress* by New York journalist Michael Braun and published by Penguin in 1964. Braun was working in the UK in 1963 and realised that something was happening. He saw them in Cambridge, York, Liverpool and London and then in early 1964, he was with them in Paris and New York. Back then, few people went to more than one show on a tour, so this is a unique chronicle from someone outside the touring party.

The book has much Liverpool humour and shows an affection for the Fabs. Bob Wooler predicts, "Brian Epstein has built his own Nemesis. As he gets more and more artists, they'll start getting jealous of one another and there will be dissension."

Harold Wilson comments, "The Tories are trying to make the Beatles their secret weapon." Look who's talking.

Hunter Davies was Atticus, a society columnist in *The Sunday Times*. His novel, *Here We Go Round The Mulberry Bush*, was being filmed. He talked to Paul about 'Eleanor Rigby' but he also asked if he would be interested in writing the film's theme. Paul wasn't but invited Hunter, a fellow northerner, to write their authorised biography. Hunter talked to the Beatles, their associates and their relatives throughout 1967, the all-changing year of *Sgt. Pepper*.

Hunter is the only outsider to have been around when Lennon and McCartney were songwriting and he saw them write 'It's Getting Better' and 'With a Little Help from My Friends'. I asked him if he wanted to help with the rhymes. "Oh yes," he said, "but I was there as a reporter."

It is an authorised book, so Hunter had to tread water. John called it a whitewash, but it was John who wanted passages removed because Mimi would read it.

Hunter did not do shorthand or use a tape-recorder. He brought a scribbled notebook to the Merseybeatle Convention in 2020 and although fascinating and being donated to the British Library, it made little sense. Still, it worked for him and he wrote an excellent book.

The first book to show that there was another side to the Beatles was *The Man Who Gave The Beatles Away* by the Beatles' first manager, Allan Williams, and published in 1975. Allan dedicated the book to Stuart and Rory, "who never quite made it, but then who did?" Certainly not Allan Williams who was sacked over unpaid commission when the Beatles went to Hamburg. When Brian Epstein wanted to manage them, Allan advised, "Don't touch them with a fucking bargepole."

Back in Liverpool for a Wings concert, Paul McCartney met Allan and commented: "Allan, we didn't swear like that." When Allan asked him for a dedication, Paul said, "I've got to be careful or it will end up on the paperback." He wrote quite brilliantly, "To Allan, Some parts of this book are partially true, Paul McCartney".

Macca may have objected to Chapter 18 in which Allan accuses Liverpool groups of returning from Hamburg with VD, thus, according to Williams, generating an epidemic in the UK.

Glenn Frankel is a Pulitzer prize winning journalist for the *Washington Post* and is writing a biography of Brian Epstein. This will contain new material about the workings of the Beatles and his relationship to them. He has the problems of writing about a gay man in the 1960s when homosexuality was illegal and attitudes very different from today's. There will be stories that merit a different slant today, but again, is anything new to be said about the Beatles?

Yes, there is.

Jane Asher was an actress and a regular panellist on *Juke Box Jury*. She was Paul Macartney's girlfriend and broke it off when she caught him cheating. She became a TV cook and has written several books but she has never told her story, not even to Hunter Davies. Why won't she talk? We don't know but as she is prepared to talk about anything but the Beatles, there may be more to this than meets the eye.

Then there's the mystery surrounding Pete Best. Pete claims he was never told why he was sacked, but he was. Eppy said, "Your drumming isn't good enough": it's just that Pete didn't believe him. I think, though, it is like *Murder on the Orient Express* with everybody having their own reason for sticking the knife in.

In January 1969 the Beatles spent a month in Twickenham Film Studios making the album and film which turned out to be *Let It Be*. The tension was increased by John bringing his missus to work – the other Beatles didn't do that and it spoiled the equilibrium within the group.

The *Let It Be* sessions had been filmed by Michael Lindsay-Hogg and the film *Let It Be* was shown worldwide. It played into the commonplace narrative: the individual Beatles were fed up with being Beatles and wanted to end the partnership.

The full *Let It Be* tapes were heard by two journalists Doug Sulphy and Ray Schweighthardt and they wrote a book in 1998, *Get Back – The Beatles' Let It Be Disaster*, the very title telling you how they found them.

And that might have been that. The Beatles *Let It Be* film would forever be seen as a disaster. The filmmaker Peter Jackson viewed the complete sessions and realised that there was wonderful stuff, both in terms of music and their relationships with each other. The sessions were nowhere as extreme as had been thought.

Jackson worked his way through the tapes, re-edited them and made a three-part documentary of feature-length films for the Disney Channel. Over seven hours we see the sessions in a new light and how they enjoyed singing snatches of rock'n'roll songs. They had disagreements, but this wasn't Noel and Liam. It meant that 50 years after the break-up, we could (and should) look at the break-up of the Beatles in a different light.

Without a doubt, the best Beatles researcher and writer is Mark Lewisohn and there is little to criticise in his work. He has written many books on the Beatles but his masterwork is *Tune-In*, issued in two editions – the key one being two hardback books in a slipcase – 1,600 pages and taking the Beatles story up to the end of 1962. That was published in 2012 and we are waiting for the next volume. He said it was going up to *Sgt Pepper* in 1967.

That's impossible.

If you cover the early years in such detail where there is relatively little recorded music to write about, I can't see Volume 2 covering more than 1963 and 1964 if in similar detail. Not only is there so much happening in the Beatles' career but they impinge on so many other aspects of contemporary life. Mark's problem is not unknown as the biographers of Pablo Picasso and Lyndon B Johnson can testify.

On a local level, Colin Hall was the custodian at Mendips in Menlove Avenue for 20 years. This is where John Lennon lived as a child and adolescent. He has written *Pre-Fab* (2018) with the Quarrymen's drummer, Colin Manley, and *The Songs The Beatles Gave Away* (2022) about the songs that Lennon and McCartney wrote for other people.

David Bedford's *Liddypool* (2009) is an amazing book about the locations of Beatle sites around Merseyside. He includes walking tours and has taken hundreds of photographs and it is a gargantuan effort. Admittedly, when you get to some sites now, you will find there is nothing of significance, but never mind. This is especially true of Southport which should have done much more to link the Beatles to their town. When Brian Epstein took over the Beatles in late 1961, it seemed that his first job was to conquer Southport.

80@80

CHAPTER 73

Days In The Life: 2016-2019

When asked if it was difficult to interview musicians, I would generally say no. Sometimes they might get a bit technical for me as a non-musician but then my role was as an everyman ensuring what they were saying would be understood by listeners.

I picked up on interviewing tips from the newsroom. If anyone came in with a story, you could get through any interview without knowing what it was about with the questions, "What's it all about then?" and "When did it all begin?" You can pick up the details you need from the answers,

One Sunday afternoon during an election campaign, Miss Whiplash came to the station when there was no one in the newsroom. I did the interview using the principles above and that worked fine. Miss Whiplash was campaigning for less police harassment for prostitutes.

There were very few interviews where I felt I had missed out. You should get it right first time as usually there isn't the opportunity to go back. One presenter, Terry Lennaine, recorded an interview with Mrs Thatcher (of all people) and found it had not recorded. He went back to Mrs T for a second go and fortunately, she didn't fly off the handle.

Another BBC Radio Merseyside presenter, Bob Azurdia,

played a brilliant trick on Paddy Ashdown, the Liberal leader. He was campaigning for a local councillor and let's say his name was Fred Jackson.

Paddy had been briefed poorly and had no idea who he was. He said, "I think Tom Moss is a great candidate. "Don't you mean Mr Jackson," said Bob. "Yes, of course that's right. It's been a long day. It's Tom Jackson, of course." "No," said Bob Azurdia, "I think you will find that it is Fred Jackson on the ballot paper", so Paddy had been caught twice within 10 seconds.

As for acquiring an interview technique, I would listen to an interview and say, "Did this interview add to my understanding of so-and-so? Were there any missed leads? Will it satisfy the listeners?" Billy Butler liked to dredge up something obscure which usually worked well as the subject realised this was not just another faceless interviewer, but the danger is that Billy might bring up something that his subject wanted to forget.

I loved *In The Psychiatrist's Chair* on BBC Radio 4 with Professor Anthony Clare. He probed gently but you got insights and information in each half-hour programme, which still sound great today. He showed Bob Monkhouse that his mother's intentions were different from what he thought. "Why did you agree to do this programme?" said Clare. "I'm writing my autobiography and I thought this might help," Monkhouse replied. It certainly did, but not as he anticipated.

An interview of mine in this area was in 2017 with Tony Sheridan Jr, the son of the maverick singer and guitarist who played with the Beatles in Hamburg. Sheridan had been an appalling father, never ever buying presents and yet once his son was working, wanting to borrow money. Sheridan was a self-centred musician who only did what he wanted but I didn't know until then how much he carried it over into his private life. Tony

Sheridan Jr was very likeable, but he had been scarred by his father's behaviour.

I had had my own run-ins with Sheridan, notably when I wrote about his need to improvise. He told me angrily, "I would never have said anything as stupid as that." But he did as I had it on tape. He was coming to the Beatles Convention and he would sort me out when he got there. I was usually doing the interviews on stage but it was better to stay away that year. It wasn't cowardice so much as common sense.

A wild area like St Pauli suited Tony Sheridan but he was in trouble when the security staff from the Star-Club decided to fight it out with another club at 2am on waste ground. Both clubs put up their best fighter and the police broke it up. Tony Sheridan was arrested for shouting "Kill him, Willie", thereby encouraging violence. Sheridan's defence was that people shout like that at football matches. Both Sheridan and the floor manager at the Star-Club, Horst Fascher, were banned from St Pauli for two years, so what did they do? Horst took Tony to Vietnam to entertain the troops.

When I was backstage at Beatle conventions, I was intrigued at how performers related to each other. The NEMS press officer, Tony Barrow had told me that in the 1960s the nervous Billy J Kramer had toured with the ever-confident Gerry Marsden. Gerry might come off stage and say to Billy, "That was a difficult audience tonight, Bill, you'll have a job winning them over." Billy would feel even worse at the prospect of going on stage.

They shared a bill at the Convention and Billy was top because he had come from America. I was backstage and Gerry was super-confident as per usual. He could tell you a joke and then he'd hear his name and bounce on stage. He did an excellent show for an audience of 60s fans but he came off and said to Billy, "Cor, it's rough out there, Bill, good luck!" I was witnessing what it was like between them 40 years ago.

I went with my friend Tim Adams to meet the soul singer, Tommy Hunt, who had recorded the original version of 'I Just Don't Know What To With Myself' in 1962. It was 11 am and he was dressed immaculately as he was on stage that evening and at his age, didn't want to dress again. Tommy showed his awards and he was delightful. He had come over for the Northern Soul explosion and had married a Yorkshire girl. They had a daughter but had split up. "Nobody can tell you what love is going to do," said Tommy, sounding like one of his records.

Mark Guerrero, known for Chicano rock'n'roll, told me he was returning to the Beatles' Convention in 2018 but this time bringing with him Chan Romero, who had recorded the original version of 'Hippy Hippy Shake'. I asked the British Music Experience in the Cunard Building at the Pier Head if they would like an evening with them and I added a Swinging Blue Jean, Ralph Ellis. The Blue Jeans never met Chan, but they had influenced each other's lives. Chan was a minister: he had been married for 58 years and he had 12 children, 53 grandchildren and 37 great-grandchildren. Mark told us that his father was Lalo Guerrero who was championed by Ry Cooder on his album, *Chávez Ravine*, so it was an unusual and informative evening with live music.

I was asked to be one of the writers for *30-Second Rock Music*, which was in a series of books that explained the essential elements of a genre in 30-second bites, although you'd have to be pretty good to read them that fast. The book was edited by Mike Evans and involved my friends Gillian Gaar and Patrick Humphries. It was a beautiful production but I was never sure about its readership. Also, the text was difficult to write as I didn't really know its audience.

Robert Kronenburg, a professor of architecture at Liverpool University, wrote a wonderful study of performance venues, *This Must Be the Place*, and this book worked well because he was as much into the music as the architecture. He found many good examples in the north west. This book could be twinned with *How Art Made Pop* by Mike Roberts, a brilliant study of how art schools had influenced rock music in the 1960s and then, as the author pointed out, Pop became Art. Mike Roberts himself had experiences of pop stardom as he had fronted the Mike Flowers Pops (who had made a cheesy 'Wonderwall') and once a year there would be a reunion.

CHAPTER 74

Ghost Stories

This is not the final chapter of *80 At 80* where I depart this earthly life. This is about my experiences of ghosting somebody's memoirs, that is, writing it for them after extensive interviews and research.

Ghosted memoirs can be published as autobiographies (which is the real ghosting) or as authorised biographies (where the author gets the credit). The Billy Kinsley book was the perfect collaboration. Billy, Merseyside's Mr Music, was very pleasant and helpful and his family was great. No family secrets or if there were, I wasn't alert enough to spot them. It was a dream project, but most collaborations have a nightmarish quality to them.

You have to write the book in the style that the subjects would choose if they had the time and inclination to do it themselves. But that's not the part that's difficult: it's the problems encountered along the way.

We'll deal with the ending first. If you get your name on the final product, the book itself, that's a bonus. People who want to tell their story have an ego, that's obvious, but as the book nears publication, that ego will manifest itself.

Pat Phoenix played Elsie Tanner in *Coronation Street*. Rachel, who worked for *Liverpool Echo*, was her ghost. She did extensive research and had to cope with Phoenix's erratic behaviour as she sometimes refused to cooperate, The book, *All My Burning Bridges,* was published by Star Books in 1974. Not only is Rachel's name missing but Pat Phoenix wrote an introduction to say how much she hated ghosted autobiographies and had written every word herself.

That is extreme, but even if you get on well with your subject, the ego may take over by the end. Manchester United's manager Alex Ferguson wrote his memoir with the BBC's Hugh McIlvenny, but he is an obvious alpha male. Look at the result. It is Ferguson's story and McIllvenny is just helping him out.

I've written separately about Bob Wooler but he was too quirky an individual for an autobiography. I knew I would be quoting him a lot but there had to be a voice of reason putting things into context.

The main problem was Bob had things he would talk about and things he wouldn't. He wouldn't talk about being gay but one week he came into Keith's Wine Bar and passed me the sheet music for Johnnie Ray's 'No One Can Change Destiny'. He had nothing more to say.

Initially, Bob had said to me, very commendably, "My sole reason for writing the book is to tell the truth. I want to have something available for researchers that they can consider as fact and not fiction. Many of the other Beatle books are little more than fiction." This was a declaration of intent, but I needed Bob's background. We must begin at the beginning.

"I suppose you mean my DOB," grumbled Bob, "I was born on 19 January. I am a Capricorn, born on the cusp. Everything is rather grim with Capricorns and, by and large, they take things too seriously. Capricorns can be irritatingly orderly and like things just so."

"And the year?"

"Haven't you read Bill Harry's *Encyclopedia of Beatles People*: 'Bob Wooler was born on 19 January 1932'?"

"That's what the book says, but I don't believe it. You're very careful not to give many details about your past, but your tastes betray your age. I think you were born earlier than that."

"Does it matter?"

"Yes, it does. It is much easier for readers to relate to you once they know how old you are."

"1932," said Bob.

"And your full name?"

"Ah, I will reveal something here. In the past, I have told people that my full name is Robert James Wooler, but that is only half-true. It is Robert Frederick Wooler, which sounds so old-fashioned."

The following week we met again at Keith's Wine Bar.

"Bob, when were you born?"

"We're not going into all that again. 1932, as Bill Harry says."

"Bob, I have a copy of your birth certificate." I passed it over.

"Oh." (Long, long pause) "19 January 1926. Allan Williams knows my actual age, and he was born in 1930. He said, 'According to Bill Harry's book, I'm older than you and it should be the other way around.' I said, 'Let it be, Allan. It suits me fine.'"

"Why is it such a secret?"

"It is very difficult to imagine that a decrepit person like myself was the disc-jockey at the Cavern. I have regarded rock'n'roll as essentially teenage music. I didn't think it was music for a person over thirty to dabble with, no matter how young thinking he may appear to be. At least, this was my view in the embryo days of the 50s. Things are very different now as rock'n'roll has become an established form of music just as jazz did eventually."

"And Bob, you're not even Bob Wooler. You were born

Frederick James Wooler. We can't have this deception. If the book is published with wrong information, someone who knows the real picture can tear it to shreds."

"No one knows," said Bob, "And you wouldn't if you hadn't gone prying. I can't stand this. The book is off." (Silence)

If you're ghosting a book, you should try and find out the problems before you begin. If they occur later in the project, you've got trouble.

Tony Cartwright had been the road manager for Tom Jones and Engelbert Humperdinck, especially during their Vegas years. He told wonderful stories and was always front and centre. Barbra Streisand lost her confidence just before opening in Vegas: she told Tony and he persuaded her to perform and of course she knocked them dead. Barbra Streisand of all people loses her confidence and a road manager from St Helens tells her she's great and all is well. It didn't ring true. Again, when he met Elvis Presley, Elvis wanted Tony's advice. It was such a shame as the stories were good without the braggadocio.

I'd walked away from the project and Tony died a few years later. His daughter got in touch to see whether the book could be published. I explained the problem and said I would show it to Barry Mason who wrote for Tom and Engelbert and knew Tony well. He thought they were the ramblings of a fantasist and unpublishable.

A few years before, that lyricist from Wigan, Barry Mason, asked me to tell his story, but he wanted a selective autobiography. He had had several relationships and two wives who claimed to have helped him with his lyrics. He refuted this and thought it a ruse to extract more money. I said if I were to do the book, I would have to talk to them but he wasn't keen.

He died in 2020 at the age of 85. I'd like to have done the

book as he had a great personality, but I needed to find out what I was getting into.

Bill Martin and Phil Coulter had written 'Puppet on a String' (Sandie Shaw), 'Congratulations' (Cliff Richard) 'Back Home' (England World Cup Squad 1970) and 'My Boy' (Elvis Presley). Bill wanted to tell his story, which included buying John Lennon's house, Kenwood, and he was a wonderful raconteur. However, he dismissed other songwriters and said nothing favourable about Phil Coulter.

Bill was reluctant to approach a publisher and he didn't want me to do it. He met executives on the golf course and he would get the deal. I would only be dealing with the minions and I wouldn't be able to negotiate anything special. Probably true, so this sounded good to me.

However, Bill would only talk with publishers when the moment was right and not now. The expenses would come out of the initial advance (when it came) and then the proceeds would be split fifty/fifty up to £20,000, and the rest would be Bill's, so effectively I would get £10,000 plus my expenses for writing the book. Fair enough, but Bill was a multi-millionaire.

Bill and Jan lived in a tall, narrow house in Belgravia with lots of stairs which kept them fit. On one of my first sessions, there was a Polish decorator working next door. When Bill asked him to do some painting for him, he quoted £500. "Far too high," said Bill and talked the poor bloke down to £350. He added, "I can't approve this myself. You'll have to talk to my wife. Can you call round in half an hour?" Bill returned and told Jan. When the decorator came round, Jan said, "Oh, that's a little high, can we say £300." The alarm bells should have been ringing in my head. This man doesn't want to give me a penny if he can help it.

Bill was insistent that we finish the book and then see a

publisher which was the wrong way round. You need to know what a publisher's requirements might be and pitch the book accordingly: for example, if there was an American market for the book, then you have more about Elvis and less about Sandie Shaw.

Bill was best known for his songwriting partnership with Phil Coulter but the two had split acrimoniously and Bill was even reluctant to mention his name. They didn't speak, although there was talk of putting their film of *The Water Babies* on stage: Bill had been writing new songs with somebody else, but the logistics of staging an underwater show hadn't been resolved. I said to Bill, "Is this a good idea? *The Water Babies* wasn't even a successful film." "Not my fault," said Bill, "The director Lionel Jeffries drank too much."

Also, Phil Coulter was an important name in Irish music and what if he were to write his autobiography and get it out first. The books might clash, as Phil would have a different view of events.

Phil might have found that working alongside Bill was torture especially if Bill wanted the credits. When I was in Dublin, I took a chance and interviewed Phil for my radio show and heard different stories about the songs, especially the poignant 'Scorn Not His Simplicity', a wonderful song about a child with learning disabilities, beautifully sung by Luke Kelly for the Dubliners and later Sinéad O'Connor. I couldn't see Bill having that empathy, especially as it was about someone in Phil's family.

Bill was a lively after dinner speaker (one of the best) and he wanted his book to be just as funny. However, when he was working as an engineer in South Africa in 1960, he witnessed the Sharpeville Massacre from the top of a pylon. This was world history but he felt disclosing this would distort the nature of the book. I disagreed, "You witnessed one of the most dramatic events of the twentieth century and it must be in." We agreed to write it up and see how it looked alongside the other material.

When I finished the text, Bill said he was very disappointed. I had done a poor job and he would have to bring his friend, a former Fleet Street journalist, Stuart Cheek (Cheeky), to finish it. He published the book himself, calling it *Congratulations – Songwriter to the Stars*. He gave me a credit as being the one to "inspire me to write a book". Well, writing the book was his idea but he certainly didn't write it – and when I looked at the book, nor did Cheeky as the text is at least 95% mine. According to Bill, Cheeky was the one "who helped me put the idea together". All rubbish; it was me. And I got little for it – nothing for my time, a few expenses – but it was certainly fun knowing such a livewire. He'd come a long way with his personality but his ability as a songwriter was not nearly as great as he thought it was.

What did Bill Martin get out of it? I don't know. This book could certainly have been published by a major publisher and he would have been ideal promoting it on the chat show circuit. He was 78 when it was published in 2017 and maybe he just wanted a book for his family and friends, and I was the stool pigeon who wrote it.

80@80

CHAPTER 75

Days In The Life: 2020-2023

Around December 2019 there was talk of this mystery disease in Wuhan and it was spreading fast, but for the first part of 2020 my *On the Beat* show carried on as normal with guests including Judy Collins, Joe Brown and Merrill Osmond. What would be my last *Juke Box Jury* in March was with Liverpool's finest country singer Ethan Allen, the museum curator Paul Gallagher and Eric's DJ, Norman Killon. Three old friends.

One of the first areas outside China to be affected by Covid was Milan. The singer Zucchero lived there but was still intending to play UK dates. I did a telephone interview with him on what would be my final programme.

Also on that show I spoke to Bucks Fizz, who were playing Pontins in Ainsdale, as they would be ideal in the run-up to Eurovision. Pontins was packed: no signs of isolation and not many face masks. I was going to broadcast the interview on March 22 but a UK lockdown was introduced. The BBC could still broadcast but I couldn't enter the premises as anyone over 75 was seen as vulnerable.

There was no arguing about it. *On The Beat* was over. I thought that even when things get back to normal, I'll never be there again. The BBC would realise that this old guy was on his own in the station on Sunday afternoons and anything could happen. I miss all the friends I made over the years, both at the station and among the listeners.

The programming on local radio changed dramatically as can be seen from *Radio Times*. There used to be editions for the different regions, and the north-west edition would have Liverpool, Manchester and Lancashire on the same page. Now there is a double page with the schedules for all 39 stations. There are three daily local programmes (6-10am, 10am-2pm and 2-6pm). After some local sports programming, there is a shared programme across the north-west and then the stations come together for late night listening with Becky Want: what is that but another national programme? During the night, the station switches to BBC Radio 2 and there is local programming again at 6am.

Weekends have local programming until the evening, again in four-hour shifts. *BBC Introducing* for local bands has survived and BBC Radio Merseyside still has its Chinese community programme, but the specialist programmes have been decimated.

The four-hour programmes of conversation, news and music don't have much room for manoeuvre. The BBC has created playlists for local radio stations so no matter where you were at 4.23pm, say, you would hear Adele.

On several occasions over the decades, BBC local radio has tried shared programming, and it has never been successful because people switch onto local radio for local programmes. Isn't that obvious? Well, obviously not to those in charge. It is particularly ridiculous in a city like Liverpool and a region like Merseyside which creates so much local news, entertainment and music.

Some of the regular Radio Merseyside presenters (Billy Butler, Frankie Connor, Linda McDermott) have a new home on Liverpool Live which broadcasts from the Baltic Triangle and sounds like Radio Merseyside with adverts, and they'll need a lot of them to survive. Good for them. I've been there a few times and been impressed.

A wild card that might save it comes from the politicians themselves. At general elections, politicians like to be in front of the public at every available opportunity, and local radio is perfect for them. As a station has to be balanced politically, that is a lot of airtime for hot air.

Similarly, the renamed commercial station Radio City, now Hits Radio, will only have a live morning programme from the city with national programming during the day. The exception is sport as everybody appreciates its local importance, so why not the rest? One thing is certain: listening figures will go down.

Lockdown itself wasn't too bad for us, at least not me. Anne's mobility isn't great and she doesn't like walking, but we live by the pine woods and so I was able to walk around there most days and hardly saw anyone. Sometimes I went for two walks which means I can't criticise Boris for breaking the law.

One benefit from Covid is that we got to know our neighbours through clapping for carers. Dave and Angela across the street are expert organisers and we have had a few get-togethers since. Ironically, Dave and Angela met each other at the Casbah. I didn't know until I met them that Pete Best's dog was named Satan. I could have used that to comic effect in one of my Beatle books, and still might.

CHAPTER 76

Liverpool Actually

The 1997 film *Love Actually* is the ultimate feel-good movie. It takes place around Christmas and is a highlight of seasonal viewing.

The British Prime Minister (Hugh Grant) is being intimidated by the US President (Billy Bob Thornton) but he fights back at a televised press conference with a brilliant speech: "We may be a small country but we're a great one too. The country of Shakespeare, Churchill, the Beatles, Sean Connery, Harry Potter and David Beckham's right foot and David Backham's left foot come to that, and a friend who bullies us is no longer a friend." Billy Bob Thornton's pained expression is priceless.

Hugh Grant could have stood as a real-life politician on that speech – and been elected. After all, Volodymyr Zelensky became President of the Ukraine after playing the President in a TV comedy series which called out corruption.

Closer to home, let me be Steve Rotheram, the Metro Mayor's speechwriter. "We may be a small city but we're a great one too. The city of St George's Hall, two cathedrals, two Liver Birds, Three Graces and three Williams - William Gladstone, William Brown Street and Willy Russell, not forgetting the Mersey Tunnels, the Williamson Tunnels, *Brookside, Z-Cars*, Tom Baker as Doctor Who, Rex Harrison, Taron Egerton, Ken Dodd, Dickie

Lewis, Paul O'Grady, Cilla Black, the four Beatles, the Cavern, Eric's, Red Rum, the Reds, Kenny Dalglish, Dixie Dean, the new stadium and the old Pier Head. Whether you come to Liverpool from the motorway, Lime Street Station or John Lennon Airport or whether you live here, you'll hear an accent exceedingly rare and You'll Never Walk Alone."

CHAPTER 77

Spanner In The Works

The other day there was a competition on BBC Radio Merseyside: which group had lasted longest with its original line-up? The answer given was Z Z Top, which went from 1969 to 2021 when Dusty Hill died. The researcher was wrong and what's more, had overlooked a local group stretching from 1963 to the present – Scaffold.

In the 1960s I loved attending Scaffold's annual shows at the Everyman Theatre on Hope Street, Liverpool. In particular, *P C Plod* with John Gorman as the hapless cop, and the evening ended with the audience singing 'All You Need Is Plod', which puts it in 1967.

Scaffold had been formed in December 1963 for a TV series, *ABC at Large*, and they predated Monty Python and the Goodies, but all three acts owed something to Spike Milligan's surrealistic humour. Scaffold combined Roger McGough's poetry with Mike McCartney's whimsical songs and John Gorman's comic pratfalls.

In July 2022 John Gorman invited me to the Athenaeum, a businessman's club in Liverpool that is as old and grand as its name and now admits women. Scaffold would be performing two shows on the same day at the Everyman in October and they'd like me to host them. It sounded like fun. John was all for the comeback, Roger less so, and Mike said, "Okay, as long as I don't have to sing." John said they would screen 'Lily the Pink' from *Top of the Pops*, but surely anyone paying to see Scaffold would expect 'Lily the Pink' live. John said that they could sing over the clip which sounded worse. Still, they had a director, Mike Haskins, who had often worked with Griff Rhys Jones and knew how to present comedy.

Although John wanted Scaffold to go ahead, he was working on a novel. He had been fascinated by all the climbers going up the world's highest mountain and he thought Richard Branson and Elon Musk had missed a commercial opportunity to open a café and night club for climbers queuing to reach the summit. His novel has the working title, *Climbing Mount Everest by Public Transport*.

I was invited to join a Zoom meeting where they would read old scripts and decide what still worked. When they did 'TIM', Roger said, "Will anyone get this? Does anybody know what a speaking clock is?" Maybe not, but that of itself could prompt humour with older folk laughing and younger ones looking bewildered.

The 60-year-old sketches had durability, but this time round I noted serious undertones. Some sketches resembled a comedy take on the menace found in Harold Pinter's plays. One sketch called *Birds* was not politically correct. "Actually," said John, "that is based on two people at Hope Hall who worked as a duo and victimised young girls with that sort of dialogue."

The show would start with the new video for 'Do You Remember', excellently compiled by Mike's son, Josh, and then I would welcome Scaffold but only Rog and Mike would come on. "You chat together for a minute, or two" said John, "and then I come in from the back as P C Plod and say 'Excuse me' and announce that there had been some bad parking and 'Will the owner of RGH 456 DHLK DUPY EJKZ, please move his car as everybody is tripping over the numberplate?'"

Mike was adamant that he didn't want to learn anything new. It transpired that he also didn't want to learn anything old and so they would perform with scripts in their hands, justifying it by saying this was how they performed at Hope Hall before it became the Everyman.

I argued for something new as otherwise diehard fans would only be hearing jokes they knew, which was my own position. I suggested that they said, at long last, what the Aintree Iron was. "You're all around 80, so why keep it a secret any longer?" I felt as though I had sworn in church.

I also said, "I'm still not sure about 'L the P'. If I was going to see a 60s band, I would expect to hear the hits rather than see videos." Mike said, "I agree but this is an old man's voice, I can't do it anymore. On the other hand, I can do that sketch about the old man perfectly. I don't have to act." With some coaxing, they would do '2 Day's Monday' and 'A Long Strong Black Pudding' live.

In September, Roger sent me a letter to read out saying that Scaffold are very sorry but they can't do the show tonight but here are Bootleg Scaffold, and on they come. They dropped this idea.

Roger lived in Barnes but he was going on holiday to Crete and would not be in Liverpool until the day before the shows. He booked into a hotel for two nights and there was an argument about whether the Everyman would pay for both nights. Perhaps more to the point, he had fallen out with John and put the phone down.

John had also fallen out with Keith, the guitarist who would be accompanying Scaffold on the live songs. John thought it was because his name wasn't on the poster. Nor's mine come to that.

There was a rehearsal on Friday, the day before the shows. At first no one was sure if Roger was on the train. His train would get in at 1pm and he was meant to get up to the Phil quickly. "We all know Spanner'll walk," said Mike. "Spanner'd never grab a taxi," said John, and then to me, "We call him that because you'd need a spanner to break into his money."

The Everyman only agreed to fund one of his hotel nights so he must have been irked by that.

Mike would have a solo spot, talking about his photographs and promoting his Genesis book about the Beatles, which cost £350. He told me, "I've always been very wary of talking about the Beatles but now I'm nearly 80 and I see six-year-olds who don't know who the Beatles are, so I've got to do my bit."

I said, "Obviously, you won't be selling it at the Everyman, but are you having leaflets?" This led to a discussion about merchandise and John said, "Roger might have some books." I said, "Whatever is for sale, you don't promote it yourselves, leave it to me. Ralph McTell's golden rule is that artists don't push the merch: you're not to look like salesmen." They found this amusing but it is brilliant advice. Scaffold signed 100 posters in advance for charity available at £25 each, all of which sold.

When Roger arrived, he hadn't brought his white suit which was just as well. We would have them on video in their white suits for 'Lily the Pink' and it would look odd to see them in the same suits in 2022 – a wonderful ad for the tailor, though.

Roger had been going through the script: "There are four sketches together here and I think *Old Folks* should go as it is the least funny."

Mike:" And very conveniently, you just happened to have written the other three."

When Mike disappeared for half an hour, he was locked in the basement. It was said to be accidental, but I did wonder…

Both shows worked fine and were filmed by Roger Appleton, but that has yet to surface. I liked the way they kept the show slightly satirical with references to Liz Truss and Rishi Sunak (in 'Lily the Pink') and Vladimir Putin (in 'A Long Strong Black Pudding'). Roger told me, "The one good thing about Putin is that he has a great name. You can do something with that."

Roger McGough read his famous 60s poem, 'Let Me Die A Youngman's Death' which now had a companion piece, 'Let Me Die An Oldman's Death'.

One revealing comment is that Roger said that Scaffold had come up at the same time as *That Was the Week that Was, Beyond The Fringe, Monty Python's Flying Circus* and *The Goodies*, but unlike them, they hadn't come from Oxbridge.

In purely comedic terms, John Gorman gave a masterclass in playing a drunk singing a variant of 'Ten Green Bottles', 'Ten Whisky Bottles'. I marvelled that an 86-year-old could throw himself about on stage and I hoped he wasn't going to get injured. John did his chocolate eclairs sketch which originally involved eating several eclairs in quick succession, but John was wary about eating more than one as his gall bladder had been removed.

In the Q&A, Scaffold were asked to explain the Aintree Iron. Mike McGear who wrote the song said that at the time, 'Our Kid' had suggested they dropped the obscure reference, which was bizarre advice for the psychedelic era. Scaffold teased the Everyman audience and at the end of the first half, I asked Mike what the Aintree Iron was, and Mike said, "Okay, here goes. The Aintree Iron is…." Blackout.

Roger was concerned about returning to London the day after the shows as trains had been cancelled due to strike action.

In the second house, he asked if anybody was going to London and could give him a lift – and somebody said his son was going and he would arrange it. Blimey, and I'd only suggested Scaffold didn't refer to the merch table.

The audiences had loved the shows but I'd seen the rehearsals and they beat anything I'd seen on TV that year. I'd liken their relationship to a Venn Diagram that is constantly changing. The tensions between the three of them are self-evident.

In the interval on the second show, John and Mike were looking at the receipts and clearly resented paying Roger his expenses in coming from London for the shows. It was Roger's fault for moving away from Merseyside and so he should pay his own expenses for coming back. But there was one thing on which they were all agreed: I wasn't getting anything. I don't call them Scaffold anymore: I call them Spanner.

Nevertheless, I am very pleased that they asked me to work on these shows, that I got very kind thank you notes from Mike and Roger and that John invited me back to the Athenaeum.

CHAPTER 78

Everybody's Talking About Jamie

Monday 29 January 2024: I was on the guest list for Jamie Webster's new album, his third, *10 For the People*, at Merseymade. There were three houses and I had a wristband for the second. I was taken to the stage before the public were let in and although I only had a fleeting word, Jamie seemed a very nice guy. He had started promoting the album on 22 January and with several performances a day, this would be his 26th gig on his *Pop Up for the People* tour. "I was singing in a church last night and it felt like *An Evening with Jamie Webster*. This is a standing audience of Scousers, so it'll be easier to get the songs across." His new album was No. 2 in the midweek charts and hopefully that would be reflected in the next album chart.

It was a full house, taking up the first floor, probably about 120 people. I was the oldest by a long way and there were a lot of kids, usually in Liverpool shirts, because of 'Allez Allez Allez'. James didn't moderate his language but then they know 'Allez Allez Allez' so who cares? Jamie didn't do 'Allez Allez Allez' which I expected as the encore, but a good proportion of the audience might have been Everton fans, so better not to alienate them.

If Jamie had come along a few years earlier, I would have had him on my show, although his language might have been a problem. He is 29 now and getting married to a girl "who makes the best roasties in the world", which might be a euphemism of course.

The opening acts were both being produced by Jamie Webster. The first set was from Jack Valero. He began 'Something You Can Do' with a Barry Gibb-styled voice but the song moved into normal levels. The children were standing at the front and one of them, a little girl called Lucy, requested Leonard Cohen, which was impressive for a five-year-old. Jack was surprised but she really wanted 'Let It Go' (not Leonard Cohen), a song from *Frozen*. She got 'Homecoming Time' instead but then he did 'With a Little Help From My Friends'. His final songs were 'Innocent Light' and the lively 'This Is a Nightmare'.

Then came a lad from West Derby, Ellis Murphy, influenced by early Dylan guitar-and-harmonica and with a spectacular 60s haircut – I notice these things now. He sang 'Not Like You', 'Thinking about Time' and 'Country Blues' (which reminded me of Timon in 1966), 'I See What I See' and finished with a new song (written that day!), 'More Than I Can See'. He went down well but when he said he was doing one more song before Jamie came on, there was an unfortunate cheer. They didn't mean to be unkind.

Jamie Webster began with a five-minute spiel about touring and how he loved coming back to Liverpool. He opened with 'Voice of the Voiceless' which had neat rhymes and a torrent of lyrics, resembling early Springsteen. He said, "I know a lot of my songs are anti-Tory and I could write a million songs like that, but instead here's one about life in the supermarket." This was a touching song about elderly people shopping together, 'Lovers In The Supermarket', the only song aimed at my age group.

This was followed by 'Looking Pretty Good to Me' which

described how he met his partner Rachel in Thailand, both Scousers on holiday. He sang a song for Rachel, 'Something in the Air' which referred to her 'shit tattoo': just the thing to put in a love song, but I liked these personal touches.

'How Do You Sleep' was about how big business makes money out of wars (Brecht's *Mother Courage* really) and the homelessness it creates. "Can you tell me when these people will be free. It's thanks to you they're labelled 'refugees'."

There was a singalong chorus to 'Sing Your Tears', which went down very well. 'On Me Oh My' had a good lyric with a 'knobhead' in there. Then his song for Liverpool itself: it is "My city, my people, my heart" on the record but his fans sang "My city, my people, my arse". He finished with 'Weekend in Paradise', which the crowd knew well. Considering the number of gigs he had been doing, his voice was still good.

I spoke to Jack Valero after the show and said I was impressed with Jamie Webster as "there's a lot of Billy Bragg and Bruce Springsteen in there, and there's quite a bit of Billy Bragg in you as well." He said, "I hope so, as Billy Bragg's my dad."

CHAPTER 79

The Beatles' Legacy

This book covers my 80 years from 1945 to 2025, and although I'd like to create a world record by not dying, that isn't going to happen. If we go on another 80 years to 2105, we will be in the twenty-second century and the world will be massively different...

...that is, if we haven't blown ourselves up. Even though we might be physically capable of living until 120, we may have wiped each other out in nuclear attacks or with deadly viruses. There are some insane and irrational people amongst the world leaders today. The expectation of life for somebody born today is perhaps not 80 years but more like 50.

For example, the West has been saying for years that Vladimir Putin must be replaced, but this assumes that his replacement will be friendlier and open to negotiation. What if they are worse? It could happen. We hope for the best, but we prepare for the worst. The biggest threat to climate change could be the escalation of warfare.

I am proud to be part of the Beatles Legacy Group which was established by the then Mayor of Liverpool, Joe Anderson in 2016 and is chaired by Peter Hooton of the Farm. Even now, over 50 years after they broke up, the Beatles are worth over £100m a year to the local economy and they support 2,000 jobs. The city must ensure that new and existing projects are of a high standard and contain correct information about the Beatles. The Beatles were way ahead of the field in everything they did but I'd like the rest of Liverpool's musical heritage to be appreciated. There is a vast difference between the rise of Buddy Holly and the Beatles. Holly was on his own in Lubbock, Texas, taking inspiration from records and radio programmes. The Beatles were very impressed with American music, true, but they were also very aware of rival bands, the network of local venues and Liverpool's reputation as a city of entertainers.

My publisher, David Roberts, thinks that *80@80* should end with an assessment of the Beatles legacy in a hundred years' time. It's a valid question but I have doubts about the world progressing that far.

Barry McGuire could be right. I think there will be no Beatles, no Stones, no anything, but assuming the world order remains roughly as it is, I will answer the question.

Firstly, copyright. Copyright laws vary around the world and may be changed, but generally, a composer's copyright lasts until 70 years after his death. McCartney's copyright will probably go into the next century, Lennon's falls away in 2050, and George Harrison's in 2071. It is possible that the 70 year period will be extended because it does penalise those unfortunate composers who die early. Look for example at the amount of 50s and 60s music used in TV advertising – the underlying message is that rock'n'roll sells.

Once out of copyright, the music is royalty free and anybody can do what they like with it. Beethoven, Mozart, Shakespeare and Dickens are out of copyright and their work can be distorted or expanded however you like. You can play fast and loose with Shakespeare's plays and give them short shrift, and if you do that, you are quoting Shakespeare. However, the integrity of the original works remains, and this hasn't damaged their status.

But behind David's request is the question, "Will anybody be interested in the Beatles in 80 years' time?" If the answer is no, the copyright laws hardly matter. I found myself alone in the Marlene Dietrich Museum in Berlin: could someone find himself alone in The Beatles Story at the Albert Dock in 2105? No. I don't think that will happen and I believe the Beatles will endure.

One, there is an enormous breadth to their songwriting. There are simple songs like Buddy Holly's which can be picked up by youngsters learning the guitar and then there are the social commentary of 'Eleanor Rigby' and the psychedelic 'Strawberry Fields Forever'. The Beatles have a wide catalogue and a host of songs that everybody can sing – Bruce Springsteen conquered stadium rock but only a handful of his songs are known throughout the world.

Two, the story of the Beatles is perfect, like a Rock Nativity. Their rise is one of warmth and friendship and there is a human interest that isn't in the early years of Sinatra or Presley. I loved the Byrds' work in the 1960s, but by comparison, their back story is dull. What's more, the Byrds never looked right: the Beatles knew instinctively how to look good together.

"The Beatles' story has a beginning, a middle and an end, and there are various periods - the pop period, the psychedelic period, the John and Yoko period, and so on," says Rick Wakeman. "It's great for young musicians of today because they can see the complete works and lifespan of the Beatles, which we could never do at the time. It got to the stage where everyone thought that everything would be a classic, and the pressure was too much for them."

Their only official biographer Hunter Davies says, "The thing about the Beatles is that the further we get away from them, the bigger they become. Look at the memorabilia and artefacts as more and more people are living off the Beatles. When Apple was at its height, no more than 50 people were employed by the Beatles. There are thousands of people in the world today living off the Beatles: the look-alike groups, the tours, the dealers, the writers and the university lecturers. It's amazing."

The Beatles are included in university courses now: there was opposition at first, perhaps because they had not had the academic training of classical composers, but surely that is one of the more remarkable factors: just how did they do it?

The Beatles had an audience that grew old with them. BBC DJ Alan Freeman told me, "The Beatles freed me from middle-age. When the Beatles happened, there I was, heading for 40, and they made me feel terribly young again. It was great. They were sensational."

The Beatles achieved things that they never could have contemplated. They more than anyone knocked down the Iron Curtain as Soviet teenagers wanted to hear this music. When Ukraine left the Soviet Union, Lenin Square in Izium with some good humour became Lennon Square. The mural of John Lennon has so far survived the invasion.

Competitively, the bar was set high in the 1960s and the Beatles wanted to be ahead of the game. It was good fortune that Bob Dylan came along at the same time. He had a different approach but they influenced each other and spurred each other to new heights.

David Bowie amassed a huge cult following but never quite had that mass appeal as he was regarded as a space oddity. The Rolling Stones mastered stadium rock but became parodies of themselves, although they, Elton John and McCartney have shown that rock is not exclusively a young man's game. Queen and Madonna became huge stadium acts, but their records have lacked the variety and ingenuity of the Beatles. Michael Jackson wrecked his own career by not appreciating how his behaviour might look to outsiders. Taylor Swift is everywhere today but again, where are the songs?

Neil Hannon of the Divine Comedy: "The Beatles had an influence on every succeeding band or artist that came afterwards. It may be a second or third generation influence, but it is still there. The Beatles changed everything and they are also the link to old-fashioned vaudeville, 20s flapper songs, Noël Coward and Cole Porter. Many of their records are not 4/4 rock'n'roll at all and are in that old tradition. Look at 'Eleanor Rigby', which was brilliantly arranged by George Martin. It has a Bach-like string arrangement and it is a remarkable track."

Since the Beatles disbanded, journalists have been asking who will be the next Beatles. No one has achieved that total breakthrough. Maybe the answer is the Beatles themselves as there have been ingenious schemes to keep the band contemporary and appealing to the next generation.

Abba created great pop records and had a wonderful image, but again there was not too much development in their music. However, they did beat everyone with *Voyage*, the AI Abba, which is doing tremendous business in London. The AI Beatles might not be far behind, but I think not. The Beatles don't like being second. But who knows? Can't you see the success of AI Woodstock?

Mark Lewisohn: "The Beatles music will never, ever die, and people in the future will always be talking about how great it was."

What was it Paul McCartney said? Ah yes, I believe in yesterday.

CHAPTER 80

Bop Til You Drop

"The cradle rocks above an abyss and common sense tells us that our existence is but a brief crack of light between two eternities of darkness."
(Vladimir Nabokov, Speak Memory)

So, I'm coming up to 80, a long way past the expected three score years and ten of a century ago and I hope to go on much further. I would like to make *The Guinness Book of World Records* by not dying but I don't think that is possible. Still, at this point in time, the oldest man in the world lives in Southport, so you never know. (Spoiler alert – John Tinniswood, the oldest man in the world, has just died aged 112.)

I do hope, though, that I don't die anytime soon as world politics today is so engrossing and I want to know how the wars are going to be resolved in the Ukraine and Gaza, not to mention the warring gangs in Haiti. I fear the worst and hope for the best.

When Donald Trump first stood for POTUS, I thought it was ridiculous and that he didn't stand a chance as he had been such an idiot hosting *The Apprentice*. However, I hoped, rather foolishly, that he would get in, not because I agreed with anything he said or wanted him to win (lord, no!) but because I was intrigued to see what would happen if he did. Now that I know, there was no way I wanted him to win a second time. It is hard to imagine a more divisive President than this man who is motivated by self-interest.

And now we have the overthrow of the brutal Assad regime in Syria. Assad had been an eye surgeon in London, presumably with compassion for those he treated, and yet he became the most brutal of dictators, worse than his father. How did that happen? I suppose it echoes Michael Corleone in *The Godfather* – you get sucked into the family business.

So much has gone wrong with the huge industries under the UK Government's control – the Post Office and the treatment of sub-postmasters, the NHS with its lengthy waiting lists, the railways and HS2, the border forces and illegal immigrants, the shortage of doctors and dentists, the children who don't go to school, the potholes in our roads, the awarding of PPE contracts and their ineffectiveness, the awarding of honours to dishonourable people, the monitoring of the water companies and the disposal of sewage. Then there are those arguments that appear to have been lost – the collapse of the high street, the closure of bank branches, the BBC's broken promise on delivering local radio, the closure of libraries and chewing-gum on the streets. Broken Britain is about right.

But again, I want to see what happens next. Can anybody get it right? The best way to sort out the world would be to get everybody living for the common good so that the ridiculous amounts spent on defence are no longer necessary, but that is an impossible dream.

I don't feel it's an achievement to get to 80. It is more by accident than anything else. My father was determined to get to

80 but I don't know why he was hung up about it. It didn't do him any good as he died when he was 79 in 1988, and my mother insisted that the obituary notice read "in his eightieth year".

Maybe my ashes could be scattered in the Mersey: I like the sound of that but in my own minuscule way, I would be adding to the pollution of the waters and also, it's a hassle to arrange. However, if that were to happen, I'd be in good company as both Clinton Ford and Lita Roza had their ashes tipped off the side of the Mersey Ferry. You arrange it beforehand, and the ferry stops for five minutes so that someone can say a few words.

It's better than the *Blue Peter* presenter John Noakes who arranged for his ashes to be put into a firework which was set off in his old school. I certainly wouldn't like my remains to be on the playing fields of Rydal.

I've just heard a new interview with the American actor Ed Asner on BBC Radio 4 and he died in 2021. It is astonishing what can be done with AI these days, and what is available for rich celebrities and their families will in time become commonplace. But why do it at all?

But what is going to become of us? Look at how much the world has changed in recent years. I can hold all the world's knowledge in my hand with a Smartphone. How many people do you see reading books on a train? What is the future of libraries? Are they only going to be for the privileged? Indeed, what is the future of work itself? It is predicted that AI will replace 30% of the workforce within 20 years. How are we going to use all this leisure time? Are the Arts going to become significantly more important – I hope so. The Culture Ministers were once big beasts but these days the role has been demoted.

The Beatles will surely remain with us. In 1997 Paul McCartney wrote a classical piece, *Standing Stone*. Standing stones are monuments to the future, like Stonehenge, something will last long after their creators have gone. Maybe McCartney was making a point about his own work.

Lots of people want to go on living because they have a Bucket List. I certainly don't want to go parachuting, skydiving, climbing Mount Everest or any of the ridiculous things that some old folks do. I can't think of anything for my bucket list – oh yes, I can, I'd like to go to Paris and see where Serge Gainsbourg lived as his home is now open to the public and we would both like to go across Canada by train. I hope I get the chance to archive my files which are being given to Liverpool Central Library. Many of my radio programmes are already with them and the British Library, which is very gratifying.

Anyway, I've not finished yet and I want to write until I hit that final full stop. Maybe I'll write a final *Echo* column in which I will thank everybody and thank Anne for being the pot of gold at the end of the rainbow. (I can do clichés as well as anybody, but it's true.)

So that's it. I'm destined to sit at home and write until I….arrgh!

P.S. If I last another 10 years, I can expand this text into *90@90* – and that's a much better idea.

Non-Index

I decided against an index as I didn't want friends and acquaintances looking themselves up to see what I'd put. I'd like them to read it in context.

I've come to realise what an astonishing number of people we meet during our lives and so there are notable omissions. The other day I met a BBC sports reporter, Charlie Lambert, whom I've known for decades and yet he isn't in the book (well, he is now) because there are no chats I remember even though he is a thoroughly pleasant guy. Not being in the book is not a value judgement. I've loved meeting every one of you, but a book can't be a list of names.

Writing this memoir has been great fun. I advise you to try it sometime.

Thank you and goodnight.

Bibliography

Some passages of text and quotes in this book have been borrowed from the many books and articles I have written over the years, underlining what my good friend, Tony Barrow, the Beatles' press officer, used to say: "Rework your catalogue."

Here's a list of just some of the books and features that have been raided for *80@80*:

Let's Go Down The Cavern, Hutchinson, 1974

Presley Nation, Raven Books, 1976

Stars In My Eyes, Raven Books, 1980

Bob Wooler, Best of Fellas (The biography of Bob Wooler) Drivegreen, 2002

The Walrus Was Ringo; 101 Beatles Myths Debunked by Alan Clayson and Spencer Leigh, Chrome Dreams, 2003

The Cavern - The Most Famous Club in the World, SAF, 2008

Everyday: Getting Closer to Buddy Holly, SAF, 2009

The Beatles in Hamburg, Omnibus, 2011

The Beatles in Liverpool, Omnibus, 2012

The Beatles in America, Omnibus, 2013

The Cavern Club, McNidder & Grace, 2016

Simon & Garfunkel – Together Alone, McNidder & Grace 2016

Bob Dylan - The Day I Was There, edited by Neil Cossar and published by This Day In Music, 2017.

Elvis Presley - Caught In A Trap, McNidder & Grace, 2017

Buddy Holly: Learning the Game, McNidder & Grace, 2019

Bob Dylan: Outlaw Blues, McNidder & Grace, 2020

The Road to Love Me Do by Spencer Leigh and Mike Jones, Beatles, Liverpool & More, 2022

Plus features and reviews for *Country Music People, The Independent, Let It Rock,* the *Liverpool Daily Post* and the *Liverpool Echo.*

Have pen, will scribble - the story of my life!

Recent music titles from Poppublishing

"A genius for absorbing influences and surpassing them through his own powerful creativity."
Billboard magazine on Stills

The biography is in stock and available now from Amazon or from the publisher at poppublishing@gmail.com

Chaperoning Kate Bush, touring with the Carpenters, befriending Phil Lynott, working with, and almost for, the Rolling Stones, Brian Southall has had the fantasy job most of us dream of.
His second memoir is in stock and available now from Amazon or from the publisher at poppublishing@gmail.com

80@80

SPENCER LEIGH

80@80

Printed in Great Britain
by Amazon